Communication
Audits

Management Applications Series

Alan C. Filley, University of Wisconsin, Madison
Series Editor

Performances in Organizations: Determinants and Appraisal
L. L. Cummings, University of Wisconsin, Madison
Donald P. Schwab, University of Wisconsin, Madison

Leadership and Effective Management
Fred E. Fiedler, University of Washington
Martin M. Chemers, University of Utah

Managing by Objectives
Anthony P. Raia, University of California, Los Angeles

Organizational Change: Techniques and Applications
Newton Margulies, University of California, Irvine
John C. Wallace, University of California, Irvine

Interpersonal Conflict Resolution
Alan C. Filley, University of Wisconsin, Madison

*Group Techniques for Program Planning: A Guide to Nominal
Group and Delphi Processes*
Andre L. Delbecq, University of Wisconsin, Madison
Andrew H. Van de Ven, Kent State University
David H. Gustafson, University of Wisconsin, Madison

Task Design and Employee Motivation
Ramon J. Aldag, University of Wisconsin, Madison
Arthur P. Brief, University of Iowa

Organizational Surveys: An Internal Assessment of Organizational Health
Randall B. Dunham, University of Wisconsin, Madison
Frank J. Smith, Sears, Roebuck and Company

Managerial Decision Making
George P. Huber, University of Wisconsin, Madison

Stress and Work: A Managerial Perspective
John M. Ivancevich, University of Houston
Michael T. Matteson, University of Houston

Organizational Behavior Modification and Beyond, 2/E
Fred Luthans, University of Nebraska, Lincoln
Robert Kreitner, Arizona State University

Communication Audits
Cal W. Downs, University of Kansas

Communication Audits

Cal W. Downs

University of Kansas

Scott, Foresman/Little Brown College Division

Scott, Foresman and Company

Glenview, Illinois   Boston   London

To Alice, Allyson, and Kevin

Working has been so much easier because of the joy and fun which they generate.

Library of Congress Cataloging-in-Publication Data

Downs, Cal W.
    Communication audits / Cal W. Downs.
        p.   cm.
    Bibliography: p.
    Includes index.
    ISBN 0-673-18275-4
    1. Communication in organizations—Auditing.   2. Management audit.
I. Title.
HD30.3.D68 1988
658.4'5—dc19   87-28392
                                                                    CIP

Foreword

The Management Applications Series is concerned with the application of contemporary research, theory, and techniques. There are many excellent books at advanced levels of knowledge, but few address the application of such knowledge. The authors in this series are uniquely qualified for this purpose, since they are all scholars who have experience in implementing change in real organizations through the methods they write about.

Each book treats a single topic in depth. When the choice is between presenting many approaches briefly or a single approach thoroughly, we have opted for the latter. Thus, after reading the book, the student or practitioner should know how to apply the methodology described.

Selection of topics for the series was guided by contemporary relevance to management practice, and by the availability of an author qualified as an expert yet able to write at a basic level of understanding. No attempt is made to cover all management methods, nor is any sequence implied in the series, although the books do complement one another. For example, change methods might fit well with managing by objectives.

The books in this series may be used in several ways. They may be used to supplement textbooks in basic courses on management, organizational behavior, personnel, or industrial psychology/sociology. Students appreciate the fact that the material is immediately applicable. Practicing managers will want to use individual books to increase their skills, either through self-study or in connection with management development programs, inside or outside the organization.

Alan C. Filley

Preface

Teaching and consulting in the area of organizational communication has been immensely rewarding to me. The blend between the academic approach to knowledge generation and the consulting orientation toward using that information in practical ways is both challenging and humbling. Thousands of books and articles have been written to "explain" how communication is supposed to work in organizations, but the more of these I read, the more I become convinced of how inadequate those explanations often are. That is why I tell students that the most important skill they will develop from my courses is the ability to analyze. Then, as they learn to analyze a given organization, they can use their knowledge to help the organization.

The purpose of this book is to explain different means of analysis, from which the reader is free to choose what will work best in a given situation. No attempt is made to rank-order the analyses in terms of utility, and I encourage readers to use bits of each that make sense. I also urge readers to develop new methodologies. Believe me, I shall continue to do so; such an attempt ensures us of growth.

My own growth has been the product of collaboration with many people. One of the most exciting times was the ability to develop the ICA audit with outstanding people like Gerald Goldhaber, Tom Porter, Gary Richetto, Harry Dennis, Don Schwartz, Phil Salem, Peter Hamilton, Sue DeWine, Howard Greenbaum, Ray Falcione, and many others. I owe much to their scholarship and stimulation. My students have also taught me a great deal as we have explored ways of making sense of data about organizations. And while I continue to analyze some organizations alone, the best times come through collaborative efforts where differences of opinion challenge, extend, and frustrate my own point of view.

In writing this book I am particularly indebted to five people. Alan Filley encouraged me to write it and then he read every word to give me constructive comments that sharpened the book's focus and enriched the materials. Phil Clampitt has worked with me on numerous projects, and has extended my original work on communication satisfaction. That is why I was particularly pleased that he agreed to write the chapter on the communication satisfaction questionnaire. Tom Porter has one of the most innovative approaches to organizational communication. Our many informal conversations at conventions has increased my respect for his work, and he has enriched my understanding of networks. I thank him for writing a chapter on networks. Ken Mackenzie has helped me sort out the difference between academia and the "real world." I find the development of practical theories to be intellectually healthy. Finally, Jack Light gave me my first opportunity as a young scholar to analyze his organization over a period of time. His offer has been one of my most rewarding experiences and certainly has had a great impact on my career.

As you read this book, keep in mind that the aim is not to provide formulas for analysis or auditing of organizations. The primary aim is to acquaint you with some tools of the trade, to describe the basic strategy of the art, and to challenge you to improve upon them.

Cal W. Downs

Contents

1
Introduction

Communication problems in the organization are not unlike the progressive development of a headache. If the initial bodily cues are ignored or not monitored, the full "throb" will hit. The result is much more time and effort lost in trying to correct the unbearable condition than would have been needed to prevent the situation in the first place. The communication audit can provide that initial sensoring or monitoring for the organization which will allow for a preventative stance regarding communication problems rather than the typical corrective stance.

> Howard Greenbaum and Noel White
> Professors

The audit process served as a catalyst for organizational change by bringing us face to face with issues only randomly perceived before. The result provided a framework for specific action steps such as:
−the investment of increased attention and energy in the planning function at all levels of the organization.
−an increased focus on the skills of giving performance feedback and recognizing excellence in staff training.

> Jeannette Terry
> Director of Staff Development
> Seminar Company

Our management team has studied the results of the audit to address several of the key issues that were brought to our attention. Efforts will be directed to maintain the areas of strength and to improve upon a select number of weaknesses. I thought it was a favorable experience.

Stephen R. Schuchart
Vice-president
Savings and Loan Company

At every level — interpersonal, organizational, and international — we depend on effective communication. When a married couple petition for a divorce, we usually say that they must have had a communication problem. When employees create a work slowdown or strike, we blame it on a lack of communication. And when international superpowers break off negotiations, their inability to communicate makes us feel uncomfortable. But as these examples illustrate, our tendency is to take communication for granted until there is some problem, and this has led to terrible mistakes. No one needs to convince us of the importance of communication: we know it intuitively; we experience its importance daily; we have faith in what it can accomplish. But we are still stuck with the habitual behavior of not paying attention to it until something goes awry.

The basic premise of this book is that organizational processes need periodic monitoring. Warren Bennis (1969) described this need graphically:

Organizational systems, like other organisms, evolve and have a life cycle. They have a dawn and, quite often in recent years, a sudden old age or stagnation periods. Given the pace of events and the turbulent environment, organizations confront tremendous problems if decline is not inevitable. Essentially, this means that organizational systems must renew themselves continuously if they are to survive in this society (p. 37).

In recent years deregulation, rapid technological advances, employee mobility, international competition, and independence of the work force have produced dynamic environments for most organizations. These changes have also created an awareness of the tremendous importance of internal organizational communication. Long taken for granted, communication can now be related to job satisfaction, productivity, team-building, and the general coordination within the organization. Therefore, periodic monitoring of how well employees are communicating is particularly important for organizations, because their very survival depends on their workers' abilities to coordinate and to exchange information. Consequently, there is a growing awareness of the need to conduct a periodic *communication audit*. Managers would not dream of making a major financial decision without basing it on as much up-to-date information as possible. Nevertheless, some managers often make decisions about people and organizational communication on the basis of an unsystematic collection of hearsay evidence, intuition, personal experiences, and three-year-old attitude surveys.

NATURE OF COMMUNICATION AUDITS

For many of us, the word *audit* elicits fear or irritation because of its association with the Internal Revenue Service. Basically, however, an audit is merely a process of exploring, examining, monitoring, or evaluating something. Accountants audit our financial records, physicians audit our health, professors audit our learning progress, and managers review, or audit, our level of performance. In other words, the auditing process is one with which all of us are familiar. The idea of conducting a *communication audit* may be new to organizations, but it follows a long tradition of management trying to obtain feedback about how well the organization is doing. A communication audit differs from other audits only in that it focuses primarily on communication, and, therefore, there are certain methodologies that may be applicable to it. A communication audit, like all others, should possess several of the characteristics described in the following sections.

Professionalism. • The investigation is conducted by *independent* auditors with training that qualifies them to make the investigation. In other words, individuals are not allowed to check themselves because they would have a vested interest in the results, and therefore the results would be suspect. Although the audit can be conducted by outside professionals or by in-house experts, there must be an element of professional independence. To be valid the investigation needs to be conducted by someone with expertise both in the analysis of communication and in the general processes of consultation.

Alan Filley (1985, p. 3) describes the characteristics of a good consultant as having (1) the ability to diagnose problems accurately, (2) the ability to serve as a facilitator or catalyst, (3) the knowledge of and skill with consulting processes, (4) sensitivity in using change processes, and (5) the ability to give people the experience of success. To these, add (6) a willingness to grow and learn from the experience and (7) a dedication to the critical review of one's own theories.

Diagnosis. • More than anything else, the audit is a diagnostic technique. It answers the questions "What characterizes this organization?" "What does it do well?" and "What needs improving?" The diagnostic design should provide for systematic observations to be made about all areas of communication that are considered important.

Skill in diagnosis is critical to obtaining a valid and reliable view of the organization's strengths and weaknesses. Furthermore, unless the auditor makes a skilled diagnosis, the proposals for change will undoubtedly be inappropriate. A common tendency for many of us is to define problems according to the solutions that we have available, but it is very important that the initial diagnosis be more open than that. The judgments should be conceptually sound, precise, accurate, and relevant to the purpose of the audit.

Evaluation. • The reason for conducting the diagnosis is to make some judgments about communication within an organization. Implied in every audit is a comparison of what is to what ought to be. There must be standards, purposes, or objectives—and sometimes the performance levels of other organizations—against which the organization can be judged. This fact needs to be emphasized. *Anyone can collect information about communication in the organization, but it takes persons with professional expertise and insights to make practical sense of that information—to identify strengths and weaknesses.* For example, "the most frequent mistake that managers make is to interpret a relative score in absolute terms, that is, without reference to some comparative standard" (Dunham and Smith, p. 71). What does it really mean if 20 percent of employees say they do not get enough feedback?

Professionals will have developed norms against which they can interpret the data obtained in an audit. From where do these norms come? One consultant specializes in banks, so he has developed an expertise that gives him special comparative insights about any new bank he examines. Another consultant has investigated a number of organizations within a midwestern city. Although the organizations are all different, he has become so familiar with the characteristics of the city that he can make estimates based on the kind of employees there. Both types of insights are practical and invaluable. Although the standards for effective communication vary from situation to situation, the entire audit is predicated on the existence of some evaluative criteria.

Unique design. • The audit must be tailored to the specific organization. Each organization has some unique features; therefore, auditors cannot easily take the procedures used in Organization X and use them in Organization Y. A good motto is, "Adapt; don't adopt." This is not to say that one cannot profit from experiences in auditing other organizations, for no audit starts from square one. Nevertheless, there must be some tailoring in the form of new or different questions or wording, and sometimes adaptation of other audit procedures.

The data-gathering techniques available include questionnaires, confidential interviews, observations, critical incidents, communication diaries, content analysis, and network studies. It is usually desirable to use a combination of these to avoid whatever biases can occur because of the reliance on one instrument. Adaptation to the organization may require using a "cafeteria approach" to find the methodologies that would be most useful in a specific organization. An audit need not involve them all.

Control. • The ultimate value of an audit is that it identifies the strengths that need to be reinforced and the weaknesses that must be corrected. This feedback gives management the information needed to propose actions that can correlate what is with what is desired.

Timeliness. • Even though an audit usually involves weeks of study, it still takes a snapshot of an organization at a particular time. The audit can be a valid assessment, but generalizations to be made from it must be limited to that particular time frame. Organizational circumstances are generally in a gradual but constant state of change. That is the reason why financial records are checked periodically, at least once a year. The communication patterns in organizations are not static either. They too need to be audited periodically to keep the information current.

MANAGEMENT RATIONALE FOR AUDITS

If comprehensive communication audits possess the six characteristics just discussed, they can provide an organization with at least five functional benefits: (1) verification of facts, (2) diagnosis, (3) feedback, (4) communication, and (5) training.

Verification benefit

When facts are verified, guesswork about the organization is replaced with valid information.

> Most managers believe they acquire a considerable amount of knowledge about worker attitudes and opinions through formal and informal interaction with their employees. Undeniably, this sort of unstructured observational testing does provide a good deal of valid information. Unfortunately, it can also provide a good deal of distorted information. The personal observations of a manager are greatly limited by his or her interpersonal sensitivity and by possible preoccupation with other responsibilities. In addition, the workers' dependence upon their managers for continued employment and income can inhibit or disguise their real feelings. . . . Indeed, this is one of the major insights achieved by managers who have participated as interviewers on survey teams in many organizations (Dunham and Smith, 1979, p. 10).

Perception plays a key role in shaping the way people communicate in organizations, and the truth of the matter is that our perceptions are oriented to our own vested interests and experiences. Our perceptions are often merely partially true and sometimes dead wrong. The way that a manager perceives an organizational chart is not necessarily the way the nonmanagement employees perceive it. Consider the following examples. Odiorne discovered that when both bosses and subordinates were asked to describe the subordinates' jobs, they disagreed on an average of 25 percent of the things they mentioned (Filley, 1978, p. 74). In another case, when bosses were asked to list the kinds of problems they thought their subordinates encountered, their list was quite different than the list made by the subordinates.

I have met many sensitive, skillful managers who have had fairly good assessments of their organizations. But some of them have been surprised by our audits' findings because their employees have not always exposed their feelings and reactions to them. Nor have the managers exposed their innermost thoughts to their employees. The result is a likelihood that some differences of opinion and perceptions exist.

In numerous studies of organizations, this pattern is repeated over and over, as people in different positions and geographical locations look at the organization and how it operates from different perspectives. Furthermore, perceptions of how people communicate are often inadequate. The organization chart, for example, is a fixture in many organizations. To some extent, the chart identifies authority and communication lines, and it is assumed that it represents who talks with whom. But communication audits have demonstrated that the real communication networks seldom look exactly like the organization charts and often do not resemble them at all. Furthermore, the pervasive informal channels through which people accomplish much of their work are generally left off altogether.

In the absence of valid information, people make assumptions about the organization and why things happen as they do. For example, during the time of airline deregulation, I conducted an audit of the reservation system of a major airline. The ticket agents were harried by frequent and often massive fare changes, and sometimes fares would change without the agents being told. They blamed their supervisors for not keeping them informed, and the resentments were quite strong. Of course, the agents believed that the supervisors had the information and were just not passing it on to them; they could not imagine that the supervisors did not have this information. The audit revealed, however, that the supervisors were not being provided with the information on time either. After an office at corporate headquarters changed fares, it was three days before the changes were put into the computer. Aside from implementing changes that could speed up the sharing of information, the audit was valuable in revealing to the employees that their previous assumptions and evaluations of their supervisors had not been entirely correct, and the results of the audit had a direct impact on their working relationships. Perhaps the most basic benefit of any communication audit, then, is that all parties— management and employees alike—can check and validate their perceptions.

Diagnosis benefit

Auditing forecasts problems. Although a proper audit identifies strengths, it also pinpoints those areas where aspects of communication need some repair before they actually break down. A typical problem identified in audits is the desire for information that some workers believe they need but are not getting. For example, upper management in a public utility developed a system of feeding information to managers with the expectation that they would in turn pass it on to the employees reporting to them. The system was designed in this way to reinforce the role of managers as providers of information. However, the audit identified major problems when the managers did not transfer the information, and the whole system had to be changed. In this sense, the audit enabled management to do a better job of planning and controlling operations.

In another sense, audits can yield information that explains or predicts critical organizational events such as dissatisfaction, lapses in productivity, union activity, turnover, and lack of teamwork. For example, when management became aware of tremendous dissatisfaction in one unit that was beginning to hamper coordination and productivity, an audit revealed two primary sources of the reactive behavior. One of them was traced to comments made at a specific department meeting. When managers are able to analyze the root of such problems, they may be able to influence their effects.

Finally, audits may diagnose areas of concern before they become serious problems.

> Unfortunately, many organizations fail to exploit the predictive value of surveys by using them only to diagnose a problem after it has emerged. It is also possible to use surveys to prevent such problems. For example, early detection of employee dissatisfaction with company policies could permit a careful evaluation of these policies and their impact on employees. . . By identifying many employee concerns at a relatively early stage, surveys allow management to work toward maintaining organizational "well-being" rather than fighting to remove "illness" (Dunham and Smith, 1979, p. 44).

Feedback benefit

As the previous example illustrates, *an audit becomes an important component in a feedback loop.* Communication (input) is designed to produce certain effects (output). Like the thermostat on a furnace, the audit feeds back some measure of performance so that adjustments can be made if the output is not exactly what was wanted. The audit may offer a comprehensive review of most of the communication in the organization, or it may examine only specific programs of interest to management. For example, audits have been used to develop new communications training programs, to assess how changes in telephone equipment and usage could save money, to test the impact of a new performance review system as a communication vehicle, to provide information about the structure of an organization that could be used to restructure it, and to determine the effectiveness of meetings and printed communications so they could be improved. Such feedback can have important ramifications for the overall communication effectiveness of the organization by providing benchmarks that keep management aware of the status of its communication systems. A 1983 survey of *Fortune* 500 companies discovered that 45 percent had conducted some form of communication audits. The basic rationale given for this practice was that "the evaluative process offered a *benchmark* for the progress and future of corporate programs" (Greenbaum, Hellwegg, and Falcione, 1983, p. 5).

Communication benefit

The audit benefits communication merely by focusing attention on it. Anyone familiar with the "Hawthorne effect" recognizes that people respond positively when attention is paid to them. A communication audit implicitly demands, "Don't take communication for granted." It sensitizes people to what they are doing and how they are communicating. In my experience, participation in an audit becomes a motivator for improved communication performance even while the audit is taking place. Audits pinpint beneficial ways to change. Some ideas come from the auditors, but most audits also enlist suggestions from those being audited. In some sense, the participants become a direct communication link between managers and other employees. Their suggestions are invaluable. Brooks, Callicoat, and Siegerdt (1979) surveyed several organizations that had conducted audits. They concluded that most organizations adopted changes in their communication practices as a result of the audit.

Structural changes included new, revised, or eliminated divisions, work units, job specifications, policy manuals, standard operating procedure, committees, committee membership, and "open door" policies. Changes in communication methods involved added, revised or eliminated schedules and formats of existing communication facilities, feedback spans, periodic and incident reports, newsletter, bulletin boards, internal office memos, group planning sessions, top management visits, meetings and presentations with employees, and employee recognition ceremonies and banquets. Training changes added or revised existing training programs to include workshops on communication practices and processes, orientation training . . . skill interviews, and skill training (p. 9).

This list certainly supports the idea that audits can be effective communication channels that yield pragmatic results.

Training benefit

The inherent training benefit of a communication audit is often overlooked. Its principal educational benefit may be to those managers who are involved in either the planning or the follow-up stages. Such participation in an audit provides an opportunity to develop skills and attain insights into the whole communication process. By working with an audit, one's awareness of communication is sharpened, and one becomes sensitized to interact with others more thoughtfully.

CONCLUSION

It should be stressed that communication is not the only process in an organization that needs auditing, and communication audits certainly do not solve all problems and create the perfect organization; nevertheless, audits offer important means of improving organizational life. The findings in the previously cited survey by Brooks, Callicoat, and Siegerdt reinforce this conclusion. Most organizations adopted some changes as a result of the audit, and 85 percent responded that the general perceptions of communication in the organization become more favorable as a result of the audit. In addition, I have never had an organization believe that the time and money spent on an audit was not productive. With the value of the audit established, succeeding chapters will explore the aspects of communication that should be examined and how the audit should be implemented.

Managing an audit from start to finish is a growth experience that is also fun, invigorating, and creative. Every organization is different, and the sense of discovery compensates for the hard work. Textbook answers do not always apply, so the auditors are left with a sense of creative problem solving. And the generally enthusiastic response of managers is rewarding in itself. For me, the audits have generated a greater understanding of, and sensitivity to, the realities with which organizations must deal.

Despite the challenge and the opportunity for growth, however, audits require planning and a lot of hard work—some of it tiring and mundane. Chapter 2 emphasizes the necessity of comprehensive planning and outlines basic considerations for that planning. The discussion is general because every audit operates a little differently, depending on the circumstances. Basically, however, there are six phases to an audit: (1) initiation, (2) planning, (3) diagnosis or fact-finding, (4) analysis, (5) evaluation, and (6) feedback.

Phases 1 and 2 are extremely important to the success of any audit because they provide the general orientation. The remaining phases, however, require much greater elaboration and analysis. Phase 3, diagnosis, covered in Chapter 3, points out the important areas that need to be investigated. Phase 4, analysis, is discussed in Chapters 4 through 9. This section focuses on various methodologies that might be useful to the auditor. Phase 5, evaluation, is described in Chapter 11. This phase is the most important one in the entire process because it is here that the analytic data are made meaningful to both auditors and managers. Phase 6, feedback, covered in Chapter 12, is the goal of the audit. It is during this phase that the organization finally discovers the usefulness of the audit. Information is provided to launch whatever adaptions the organization needs in order to make improvements.

REFERENCES

Bennis, Warren. *Organizational Development*. Reading, Mass.: Addison-Wesley, 1969.

Brooks, K.; Callicoat, J.; and Siegerdt, G. "The ICA Communication Audit and Perceived Communication Effectiveness Changes in 16 Audited Organizations." *Human Communication Research* 5 (1979): 130–137.

Dunham, R. B., and Smith, F. S. *Organizational Surveys*. Glenview, Ill.: Scott, Foresman, 1979.

Filley, Alan C. "Introductory Notes for Business 838." Unpublished manuscript, 1985.

Filley, Alan C. *The Compleat Manager*. Middleton, Wisc.: Green Briar Press, 1978.

Greenbaum, Howard; Hellwegg, Susan; and Falcione, Ray. "Evaluation of Communication in Organizations." Paper presented at a convention of the International Communication Association, Dallas, May 1983.

2

Initiating and
Planning an Audit

PHASE 1: INITIATION

Audits can be initiated either by the consultant or the client. Sometimes auditors market their audit services just as they would market training programs, that is, through advertisements or personal contacts. In most cases, however, the clients make the initial contact because they are looking for help with a problem generally considered to be in the area of communication.[1] Once the contact has been made, the goal is to determine whether or not the auditor's technology is suitable for the organization's purpose. The ethical auditor must pursue these deliberations with the realization that sometimes one may have to refuse the assignment because of lack of expertise or because of the unsuitability of certain goals. However, if there does seem to be a fit between auditor and client, the guidelines discussed in the following sections will complete the initiation phase.

---

[1]Auditors often have a reasearch component in their audits. There may be specific questions that they wish answered, not for the improvement of the organization, but for the refinement of their own theories. My own Communication Satisfaction Questionnaire, discussed in Chapter 7, was partially developed this way. Similarly, Rogers identified his primary goal in one audit as the development of a "research protocol for studying information diffusion." Cumulatively, such audits have been worthwhile in developing research tools that try to discover the keys to effective organizational communication. For example, summarizing the results across several audits, Goldhaber and Rogers (1979, pp. 16–17) concluded that communication behavior was *strongly* related to job tenure, organizational tenure, and age. The demographics that were *moderately* related to communication behavior included education, supervisory status, communication training, and the number of people with whom one communicated.

Meet with key people

The first phase of every audit ought to include several preliminary meetings with key representatives from the organization. More than one meeting is desirable, because the ideas of both auditors and clients can go through an incubation period. Basically, these meetings should accomplish four things: (1) accommodate the client's purposes, (2) define the scope of the audit, (3) familiarize the audit team with the organization, and (4) familiarize management with the audit procedure.

Accommodate client's purposes

An audit can be time-consuming and expensive, so the decision to conduct one should not be taken lightly. It must be emphasized that there is no one purpose for an audit, and each client may have a special objective in mind. For example, one manager of a manufacturing plant wanted to treat the audit as a basic attitude survey; another wanted to test a particular communication system; and still another wanted an audit to serve as the basis for some training in teamwork. Each of these audits would be set up differently because of the different purposes. While the auditor should have the expertise to design a general audit, the client's objectives need to guide the design.

Get consensus about project

One problem sometimes encountered is that influential members of the client organization have different goals for the audit. For example, I was retained by a corporate-level manager to audit a plant for the express purpose of developing a new communication system. I assumed that all managers knew about and agreed upon the basic purposes. However, midway through the audit I realized that the plant manager always talked of training as being the end result; in fact, he always changed the subject when talk centered on a new system. Eventually, we had to face the issue of differences in purposes, but the differences were never really reconciled. This situation demonstrates the necessity of clearly identifying the objectives at the very beginning and securing agreement with them. The purposes then determine the scope of the audit.

Define scope of audit

Since communication is a broad concept, the focal points are virtually limitless. One could legitimately explore all areas to be described in Chapter 3, but this may not be practical. Therefore, the scope needs to be clearly defined.

Some audits, for example, are designed to be comprehensive analyses of an entire organization. Others limit themselves to a particular communication unit in the organization. Some audits focus on internal communication only; others include external communication with clients. Finally, some audits forcus primarily on the communication networks, while others evaluate the kind and number of messages exchanged. In other words, scope is determined by what the organization values most at the time and by where management thinks problems can be uncovered. It may be desirable to fashion a broad format in general but to conduct an in-depth examination of issues of special concern. Of course, defining an audit's scope has political ramifications, because auditing or investigating any aspect of a work unit can be threatening to those people being investigated.

Familiarize audit team with organization

While audit techniques can be fairly standardized, a general survey of the company is needed before starting to plan the actual mechanics of the audit. It is helpful, for example, to have people describe both the structure of the organization and some of the key players. A physical tour of the facilities gives an overview of the work processes, the employees, and the general climate. Finally, printed reports, brochures, and statements of values provide useful indicators of what is important to the organization. A practical way to assess how much you know about the organization is to try to develop a comprehensive description of it. After sketching out the description, examine it closely to see if there are any obvious gaps.

Familiarize management with audit concept

Be prepared to summarize how an audit is conducted and how it can benefit the organization. Two resources are useful persuaders. Refer to previously satisfied clients and then walk the prospective clients through a typical methodology from a previous audit. Without violating confidentiality, parts of a previous audit report can demonstrate the kind of information that can be generated. Once the decision to conduct the audit is finalized, there are numerous details to be decided concerning how auditor and client will relate to one another. Thus the auditor moves into Phase 2, the planning stage.

PHASE 2: PLANNING

Make financial arrangements

There are many costs involved in an audit other than just the employees' time. These include telephone calls, postage, computer time for analysis, secretarial help, duplication expenses, travel costs, and the charge for supplies. These costs are not always predictable, but managing an audit involves managing a budget. It must be determined who will pay for expenses and how. Furthermore, one needs to work out in advance exactly what the consulting costs are going to be and whether to charge by the project or by the day or time. I prefer the latter because it gives me greater flexibility.

Decide nature of final report

From the outset it should be clear as to what information is going to be provided to whom. Normally, I arrange to give comprehensive oral and written reports to management, and there is generally no difficulty with this. A second approach is to meet with individual managers and give them oral and written reports about their units. In some cases, managers have asked the auditor to be present as they discuss the audit in a meeting with their units. A third possibility is to prepare a written report of one to two pages to be circulated to all employees. During the audit process, employees typically ask what is going to happen to the information, and the fact that many have participated in other surveys deters their motivation to participate. In fact, in her survey of the uses of information collected in attitude surveys, Davis (1986) found that organizations typically do not use or report in detail the results of their surveys. Therefore, the promise of a report can be a positive motivator to participate in the audit. Consequently, when employees ask about the possibility of seeing a report, you want to be able to answer yes or no, but you can only do this if you have made the agreement in advance. Any report to employees should not be too detailed, and management should have the opportunity to review the report and to make changes. An audit is designed to help solve problems, not to create them by reporting information that should not be widely circulated.

Clarify auditor-client relationship

How the auditors and clients are to work together is one of the most important decisions to be made. And because there exists a variety of consulting styles, this relationship needs to be clarified early. How much is management to be involved in implementing the audit? What expectations does management have about focusing the efforts of the auditors? What kinds of discussions are to take place between managers and auditors during the analysis and evaluation phases? Basically, there are three approaches that can be used (Goldhaber, 1979).

A *purchase* model occurs when the client organization diagnoses a specific problem and contacts the auditors to solve it. In such an instance, the managers decide where the focus of the audit shall be and then may leave the other decisions to the auditors. For example, managers in one organization decided that they had a teamwork problem, contacted us, and then had nothing to say about the audit until the final evaluation was given. After the audit, a teamwork seminar was presented, and the relationship was terminated. In this case, the involvement of management throughout the process was minimal.

A *medical* model occurs when the client organization (patient) describes the symptoms and asks the auditors (doctor) to diagnose the problem. Usually the auditors are expected to determine what is wrong and to suggest remedies. Again, in this model, management leaves the auditors alone. As an example, one of our clients believed that the employees needed to be more involved and contribute more creativity to their jobs. Therefore, an audit was conducted with the specific purposes of identifying obstacles to job involvement and designing a new model of employee participation.

A *process* model demands that auditors and clients work jointly in all phases of the audit. They plan together, they discuss the analysis together, and they discuss ways of implementing new procedures together. One major assumption behind this approach is that no outside auditors can ever completely understand the nuances of the organization in the way that its employees do. Therefore, the auditors function as important resource advisors, but the managers must be the doers. They are ultimately responsible for all decisions and their implementation.

As an auditor, you may have a preference in regard to how you like to operate. Nevertheless, you must clarify this preference and win acceptance for the approach from management. I learned a valuable lesson about this through a failure. I was hired to do a second project for a company because the first was very successful, and they had liked the audit process I had previously used. Consequently, I started the project assuming the guidelines were the same. However, I soon learned that my assumption was incorrect. I was dealing with a different plant manager; and when I wanted to discuss preliminary findings, he was uneasy. When I asked for his input on directions to explore, he was vague and would change the subject. Actually, he wanted me to present solutions, and my credibility actually suffered when I did not make outright decisions. Furthermore, this situation was complicated because I was being paid by a top-level manager who had one set of expectations, while I had to work with a plant manager who had a different set of expectations. Apparently he was insisting on a medical model while I was trying to use a process approach.

Arrange liaison with organization

Every audit requires a great deal of coordination within the organization itself; therefore, it is useful to have a liaison employee or committee of employees to handle these details. Such people are invaluable as they publicize the audit, win support for it, schedule interviews, arrange conferences, or dispense questionnaires. Furthermore, it is useful to have some person(s) designated to be the contact(s) when problems occur. One of my best liaison experiences occurred in the audit of a university. A committee of approximately twenty people functioned well in assisting in the entire design and follow-up of the audit. Most often, however, we only deal with one or two individuals. Since much of the coordinating work is clerical, a good secretary or assistant can be helpful.

The relationship with the liaison individual(s) is crucial to the success of the audit, and it is imperative to explain the purpose and procedures thoroughly. Watch for signs of lack of support and try to countermand them. Once a liaison manager assigned much of the coordination to an assistant who obviously was fearful of the project. She created obstacles by developing unnecessarily complicated schedules, not assigning enough interview rooms, insisting that she talk to only one member of the audit team, and informing us that certain key people could not be interviewed. The problems were circumvented by going around her to her boss, so the audit did not suffer. But when she volunteered to dispense the questionnaires, we politely made other arrangements because we feared the impact her negative attitude might have on the respondents.

Determine focal areas

Although the general purpose may be to find out the organization's strengths and weaknesses, there are some specified focal points in communication. Some of these will be worked out in advance with management. Selection of focal areas is discussed in detail in Chapter 3. However, you may ask the following valuable questions:

1. What do you need to know for the analysis?
2. What would you like to know?
3. What information is it possible to get?
4. What are your priorities? Those of management?

The focal points of the audit will shape the choice of instruments, which is the next step.

Select audit instruments

Each of the following research techniques has proved to be a reliable form of auditing communication: (1) observations, (2) interviews, (3) questionnaires, (4) critical incidents, (5) network analysis, (6) content analysis, and (7) communication diaries. Each has special utilities that make it somewhat different from the others, and these unique features are depicted in Exhibit 2.1. Why not use them all? There is, of course, a point of diminishing returns

EXHIBIT 2.1   Potential Audit Technologies

Type	Time	Cost	Yield	Disruption
1. Observation	Variable	Relatively inexpensive cost of observer	Data from people processes, environment, and task processes	Little if observer remains unobtrusive
2. Interviews	30 to 60 minutes	Expensive; pay interviewers; pay workers for interview time	Perceptions of employees; probing allows in-depth coverage of many topics	Time away from job.
3. Questionnaire	20 to 30 minutes	Relatively inexpensive; mass-produced questionnaires can be filled out at will; principal costs are employees' time and analytic time of auditor	Standardized; quantitative data about many topics; general overview of many aspects of the organization	20 to 30 minutes
4. Critical Incidents/ Communication Experiences	Usually built in as part of interview or questionnaire	a. Relatively inexpensive b. Depends on whether collected in questionnaire or interview	Specific examples of perceived behavior, but many refuse to give them	Little
5. Network	20 to 30 minutes	Paid time to employees for filling out questionnaire; very expensive to analyze with computers	Structural information	30 minutes
6. Content Analysis	None	Many hours to code and analyze	Kind of information processed through the organization; evaluation of channels	None
7. Communication Diaries	Variable	Expensive; takes worker time to write a report of everything	Interaction networks; content of messages; channel evaluation	Great; most treat it as a nuisance

in collecting information. After a while no new ground is being explored, because the auditor keeps discovering the same information. Furthermore, there are limits to time and financial resources. Each technique will be analyzed in detail in later chapters, and the question of choosing which is appropriate under certain circumstances will be answered at that time. At this point, however, there are two general recommendations in making choices among them.

First, use multiple techniques when possible. From the viewpoint of pure research, one criticism of audits is that the validity of the findings is questionable when only one instrument is used. Situations differ, of course, as do the purposes of audits. For more limited projects, I have relied on only one technique—generally the interview—and the results have worked out. However, for more elaborate audits, data derived from at least two techniques are desirable. The more measures used to collect data, the more reliable are the data; they supplement one another so that the consistency of findings can be tested. For example, questionnaires provide important numerical information that can be analyzed statistically, whereas interviews give qualitative data that are rich in terms of in-depth explanations of responses. By using both, auditors can ensure that their estimates of the organization are likely to be realistic.

Second, focus on actual behaviors as well as perceptions. Since employees behave according to the ways they perceive situations, it is useful to tap their perceptions. Nevertheless, we find many instances when the perceptions are not consistent with the facts (perhaps a communication problem in itself) or when the perceptions among employees vary widely. That is why interviews, content analysis, critical incidents, or observations may be good supplements to questionnaires. Also, multiple techniques are useful since subjects respond differently to different ways of collecting information. There are nearly always problems of reconciling seemingly contradictory information.

Choose employees to be audited

In small organizations of less than two hundred, all employees can be canvassed, but collecting data from a more limited sample is perfectly acceptable. The decision to sample or to canvass employees depends on a number of factors. First, cost is a primary one. It is less expensive to sample than to collect data from everyone. Second, the choice of audit technique is important, since more people can be observed or be surveyed by questionnaires than can be interviewed. However, some standard techniques for compiling a communication network often demand that each employee be audited; failure to do so leaves gaps in the network. If multiple methods are used, canvassing can be used with some while sampling is used with others. For example, it is common to give questionnaires to everyone but to interview only a small number. Third, expectations of the employees are a concern. Any sampling may leave out people who wish to participate while selecting others who, feeling they have been targeted for some negative reason, may be uncooperative. One way to avoid either circumstance is to include everyone.

Ultimately, the decision to canvass or to sample may be most affected by how management wants to use the audit data. If it is to be used as a catalyst for action, canvassing the employees is helpful. It should be remembered that a sample does not necessarily give less information than a canvass. If reliable procedures are used in its selection, a sample permits an auditor to generalize about the entire organization while auditing only a portion of the workers. The following guidelines may be helpful in deciding who should be included:

1. Stratified sampling is necessary for the data to be truly representative of all dimensions of the organization. Stratification simply means that employees are included from every level, every work unit, and every shift. The essence of representativeness is that you will get the same information by taking a sample that typifies the organization as you will by auditing everyone.

2. Avoid making the sample too small. While there are no guaranteed formulas for deciding exactly how many people should represent the organization, it is better to have too many people than too few. Some guidance may be obtained from a table developed by Krejcie and Morgan (1970) to estimate the approximate sample size from a given population. This is reproduced in Exhibit 2.2.

3. Include all key people. There are some who are in positions to give more of an overview of the organization; make certain all of these people are included. Although it would be a mistake to audit *only* the key people, we have found that auditing a number of them can give a fair assessment of the organization.

4. Do not overlook part-time employees. Organizations seem to be hiring more and more people for less than full-time work. Since they can have a significant impact on the communication in the organization, part-time workers should be included.

Forecast time sequence

Most audits are conducted over a period of several weeks, often making coordination difficult. Therefore, it is helpful to set up a check list of procedures with target dates. Such targets not only help the auditors keep on track, they also give the clients *a sense of progress*. Operating without such a plan creates a lack of definition for many clients, who experience anxiety wondering when—and if—things are going to happen.

Time is a factor in other ways, too. Employees take time away from their jobs to participate, and this needs to be coordinated well in advance. Furthermore, schedules must allow enough time for participation to be meaningful.

EXHIBIT 2.2   Table for Determining Sample Size from a Given Population

N	S	N	S	N	S
10	10	220	140	1200	294
15	14	230	144	1300	297
20	19	240	148	1400	302
25	24	250	152	1500	306
30	28	260	155	1600	310
35	32	270	159	1700	313
40	36	280	162	1800	317
45	40	290	165	1900	320
50	44	300	169	2000	322
55	48	320	175	2200	327
60	52	340	181	2400	331
65	56	360	186	2600	335
70	59	380	191	2800	338
75	63	400	196	3000	341
80	66	420	201	3500	346
85	70	440	205	4000	351
90	73	460	210	4500	354
95	76	480	214	5000	357
100	80	500	217	6000	361
110	86	550	226	7000	364
120	92	600	234	8000	367
130	97	650	212	9000	368
140	103	700	248	10000	370
150	108	750	254	15000	375
160	113	800	260	20000	377
170	118	850	265	30000	379
180	123	900	269	40000	380
190	127	950	271	50000	381
200	132	1000	278	75000	382
210	136	1100	285	1000000	384

Note: N is population size; S is sample size.

Time schedules also have to be arranged around space requirements, work loads, and important key events. Forecasting key events that may affect the audit is very helpful. Some things we have encountered that compete with the audit are personnel changes, recent attitude surveys, reorganization, productivity campaigns, and vacation schedules during the summer.

Publicize audit

The last step in planning is to determine how to let employees know about the project. An aspect of organizational communication that is often criticized is the lack of timely information about new things. Since the audit is a major communication in itself, every effort should be made to publicize it in advance. The publicity should cover who is conducting the audit, a simple overview of some of the procedures, and why it is being done. To give it legitimacy, we have found it useful to have a minimum of three forms of publicity. First, a member of management and an auditor should explain the audit to all managers and supervisors in meetings. This gives it management's blessing, allows the coordinators to answer questions, and equips the supervisors to answer any questions from their subordinates. Second, a top manager should send a letter or memo to all employees announcing and supporting the project. Third, an announcement should be featured in the newsletter or house organ, to keep people informed while securing support. Furthermore, the announcement should be couched in terms that will allay fears and present a feeling of urgency. We find most people receptive to the possibility of improving communications.

In some ways, the publicity campaign is the most critical aspect of the audit. It sets expectations, it secures cooperation, and it provides a good example of communication. This process must not be neglected.

Formalize audit arrangements

The initiation and planning stages of managing an audit rely heavily on oral discussion. However, after auditors and clients have explored the issues and have agreed on the elements of the audit, the agreement needs to be documented. One way to do this is to sign a formal contract, and one example is given in Exhibit 2.3. The benefit of a contract is that it spells out exactly what the responsibilities of each party will be during the audit. On the other hand, some consultants use letters to document the arrangements. Such a letter is included in Exhibit 2.4. Notice that it sets out the consultants' expectations and requirements after prior meetings with managers. Some consultants have conducted audits merely on the basis of oral exchanges, and this can work well. However, specificity of detail and documentation for future reference are important, and generally the arrangements should be formalized in writing.

EXHIBIT 2.3   Sample: Contract in Apex Organization

---

1. Management Responsibility and Personnel
   The Communication Audit of Apex will be directed by Dr. Cal W. Downs. The audit team will consist of Mary Doe, Harry Poe, and Pat Washington. They will work with a liaison group, designated by management, in the planning, administration, interpretation, and follow-up of the communication audit.

2. Audit Procedures
   a. Thirty employees will be interviewed during the initial stages of the audit. Those interviewed will be selected by the auditors to represent every aspect of the organization.

    b. All employees will be surveyed by a questionnaire. Included on the questionnaire will be information about communication relationships, information exchange, networks, outputs, channels of communication, and suggestions for improving the organization.

    c. A second round of interviews will include thirty interviews. This will be conducted after the questionnaire data has been analyzed in order to probe for significant findings.

3. Audit Timetable
    a. March 15–20—First round of interviews to be completed.
    b. April 8–17—Questionnaires will be administered and analyzed.
    c. May 1–15—Second round of interviews to be completed.
    d. June 2—A report will be presented orally and in writing to management.
    e. June 12—A two-page report will be circulated to all employees.

4. Audit Budget
A breakdown for the cost of the audit is as follows:
    a. Director's Salary   _____
    b. Staff Salaries   _____
    c. Other Expenses:
        (1) Computer   _____
        (2) Supplies   _____
        (3) Postage   _____
        (4) Binding of Report   _____
        (5) Travel and Sustenance   _____
        (6) Miscellaneous Expenses   _____

Payment should be made in two equal installments. The first is due on _____, and the second is due on _____.
In addition to these expenses, Apex is committed to publicizing the audit, reproducing all audit instruments, printing all audit-related reports, supplying space and facilities for administering the audit instruments, supplying organizational outcome data to be used in the analysis, supplying a liaison committee, distributing the final report, and collecting printed documents appropriate to the communication analysis.

5. Audit Products
Apex will receive a formal printed report and thorough oral presentation of it on _____. This report will include: (1) a description of all procedures, (2) a frequency distribution of all answers on the questionnaire, (3) a summary of major findings, (4) an assessment of the organization's major strengths, and (5) recommendations for future action to improve communication.

EXHIBIT 2.4   Sample Letter Formalizing Audit Arrangements

April 10, 1987

Mr. John Smith
Apex Corporation
151 Junction Avenue
Los Angeles, California 95131

Dear Mr. Smith:

It was good to talk with you on Monday. As I think I mentioned to you earlier, I prefer to start working with a company by interviewing most or all of the people in it. Where the number is great, I generally have individual interviews with managers and group interviews with some of the employees. In large organizations I also like to give everyone a questionnaire. Where the number is small, I use individual interviews with everyone.

The interviews do three things. First, they acquaint me with the organization structure and communication processes. Second, they acquaint me with the people, demonstrating to them that I can be helpful and trusted. Finally, they give me people's perceptions about the strengths of the organization and obstacles to their performance and satisfaction. The questionnaires give information that can be used to cross-validate the interview information.

After collecting the information I prepare a report that is presented to you in written and verbal form. It is an important document since it serves as the basis for our plans for change. I like to arrange a two-hour meeting for us to discuss the findings.

I am enclosing a draft memo that you may want to revise and distribute to your people. I am also scheduling May 10 and 11 to be with your company. Depending on our further discussions in Los Angeles this week, we may want to use the first day for individual interviews and the second for group meetings. Rather than scheduling the time of interviews (they average about an hour), I'd suggest that you alert people that I will be conducting a private, confidential interview and then call them as each preceding interview is completed.

I would like to be able to tell those interviewed that they will receive a report, either verbally or in writing. Also, it should be made clear to people that I am not there to make judgments or evaluations of individuals.

My charges for this work are _____ a day plus expenses.

If you have any questions please call me at my office (212) 263-1664 or at my answering service (212) 251-8633. I look forward to seeing you in Los Angeles.

Sincerely,

Arthur Consultant

AC:re

REFERENCES

Argyris, C., *Intervention Theory and Method.* Reading, Mass.: Addison-Wesley, 1970.

Davis, Mary. *Employee Attitude Surveys: A Study to Discover the Use of Resulting Data.* M.A. Thesis. University of Kansas, 1986.

Goldhaber, G. *Organizational Communication.* Dubuque, Iowa: Wm. C. Brown, 1979.

Goldhaber, G., and Rogers, D. *Auditing Organizational Communication Systems.* Dubuque, Iowa: Kendall-Hunt, 1979.

Krejcie, R. V., and Morgan, D. W. "Determining Sample Size for Research Activities." *Educational and Psychological Measurement* 30 (1970): 607–610.

3
Phase 3: Choosing Focal Areas for Auditing

Every communication audit must be focused. Chapter 1 pointed out that the best audits cover communication broadly but that they also can be designed to investigate some special areas in depth. Basically, the data to be collected should focus on the most important elements in the organization: the people in positions, the task processes, the structure relating task processes, the structure relating people in networks, the communication channels used, and the types of information exchanged. Furthermore, the auditors need to determine what observations can be verified and must secure the perceptions of the employees. In developing focal points, auditors are in essence setting the parameters for the kinds of observations they will be able to make for a comprehensive audit.

In this chapter, eleven guidelines are given to mold the investigation. While the content of different audits may vary, these guidelines form a general pattern that has widespread application.

1. Start with a process perspective.
2. Relate communication to the other important organizational processes.
3. Examine how the task processes impact communication.
4. Determine the adequacy of information exchange.
5. Check the directionality of information flow.
6. Assess how well the communication media are used.
7. Be sensitive to differences in communication functions.
8. Check the quality of communication relationships.
9. Plot communication networks.
10. Review the organization as a complete system.
11. Relate communication to organizational outcomes.

These are discussed in detail in the following sections. The objective is to provide both a theoretical and practical rationale for each.

STEPS IN CHOOSING FOCAL AREAS

Start with process perspective

Although communication is widely accepted as being very important to organizational effectiveness, it is often oversimplified, considered to be a mere message exchange or a simple technique formula that, if followed, can automatically mold a person into an effective communicator. It has been implied that if you communicate "just right," the receiver will have no alternative but to do what you want. Neither approach to communication is helpful because neither is correct.

On the contrary, communication is one of the most interesting organizational phenomena to investigate precisely because it is so complex and multifaceted. Understanding this complexity is a necessary prelude to targeting the focal areas for any audit. Consequently, this section gives managers a brief rationale for considering communication as a process.

From the beginning of an audit, communication should be thought of as an ongoing, dynamic process—a description that is intended to differentiate it from a static, linear, finite phenomenon. Popularized by Berlo in 1960, the term *process* conveys the general ideas that (1) there are many components interacting together, (2) the outcomes of the interactions are determined by some unspecified contingencies, and (3) the interactions do not have a finite beginning or end. In other words, every communication is rooted in both a historical as well as a current situational context. Therefore, to understand any current communication interaction, one may need to understand both its history and the impact of noncommunication variables in the situation.

In one of the earliest models, Lasswell (1948) described the communication process as "who says what through what channels to whom and with what impact." Shannon and Weaver (1949) made major contributions in developing a model of communication, outlined in Figure 3.1. Berlo (1960) emphasized many of the same concepts in his famous SMCR model, in which Sources encoded Messages and sent them through Channels to be decoded by Receivers, who then responded with Feedback to the Sources. Building on Berlo, the model of communication in Figure 3.2 visually depicts each person as both a sender and receiver, and the two people maintain an ongoing interaction with one another as well as with others. This model tries to show the general dynamic context in which any given message exchange may be viewed.

These models depict communication as a basic interpersonal process, but they also have important applications to organizations. In particular, any

FIGURE 3.1   Shannon and Weaver Model

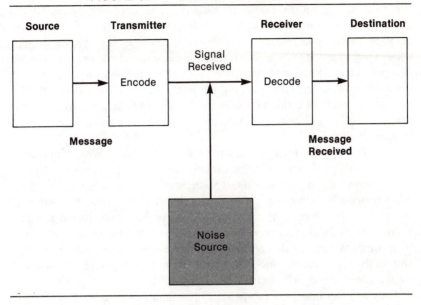

FIGURE 3.2   Downs Communication Model

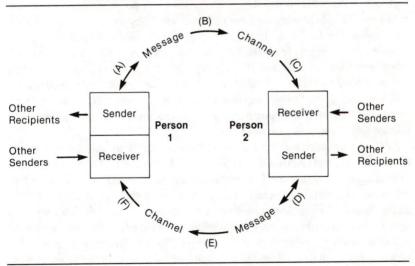

auditor ought to pay special attention to two important sub-processes: filtering and feedback.

The models call attention to the unique processes of encoding (deciding what and how to communicate) and decoding (interpretation of messages) inherent in each individual. It is important to know that messages sent throughout organizations are not necessarily the ones received, because they are filtered through a person's motivations, listening habits, and perceptions. This filtering phenomenon is not merely a capricious notion by which a person decides what to pay attention to or how to interpret a message. The filter is the essence of a person's total frame of reference, and understanding how messages are filtered is a means of understanding the total context of the individual. For example, in audits it is often useful to probe how key managers filter. In doing so, one can begin to understand how choices are made about communicating.

Probing this filtering phenomenon can also show how communication is related to noncommunication variables such as costs, competitors, goals, and images of organizational values. Sometimes communication is linked inside a person's head to some very unexpected variables. Although it is important to audit the filtering of key people in the organization, filtering occurs at an organizational level as well, and this too should be audited. Different levels of management will have access to different messages, as will different units in the organization. Such differences often have profound ramifications for the coordination and control of the organization.

Another important sub-process of communication is feedback, which refers to the communicated response to messages. In the model presented in Figure 3.2, the letters A and D refer to times when people monitor their *own* messages. They hear what they say and read what they write, often correcting themselves. The D-E-F continuum represents responses to messages by other other people. It is this feedback loop that develops two-way communication, which has been demonstrated to be more effective and more satisfying than one-way communication. In their survey of the studies of feedback, Downs, Johnson, and Barge (1984) concluded that feedback does affect levels of performance. Therefore, the communication of feedback is one of the most important organizational processes.

As auditors explore feedback, they are likely to analyze both its interpersonal and its organizational applications. For example, I have encountered several cases in which the factors that inhibited feedback between two key organizational members affected the functioning of the total organization. In addition, auditors can sometimes point out instances when the addition of a new feedback channel in the organization could enhance the coordination of work. Again, the exploration of the factors affecting feedback demonstrates how communication is interrelated to many other aspects of the organization.

Detailing all aspects of the communiation process is not my intent, but the areas of filtering and feedback have been discussed to stress the importance of the process perspective for an auditor. In summary, the concept of process leads the auditor (1) to investigate the full context in which communication takes place, (2) to search for the historical antecedents that have led communication patterns to take place as they do in this organization, (3) to be open to any unexpected variables that might be operating on communication, and (4) to recognize communication techniques but never to consider techniques as the essence of effective communication.

Relate communication to other organizational processes

Communication has always been basic to organization. It links its members, it connects the organizations to an environment, it coordinates efforts, and it provides the information necessary for production to take place. Writing in 1938, Chester Barnard, an executive, claimed that the "first function of an executive is to establish and maintain a system of communication" (p. 226). He also suggested that "In the exhaustive theory of organization, communication would occupy a central place, because the structure extensiveness and scope of organization are almost entirely determined by communication techniques (p. 91)".

Executives spend up to 80 percent of their time in some form of communication, and my surveys indicate that the ability to communicate is one of the key factors determining whether managers get hired or promoted. The same surveys point to communication as one area in which young professionals are most deficient. Thus it would seem that communication is an area where managerial behavior can make a significant difference in influencing organizational life.

One can see how pervasive communication processes are throughout the organization, and this pervasiveness has important implications for anyone planning an audit. Although we sometimes talk of organizational communication as if it were a separate, self-contained process, it really is not. Investigating communication can actually lead to a consideration of almost any other variable. Consider the following possibilities. The way one communicates may define one's *leadership style*. The *organizational structure* influences communication linkages and determines who gets what information. Communication is the means by which management accomplishes *decision making, control,* and *coordination*. The degree of *teamwork* may be tied to communication relationships. These examples emphasize that any aspect of an organization may have implications for effective communication, and the most effective audits will consider the greater complexity (Likert, 1967, pp. 26–29). Futhermore, *audits should be open enough to permit observations about the unexpected*. If they are arranged too tightly, the potential for discovery is limited.

Examine the effects of task processes on communication

Many communication specialists, like organizational psychologists, are trained to examine variables of motives, attitudes, expectations, human relations, and styles. And often there is little concern for the structure of *work;* it seems to be a given. On the other hand, no communication audit can be complete without understanding the task processes necessary for directing, controlling, and coordinating work assignments. Since there are usually many tasks to be performed in an organization, it is desirable to see how these tasks are coordinated. The organizational logic is a listing of the task processes and a description of how the organization functions. Mackenzie (1986) calls task processes the primary data for the analysis of an organization. By analyzing the tasks and how they fit together, auditors begin to understand the demands made on the communication system.

For example, in an audit of a plant, I was asked to focus on the apparent lack of teamwork. Now, lack of teamwork is generally considered to be a bad thing. But before I could begin to work on the communication that might improve teamwork, I had to determine exactly how these employees were expected to coordinate their tasks. What did they do that required teamwork? As it turned out, the employees were unclear about their own task processes, and this uncertainty inevitably led to some interpersonal problems.

Determine adequacy of information exchange

One ultimate aim of communication is to circulate information, and there are three issues that are related to how adequately this is accomplished: (1) type of information, (2) timing, and (3) load.

Every audit ought to explore whether people get *the information that they need to perform.* This can relate directly to the need for information for each task process. The auditor can gauge adequacy in two ways. First, most employees are sensitive to the fact that they do not get certain information, and they generally are willing to share this with the auditor. In addition, employees are sometimes unaware of the existence of information that could be useful; the auditors may become aware of this information through their own observations. Auditors need to make mental notes of what is available and not be tied to employee perceptions only.

Since information is most useful if it is received *on time,* the auditor can look for ways of developing a timely distribution system. This sounds easier than it often is. For example, a particular problem that plagues many companies is how to inform their own employees about a story before it is published in the press. Many employees feel cheated if they initially get their information through the newspapers; the timing is not right for them. In working with a public utility, we tried several different formats to solve this problem—but none of them was completely successful. Some problems we must learn to accommodate.

The communication *load* can be an important variable in assessing adequacy of information exchange. Load refers to the frequency and amount of communication that takes place. An optimal load is dictated by the receiver's ability to process an amount of information. Unfortunately, no one has come up with a good definition of optimal load; instead, we are more likely to define it by what it is not. *Underload* occurs when people think they need or could use more information. *Overload* occurs when people have more information than they can possibly process. In such instances, more communication is certainly not better communication.

Although the most common complaint in organizations is that employees do not get enough communication, there will usually be tension in moving from underload to overload. For example, a public service company had the following experience. After an audit, the consultant proposed a new suggestion system, and the employees were assured that these suggestions would be reviewed and a written reply sent to them. As the suggestions were received by the coordinator, they were placed in red folders and sent to the appropriate person to review. The impetus for this program was to draw out the employees—that is, to remedy an underload of suggestions. However, the program had been sold so well that one could walk by certain officers and see stacks of those "damn suggestions" on the desk. Replying to the suggestions took far more time than anyone had predicted. The new overload interferred with other work and caused a great deal of resentment.

Load may also be related to technology. Computers and new software make it possible to process a greater load of communication. But technology is also a mixed blessing. In an audit of a university, an employee identified the photocopier as the organization's greatest communication problem. Many people copied things profusely and sent them out indiscriminantly. The recipients had to read some of the messages at least partially to know that they did not want them. Therefore, the recipients felt overloaded because reading irrelevant information was taking up their time. In a real sense, the best most audits can do is to measure whether people feel underloaded or overloaded, but this is important information because it reveals how people are responding to message exchanges.

Check direction of communication flow

Because hierarchy is an inherent part of every organization, it is common to analyze communication in terms of the direction in which it flows, and the most common labels are (1) downward, (2) upward, and (3) horizontal.

Downward flow. • *Downward* communication refers to those message systems that proceed vertically down the chain of command from managers to subordinates. It takes the forms of orders, company publications, performance judgments, job instructions, company orientations, and training for the job. Employees receive a great deal of information from many different sources, but how much of this communication is effective has always been disputed. Investigators have found that "managers are more likely than . . . workers to think that downward communication is taking place" (Farace, Monge, and Russell, 1977, p. 149). Furthermore, there has long been a difference between management's perception of what employees *need* to know and what the employees say they need and *want* to know. This difference calls attention to two functions of downward communication. First, of course, employees need to have the information necessary to do their jobs, and in many organizations such information is late or lacking. However, good downward communication is not limited to immediate work assignments, and this is the part that many organizations neglect. In previous audits we have encountered whole units that wanted some downward recognition of their efforts, some sense of how they fit into the total organization, or an idea of how the company planned to meet some general economic problems. When employees do not get such information, many feel left out. Furthermore, they wonder why such information is being filtered out or distorted (Davis, 1968). These feelings arise particularly when important changes take place (Janger, 1962).

In summary, downward communication may be informal as well as formal; goes beyond task information; focuses on the employee, the unit, and the company; often does not meet the expectations of employees; and must be constantly adapted to changing circumstances. An audit provides an important means of testing how efficiently and effectively the organization is meeting the comprehensive need for information.

Upward flow. • Communication also flows from employees *up* the chain of command, either formally or informally. Whereas many people initially think of downward communication whey they think of effective communication in organizations, some of the most important information processing goes from employees at one level to their superiors. Task-oriented reports, for example, are commonly sent upward to provide feedback about performance, and without an effective system of reporting upward, no organization could possibly function long. Other forms of upward communication include suggestion systems, teams, quality circles, goal setting, and a host of techniques of participative management. Even a job performance review can have an upward dimension as an employee communicates impressions of his or her own performance levels and the goals that are relevant to the job.

Upward communication plays an important informational role in the organization, but the freedom to initiate communication with superiors also characterizes the *communication climate* for that organization. In this sense, upward communication is important not only to the organization but also to the individuals. Being able to communicate upward gives one a stake in the organization and contributes a sense of dignity or importance. In terms of organizational outcomes, upward communication affects not only productivity but satisfaction as well.

Upward communication is often deliberately filtered by employees. There is an old observation that bad news does not flow up because people are afraid of being negatively associated with it, and Downs and Conrad (1977) found a real reluctance on the part of subordinates to confront their bosses. Such filtering is done out of a need for self-preservation related to mobility aspirations and trust of managers (Read, 1962; O'Reilly and Roberts, 1974), but since it may be dysfunctional in terms of the overall organizational health, it is a much needed area for auditing.

Horizontal flow. • While communicating vertically is likely to be considered more important in most audits, much of the communication on the job takes place *horizontally* with peers, colleagues, or fellow workers with whom one does not have a hierarchical relationship. Many of these horizontal interactions take place informally for social reasons. Nevertheless, horizontal communication is also absolutely necessary for coordinating task processes.

Recently I conducted two audits where management specifically requested that horizontal communication be the major focus. In the first audit of a manufacturing plant, designers cut down on communication because they thought the engineers "looked down" on the rest of them. And in a second organization, six units were combined into one department, but one unit considered itself more professional than the rest and resisted being identified with the new department. Knowledge can give power, and some people are reluctant to share their power. On the other hand, horizontal communication is sometimes neglected not out of intent but out of *carelessness*. For example, in a university, the people responsible for a change in the school calendar "forgot" to notify the people who ran university student housing. These examples demonstrate that some of the richest data in any audit may be found by investigating the teamwork and horizontal coordinating patterns.

Assess how well communication media are used

Messages have to be transmitted through some channel or media, and these ought to be audited comprehensively. First, make a comprehensive list of all channels used in the organization. Include institutionalized oral interactions as well as written media. A representative list might include newspapers, house organs, special memos, bulletin boards, meetings, interviews, telephone calls, and training programs.

Next, gauge employee reactions to media. Over time, people develop a general belief that some media give important information while others do not. By identifying these reactions the auditor can evaluate the appropriate matching of messages to media. In addition, the auditor's actual observations can be an important resource. For example, I have found it quite instructive to attend some meetings to observe the communicative patterns. My observation data provide a rich supplement to the perceptual accounts received from employees. On one occasion, I needed to examine the job performance review system. Obviously, I could not sit in on all of the actual interviews, so I did the next best thing—I read the evaluations of every employee for the last two years. That gave me a sense of how well the review system channel was being used.

One issue that often arises is a need to determine when written channels should be used and when oral ones should be used. Oral communication has the advantage of being more satisfying interpersonally (Conrath, 1973) and more adaptable to the receiver through feedback, while written messages are best for keeping documentation and for mass distribution. The issue of channel choice is an important one, and many differences exist among managers. One old guideline is to use *multiple channels* to make certain the message gets across. In fact, a number of experiments have demonstrated that business managers believe channels fall in the following order of effectiveness: oral followed by written, oral only, and written only (Level, 1959). The *redundancy* or repetition in a system is a useful way to analyze channels.

The informal channel is one of the most important channels to audit. Although the distinction between formal and informal channels is not always clear-cut, the informal channel generally refers to the grapevine or rumor mill, or to social interactions outside the formal structure. Davis (1952) has studied how informal networks build, and many others have analyzed their characteristics. Our audits have determined that informal channels are exceptionally fast but that members generally prefer hearing information through formal channels because of the potential unreliability of information that is circulated informally. The formal and informal channels are often analyzed as if they are competitors, and unfortunately they sometimes are, but informal channels can also reinforce the formal channels and build strong organizational ties. I have never seen an organization without informal channels, but if I were to find one, I would wonder about the health of the organizational relationships.

Be sensitive to different communication functions

Not all communications have the same function in the organization, and some functions may be more important than others. While the following five functions are not discrete or mutually exclusive, they do provide a general way of thinking about differences in communication function.

1. *Task/Work Function.* Organizations succeed by getting work done, and an important aspect of communication is its ability to inform, to instruct, to command, to solve problems, to identify goals, and to announce controls. Supervisory instructions, problem-solving meetings, and policy announcements illustrate the ways communication fits the task function. Most of these ways represent some form of downward communication, but many of them will also require important feedback to be reported upward.

2. *Social/Maintenance Function.* Organizations are not merely where we work; they are also where we spend much of our lives, interacting with fellow human beings. For many people, work is their principle means of self-identification. Therefore, the immediate goals of maintenance communication are to enhance the individual's feeling of self-worth, to place high value on cooperative interpersonal and group interactions, and to keep organizational personnel functioning well together. Interpersonal relationships often suffer as peo-

ple clash trying to accomplish a task; as a result, work may grind to a halt. When this happens, maintenance leadership is necessary to smooth over the disrupted interpersonal relations. Staff socials, some meetings, personnel news in newspapers, and teamwork seminars are oriented toward the maintenance functions.

3. *Motivation Function.* There are times when compliance with a management goal cannot be ordered or commanded. Therefore, persuasive communication is designed to influence, to win approval, and to motivate. Examples of this come in appraisals between supervisors and subordinates, posters emphasizing safety habits, and speeches given by managers in organization-wide meetings to motivate people to be more productive.

4. *Integration Function.* Communication can build links so that members identify with the organization, express its values, participate willingly in its processes, feel pride in working there, and know what is going on. This is also the role of many Monday morning meetings— to let people know what is happening and to give them a sense of belonging. Other forms of integrative communication include social functions, orientation programs, training seminars, state-of-the-organization presentations, and participation in some decisions. Whenever the integrative function suffers, employees begin to think less of their jobs and their organization, and the lack of full integration can lead to a host of work-related problems.

5. *Innovation Function.* Change is necessary for organizations to improve or to adapt to the environment. Increasingly, organizations are trying to tap the resources within their employees for suggestions. Sometimes they institute formal systems, but more often they look for more subtle ways of programming new ideas. Suggestion systems, problem-solving meetings, quality circles, and goal setting are all means of being innovative.

These five communication functions, in combination, characterize the healthy organization. Although auditors differentiate among them for analytic purposes, none of them really stands alone. The maintenance and integration functions have some obvious similarities. The task-oriented function may seem the most important, but a weakness in any of the other areas may impinge on it. The functions are not mutually exclusive; in fact, there is some obvious overlap. Performance reviews, for example, may function in all five categories at the same time.

In a total audit, it is useful to audit all five functions. However, I have audited them individually, too. For example, a manufacturing plant was producing 50 percent more than it had the previous year, so the task function seemed to be working well. Management wanted to devise better ways of securing and implementing employee ideas, so they wanted a communication audit that would identify problems in the *innovative* function and suggest ways of improving it. In the actual audit, however, it became important to look also at the *integrative* linkages with the organization, because integration often seems to be a precondition to innovation. The audit revealed many strengths, but it also revealed some important problems. First, a rushed, high-pressure climate had been created by the production increases, and this had led to a certain alienation, specifically, apprehension about the job and a sense of not being kept informed. Second, integration and motivation suffered because of a new policy in hiring managers stating that most promotions would no longer come from within. The belief that promotions were blocked caused resentments, and this had to be overcome before employees would be willing to share their activities and their innovative thoughts. Finally, while the innovative and integrative functions were important, they always had to be viewed in terms of how they were related to the task function.

Check quality of communication relationships

Every message exchange takes place among pepole in some kind of relationship context. Each new interaction affects the relationship by strengthening, maintaining, or weakening it. Furthermore, the nature of a relationship may have a crucial impact on the response to any message. For example, there is a notable difference between the way organization members respond to orders from people they like and the way they respond to those from people they do not like. In general, dysfunctional, negative relationships inhibit communication. For these reasons, relationships are among the most important communication phenomena to be audited. We shall consider the superior-subordinate relationship, the team relationship among co-workers, and the relationship among managers.

Superior-subordinate relationships. • For most organization members, the *supervisors are structurally the most important communication links in the organization.* Therefore, auditing the relationships between supervisors and subordinates is a crucial focal point of any audit. Such relationships can be analyzed in terms of three elements. First, interpersonal trust "influences the quality, level, content, and directionality of communication" (Klauss and Bass, 1982, p. 23). Since it determines how much credibility one person has with another, levels of trust have been found to be significant indicators of communication effectiveness. By asking employees to describe the levels of trust in the organization, auditors can get them to identify many communication strengths and weaknesses of the organization. The lack of trust is invariably rooted in some difficulties with communication. Second, message exchange is largely determined by the superior-subordinate relationships. This seems particularly true for upward communication. For example, when supervisors are not seen as being open, employees curtail the number of ·messages that they send upward. Third, the communication style of the supervisor affects the relationship with employees. In addition to describing the style, the audit should measure the response to it. In fact, the response to the style is a key element in the audit. Both Laird (1982) and Clampitt (1983) found that "productive style" was idiosyncratic to organizational cultures. This simply means that what is effective with one group of subordinates may not be effective with a different group. Therefore, auditors must interpret the appropriateness of a given style on the basis of the people's response to it.

Co-worker relationships. • Relationships among co-workers affect both productivity and satisfaction. It is interesting to note how often people voice displeasure over a lack of teamwork. Recently, in an audit of a manufacturing plant, I encountered one unit in which people would laugh if they observed another employee having problems with a machine, and no one would offer to help. Obviously, these relationships were strained and unhealthy. We had to look for root causes of this behavior, because it was not characteristic of the rest of the organization.

Manager relationships. • The relationships among managers have a profound impact on the communicative health of the organization. These relationships often set the tone for the rest of the organization. Therefore, if one is going to improve organizational communication, there may be a need to audit the relationships among top managers. On one occasion, I was asked to consult with an organization because "those people down there need to learn to communicate." At the same time, some of the top managers were so competitive that they were not even speaking to one another. There was not much that could be done below until the problem at the top was addressed.

Rules governing relationships. • An important way to investigate relationships is to be sensitive to the rules that seem to dictate how, when, and about what people communicate. In one sense, all communication is rule-governed, because people rarely communicate in totally random or erratic ways. Rules may not be explicit, and the organization members may have difficulty articulating them. Nevertheless, they are there, and one of the most interesting ways to audit communication is to try to discover what rules people follow. If you think about your own behavior, it is likely that you can identify some rules about formality, open-door policies, privacy of interactions, what to say to your supervisor, when to say it, when it is permissible to touch, what "proper" language usage is, and how to control certain situations. If, for example, you use profanity with some people and not others, what rule are you following? As these examples indicate, rules may involve procedures or content, but in both instances they regulate relationships.

Different rule expectations are inevitable in organizations, and communication problems are the result. Stetler (1972) found great problems between local health nurses and their supervisors because of different expectations about frequency of initiation of contact. After feeding back the results of the study, the nurses and supervisors were able to iron out some differences. Laird

(1982) discovered how a manager's stopping by a subordinate's desk was interpreted by some as a friendly gesture but by others as close supervision. We have also encountered many situations in which managers thought they had open-door policies, but either no one came in to see them or the subordinates had learned not to send bad news upward. Potential rule conflicts can be found in every aspect of the choices people make about communicating. Coordinated Management of Meaning (Pearce and Cronin 1980) offers some interesting perspectives on communication rule. It assumes that an adequate analysis of communication interactions must include an examination of the meanings that individuals attribute to interaction. Thus Coordinated Management of Meaning investigates what people mean by what they do and how that may agree or disagree with the impressions that others have of their communication behavior.

Plot communication networks

As interaction patterns stabilize in an organization, they develop structures called communication networks. Some networks are formal because they follow the organizational structures. For example, if it is accurate, the organization chart is a description of a communication network because it prescribes who has contact with whom. Other networks are informal in the sense that interactions are based on friendships and social ties rather than position or work processes. Auditing these networks can contribute insight into the way an organization processes information. It is important to remember that every organization may have many different networks operating. In fact, it is possible that different types of information are processed through different and unique networks. Conrath (1973) found that these network structures may also be linked to specific channels of communication. Face-to-face interaction was associated with the physical structure, telephone interactions with the task structure, and written communication with the authority structure.

Networks are fascinating because they enable the auditor to identify the information pathways, to determine real or potential bottlenecks, to determine how the communication linkages match the needs of the task processes, and to analyze the roles that specific people occupy. And a range of technologies now permits auditing organizations of various sizes. Networks for ten to twenty people can be plotted by hand, and current computer software has allowed us to plot networks in an organization of thirteen hundred employees.

One innovation of network analysis is the emphasis on roles (Farace, Monge, and Russell, 1977). Basically, communication roles are characterized by how they link together to form the structure. *Isolates* are members who get little information and have few contacts. *Group members* are those who have a majority of interactions with each other. *Intergroup links* or bridges are members of groups who also connect with other groups. *Liaisons* are people who interact with several groups but who are not actual members of any group. It is their role that is the most fascinating, since they have been found to be more gregarious, more influential, more likely to hold higher official positions, and perceived by others to have a greater number of contacts in the system (Goldhaber, 1979). Again, no value judgments are placed on these roles, but the mere identification of who plays which kind of role gives one an understanding of how the organization operates. In a new development involving task-related communication networks, Mackenzie (1986) has identified *virtual* positions that float among task processes and that may or may not be recognized and regulated by management.

In summary, plotting networks can give the auditors some of their most illuminating insights into how the organization really works. The specific techniques for plotting them are covered in chapters 8 and 9.

Review organization as communication system

One branch of organizational theory, called systems theory, has made several important contributions to the ability to conduct meaningful communication audits. Representative writers about systems theory include Ruben (1972), Katz and Kahn (1978), and Weick (1969).

In systems theory, one is conditioned to look holistically at the unit being audited. The *system* is the total unit or organization being examined, but it is made up of many *subsystems* that can be defined differently according to one's purpose. For example, in a general audit one may examine a total system, but one also has to look at its parts or subsystems such as the performance review subsystem, the quality circle subsystem, the suggestion subsystem, and the various publications that form another subsystem. The systems perspective calls attention to the way things are related, and it underscores the fact that the isolation of any one variable often distorts one's perceptions.

Every system operates in at least one *environment* or *suprasystem*. Sometimes there may be a number of ways to characterize the environment(s). Society in the United States, for example, can be broken down into the economic environment, the social environment, the legal environment, and so on. These environments sometimes dictate communication choices, and the auditor needs to be aware of this. For example, the way that management bargains with its employees is shaped by a legal system, and although it may be ideal to communicate through extensive training programs, the economic environment of the time may curtail this option.

An important way to distinguish how systems operate within their environments is to label them as *closed* or *open*. The closed system is insulated and has apparently impermeable boundaries so that it does not react to and is not influenced by what goes on around it. There are not many totally closed environments, but there are many whose response to environmental change is slow. For example, American automobile manufacturers have been accused of being oblivious to the public's changing preferences in size and quality of cars. When Japanese cars competed so well, the manufacturers began to adapt, but their slow reaction time created some economic problems for them.

An open system is one in which communication enables the organization to sense its environment and to adapt to whatever changes are taking place. Similarly, the open system may interact freely with the environment in terms of trying to change or modify it.

The system perspective calls attention to several different communication formats. In Figure 3.3 there are six formats, each of which may be important: (1) individual to individual within the same work unit, (2) individual to individual across work units, (3) unit to unit, (4) individual to organization, (5) work unit to organization, and (6) environment to each of the other components. Checking different formats during an audit is important because they are all interrelated. Participation in work group meetings, for example, is one of the most common forms of communication in all organizations. Yet the commitment to one's own work unit may have some bearing on the communication patterns with other units. Identification with one's own unit is normally considered to be a good thing, but there are instances in which the identification is so great that it isolates the unit or blocks coordination with other units when cliques form or competition arises.

FIGURE 3.3   Visual Representation of Initial Geometric Coordinates

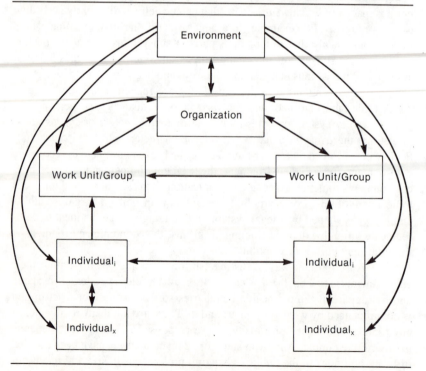

Although one format may be emphasized more than others for a particular audit, the system perspective reminds auditors that the different formats affect one another interdependently.

Relate communication to organizational outcomes

Organizations exist to accomplish definite outcomes, and communication enables the organization to achieve its purposes—productivity, satisfaction, profitability, and positive labor-management relations (Likert, 1967). A good audit cannot overlook the relationship between communication and its outcomes; in fact, the degree to which these outcomes are achieved is an important standard for judging the adequacy of the communication system.

Satisfaction. • Why is it important to examine satisfaction in a communication audit? A satisfied work force is tremendously important to most organizations because difficult problems may arise if dissatisfaction becomes intense and widespread. Therefore, one way to identify potential problems is to discover what satisfies people and what does not.

There is also a correlation between satisfaction and longevity on the job. Dissatisfied workers tend to leave, and replacing them can be expensive. It is desirable to maintain a general level of satisfaction, at least among high performing people.

If communication is supposed to have an impact on satisfaction, then it is proper to investigate how effective the communication is. As one of the most important end products of our organization members, satisfaction has been thoroughly researched. Literally thousands of studies have been generated, and in recent years the link between communication and satisfaction has been explored in detail. Frequently, the results among the studies turn out to be contradictory. Although my purpose is not to give an extensive review of the literature, it may be useful for auditors to note that positive links have been discovered between job satisfaction and the following:

1. Openness in communication (Burke and Wilcox, 1969)
2. Communication relationships (Downs and Hazen, 1977)
3. Load (O'Reilly and Roberts, 1974)
4. Communication apprehension (Falcione, McCrosky, and Daly, 1977)
5. Nonverbal behavior (Sundstrom, Burt, and Kamp, 1980)
6. Communication style (Richmond, McCrosky, and Davis, 1982)
7. Amount of feedback (Downs, 1977)
8. Congruence of communication rules (Hatfield and Huseman, 1982)
9. Communication climate (Downs, 1977)
10. Accuracy of communication (O'Reilly and Roberts, 1974)

In a real sense *most communication audits are heavily based on satisfaction.* In interviews and on questionnaires, organization members share their perceptions about what they like or do not like. Therefore, satisfaction becomes a standard by which the organization is judged by its own people. However, auditors need to exercise caution here. Sometimes people become dissatisfied over procedures that enhance productivity. For example, when a plant policy was changed to hire mostly college graduates as supervisors, much dissatisfaction was expressed. In looking at the situation, however, the auditor decided that in the long run, this change would enhance the health and productivity of the organization.

Because this discussion has emphasized the importance of satisfaction, some considerations about how to measure it are in order. There are several possibilities. One is to ask people how satisfied they are with their jobs. The responses do not tell auditors much, other than how to classify people as being either satisfied or dissatisfied, yet even this can be useful. I once conducted an audit of a plant described by management as "heaven on earth." The audit asked people merely to respond on a 1 to 7 scale to the question, "How satisfied are you on your job?" The results showed that fully one third of the employees, mostly on the third shift, had some level of general dissatisfaction. The scale itself, however, did not reveal reasons behind these results.

Some auditors find it useful to use instruments that measure *facet* satisfaction. One of the most frequently used is the Job Description Index, which contains seventy-two items grouped into five dimensions: work, pay, supervisor, promotions, and co-workers (Smith, Kendall, and Hulin, 1969). The index has a modified adjective checklist format, and it is "especially appropriate for employees with relatively low levels of literacy and requires only ten to fifteen minutes to administer" (Dunham and Smith, 1979, p. 77). A similar instrument is the Minnesota Satisfaction Questionnaire (MSU), developed by Weiss, Davis, England, and Lofquist (1967). Requiring a moderate level of literacy and from twenty to forty minutes to administer, it has one hundred items that measure satisfaction with each of the following:

Ability Utilization	Moral Values
Achievement	Recognition
Activity	Responsibility
Advancement	Security
Authority	Social Service, Social Status
Company Policies	Supervisor; Human Relations
Compensation	Supervision
Co-Worker	Variety
Creativity	Working Conditions
Independence	

Still another possibility is to devise an original rating scale of satisfaction. The research by Wanous and Lawler (1972) is particularly useful since it surveyed nine different formulas for developing rating scales to measure facet satisfaction.

Profitability and costs. • As important as it is, communication is costly. Sometimes alternatives for communicating may be judged on the costs involved. For example, comparing the cost of a house publication with employee reactions to it is one way to determine whether or not the organization is getting its money's worth. Similarly, one of the most frequently used communication channels is the meeting; it is also one of the most frequently selected solutions for communication problems. One consultant added all the salaries of each person attending a meeting and plotted out how expensive that meeting was. The participants in the meeting had never thought of the costs involved. Still, a meeting may be more cost effective than trying to meet individually with each person.

In another example, a state hospital had to cut costs during an economic downturn. One of its major monthly costs involved a huge telephone bill. The usage of each telephone was audited, and the type of equipment was then judged in view of its usage. The auditors found easy ways of saving several hundred dollars a month by making equipment changes. These illustrations point out that consideration of expense is a legitimate and necessary aspect of a communications audit.

Productivity. • There is considerable evidence that communication can be directly related to productivity. As Clampitt (1983) audited several organizations, employees generally could explain how certain communication factors facilitated or detracted from productivity. Jacobs and Jillson (1974) and Judson (1982) surveyed executives who pinpointed ineffective communication as an important reason for lagging productivity. Furthermore, a number of case studies demonstrate how effective communication can improve productivity. Glaser (1980) found a dramatic increase in productivity after new participative management and upward communication programs were introduced. Tubbs and Widgery (1978) measured the impact of a new communication program in General Motors and noted a 0.7 percent productivity increase and a savings of $7 million in production costs. Tubbs and Hain (1979) conducted several studies that found a positive relationship between communication and organizational effectiveness. In one study, they found that departments with the best ratings on grievances, absenteeism, and efficiency had the highest communication effectiveness scores. And in a comparison of two plants, the more productive one received the higher ratings on communication effectiveness.

On the other hand, *beware of formulating the cause-and-effect relations too rigidly.* Work processes depend on complex interrelations among communication, employee motivation and performance, availability of raw materials, organizational design, and economic climate. Because communication is just one of many variables affecting productivity, one needs to be careful in claiming that a given communication phenomenon will always affect productivity in a certain way.

This small sampling of research data suggests that the perceived link between communication and productivity is very strong. However, specifying exactly how particular components of communication influence behavior is not always easy. It has been related to: people's roles in the structural networks (O'Reilly and Roberts, 1974); use of communication vehicles, such as teams or quality circles; group relations (Downs and Pickett, 1977); supervisory communication styles (Bednar, 1982); and sending of feedback messages (Downs, Johnson, and Barge, 1984). Such research merely points out that any aspect of communication may be related to productivity, and the auditor must look for the connection in a particular instance. In doing so, there are several factors to keep in mind.

First, the influence of environment can be significant. Factors such as federal regulation, changes in energy costs, amount of capital investment, competitors, and general economic climate certainly affect levels of productivity. An organization may be communicating very well and still have poor productivity because of environmental factors.

Second, the link between communication and productivity may not be direct but may operate in a two-step approach. It is possible for communication to affect motivation, which in turn affects productivity (Hawkins and Penley, 1978). As an example, consider that employee X makes a suggestion about a new work procedure. If the idea is accepted and it works, the communication affects productivity directly. But suppose the idea was not accepted. Communication still took place, but now whether or not it affects productivity has nothing to do with the fact that messages were exchanged. The impact on productivity is directly related to how X handles rejection. In this situation, some Xs think that "communication" did not take place, even though messages were exchanged. In other words, communications may affect the images members have of the organization, and these images then affect the way they behave.

Third, organizations have multiple productivity goals, and it is important to sort out the most important. Some ways that productivity has been measured include input/output ratios, quantity of work, quality of work, absenteeism, project success, number of errors, number of grievances, and performance ratings. This list suggests that there are problems in defining and measuring real productivity, particularly at the individual level. It is probably best, therefore, to relate communication to unit or organizational productivity.

However, auditors have a number of alternative measures of productivity. While the term *productivity* conjures up connotations of quantification and specific measurement, there is in fact no clear, standardized definition for it. The productivity of a savings and loan institution may need to be measured differently than that of an automobile manufacturer. Within the automobile manufacturer, the productivity of line units may be measured differently than the office workers, the legal staff, the design units, and the managers. In audits of a service organization and a chair manufacturer, Clampitt (1983) found that the employees in the two organizations had very different impressions of the productivity associated with their jobs.

In selecting a measure of productivity, any auditor would do well to be guided by the measures that the organization already uses. Management will have access to some productivity data that can be useful. However, if auditors want to design means of collecting additional data, an important resource would be Paul Mali's *Improving Total Productivity* (1978).

CONCLUSION

Diagnosis begins with a focus. Although it is appropriate to audit a limited aspect of communication, this chapter has been written from the perspective of conducting a thorough audit of communication in general. Covering all areas referred to in this chapter would give a comprehensive impression of what the organization is; such a general overview is described in terms of a communication *climate* or an organizational *culture*. While these are nebulous concepts (Albrecht, 1979; Hellreigle and Slocum, 1974; and Joyce and Slocum, 1984), the general assessment of climate is an attempt to discover those stable characteristics of the environment, whether or not created purposefully by the organization, in which communication takes place. To the extent that such climates or cultures "provide a common frame of reference for participants, they would be expected to exert potent influences on individual performance and satisfaction" (Joyce and Slocum, 1984, p. 736).

The eleven guidelines can help auditors think about general areas for investigation. I have always found it useful to know what areas have been examined in the past, and I am usually guided by some of this information. It helps me make some reasonable choices in analyzing a rather complex process. On the other hand, every audit can be somewhat different, and the examples given here have been designed to show how one must often choose what is important to examine. Make the choices in collaboration with the management. Keep the areas manageable. Then use instruments that give you the best information possible in those areas. The next few chapters examine these instruments.

REFERENCES

Albrecht, T. L. "The Role of Communication in Perceptions of Organizational Climate." *Communication Yearbook 3,* edited by D. Nimmo. New Brunswick, N.J.: Transaction Books, 1979.

Barnard, Chester. *The Functions of the Executive,* Cambridge, Mass.: Harvard University Press, 1938.

Bednar, D. A. "Relationships Between Communicator Style and Managerial Performance in Complex Organizations." *Journal of Business Communication* 19 (1982): 51–76.

Berlo, David. *The Process of Communication.* New York: Holt, Rinehart & Winston, 1960.

Burke, R. J., and Wilcox, D. S. "Effects of Difference and Degrees of Openness in Superior-Subordinate Job Satisfaction." *Academy of Management Journal* 12 (1969): 319–326.

Clampitt, Phillip. *Communication and Productivity.* Ph.D. diss., University of Kansas, 1983.

Conrath, D. W. "Communication Patterns, Organizational Structure, and Man: Some Relationships." *Human Factors* 14 (1973): 459–470.

Davis, Keith. *A Method of Studying Communication Within the Management Group.* Unpublished Ph.D. diss., Ohio State University, 1952.

Davis, K. "Success of Chain of Command Oral Communications in a Manufacturing Group." *Academy of Management Journal* 11 (1968): 379–387.

Downs, Cal. W. "The Relationship Between Communication and Job Satisfaction." In *Readings in Interpersonal and Organizational Communication,* edited by R. C. Huseman, C. M. Logue, and D. L. Freshley. Boston, Mass.: Holbrook Press, 1977.

Downs, C., and Conrad, C. "Effective Subordinacy." *Journal of Business Communication* 19 (Spring 1982): 27–38.

Downs, Cal W.; Johnson, K. M.; and Barge, Kevin. "Communication Feedback and Talk Performance in Organizations: A Review of the Literature." In *Organizational Communication Abstracts,* Vol. 9, edited by H. Greenbaum, R. Falcione, and S. Hellwegg. Beverly Hills, Calif.: Sage, 1984, 13–48.

Downs, Cal W., and Pickett, T. "An Analysis of the Effects of Nine Leadership-Group Compatibility Contingencies upon Productivity and Member Satisfaction." *Communication Monographs* 44 (August 1977): 220–230.

Falcione, R.; McCrosky, J. L.; and Daly, J. S. "Job Satisfaction as a Function of Employees' Communication Apprehension, Self-esteem and Perceptions of Immediate Supervisors." In *Communication Yearbook*

1, edited by B. Ruben. New Brunswick, N.J.: Transaction-International Communication Association, 1977.

Farace, V.; Monge, P.; and Russell, H. *Communicating and Organizing.* Menlo Park, Calif.: Addison-Wesley, 1977.

Glaser, E. M. "Productivity Gains Through Worklife Improvement." *Personnel* (1980): 71–77.

Goldhaber, Gerald. "Auditing Organizational Communication Systems." Dubuque, Iowa: Kendall-Hunt, 1979.

Hatfield, J. D., and Huseman, R. C. "Perceptional Congruence About Communication as Related to Satisfaction: Moderating Effects of Individual Characteristics." *Academy of Management Journal* 25 (1982): 349–358.

Hawkins, E., and Penley, L. "The Relationship of Communication to Performance and Satisfaction." San Francisco: International Communication Association, 1978.

Hellreigle, D., and Slocum, J. "Organizational Climate: Measures, Research, and Contingencies." *Academy of Management Journal* 17 (1974): 255–280.

Jacobs, S., and Jillson, J. S. *Executive Productivity.* New York: AMACOM, 1974.

Janger, Allen. "Announcing an Organizational Change." *Management Record* 24 (October 1962): 8–11.

Joyce, W. F., and Slocum, J. W., Jr. "Collective Climate: Agreement as a Basis for Defining Aggregate Climates in Organizations." *Academy of Management Journal* 27 (1984): 721–742.

Judson, A. S. "The Awkward Truth About Productivity." *Harvard Business Review* (September 1982), 93–97.

Katz, D., and Kahn, R. *The Social Psychology of Organizations.* 2d ed. New York: Wiley, 1978.

Klauss, R., and Bass, B. M. *Interpersonal Communication in Organizations.* New York: Academic Press, 1982.

Laird, Angela. *Coordinated Management of Meaning: An Empirical Investigation of Communication and Productive Action in Two Organizations.* Ph.D. diss., University of Kansas, 1982.

Lasswell, H. D. "The Structure and Function of Communication in Society." In *The Communication of Ideas,* edited by I. Bryson. New York: Harper, 1948.

Level, Dale. *A Case Study of Human Communication in a Bank.* Ph.D. diss., Purdue University, 1959.

Likert, R. *The Human Organization.* New York: McGraw-Hill, 1967.

Mackenzie, Kenneth D. *Organizational Design.* New York: Ablex Publishing, 1986.

Mali, Paul. *Improving Total Productivity.* New York: John Wiley & Sons, 1978.

O'Reilly, C. A., and Roberts, K. "Information Filtration in Organizations: Three Experiments." *Organizational Behavior and Human Performance* 11 (1974): 253–265.

Pearce, W. B., and Cronen, V. E. *Communication Action and Meaning: The Creation of Social Realities.* New York: Praeger, 1980.

Read, W. H. "Upward Communication in Industrial Hierarchies." *Human Relation* (1962): 3–15.

Richmond, V. P.; McCrosky, J. C.; and Davis, L. M. "Individual Differences Among Employees, Management, Communication Styles, and Employee Satisfaction." *Human Communication Research* 8 (1982): 170–188.

Ruben, B. "General System Theory: An Approach to Human Communication." In *Approaches to Human Communication,* edited by Richard W. Budd and Brent D. Ruben. Rochelle Park, N.J.: Hayden Book Co., 1972.

Shannon, C., and Weaver, W. *The Mathematical Theory of Communication.* Urbana: University of Illinois Press, 1949.

Smith, P. C.; Kendall, L. M.; and Hulin, C. L. *The Measurement of Satisfaction in Work and Retirement.* Chicago: Rand McNally, 1969.

Stetler, Cheryl B. "An Exploratory Study of the Area Nurse Role." Master's thesis, University of Kansas, 1972.

Sundstrom, E.; Burt, R. E.; and Kamp, D. "Privacy at Work: Architectural Correlates of Job Satisfaction and Job Performance." *Academy of Management Journal* 23 (1980): 101–117.

Thayer, Lee. *Communication and Communication Systems.* Homewood, Ill.: Irwin, 1968.

Tubbs, S., and Hain, T. "Managerial Communication and Its Relationship to Total Organizational Effectiveness." Paper presented at the Academy of Management convention, August 1979, Atlanta, Ga.

Tubbs, S. L., and Widgery, R. N. "When Productivity Lags Are Key Managers Really Communicating?" *Management Review* 67 (1978): 20–25.

Wanous, J. P., and E. E. Lawler. "Measurement and Meaning of Job Satisfaction." *Journal of Applied Psychology* 50 (1972): 95–105.

Weick, K. *The Social Psychology of Organizing.* Reading, Mass.: Addison-Wesley, 1969.

Weiss, D. J., Davis, R. V., England, G. W., and Lofquist, L. H. *Manual for the Minnesota Satisfaction Questionnaire,* Minnesota Studies in Vocational Relations Center, Work Adjustment Proejct, 1967. Cited in Randall B. Dunham and Frank J. Smith, *Organizational Surveys.* Glenview, IL: Scott, Foresman and Co., 1979.

4

The Interview: The Most Basic Audit Technology

Interviews and questionnaires are the two most basic audit methodologies, and they can be combined in the same audit quite compatibly. Interviews are reviewed in this chapter, and the different alternatives for questionnaires are discussed in Chapters 5, 6, and 7.

For many auditors, the interview has played a supplementary role. However, it is my favorite method, and if I am confined to using just one means for learning about the organization, I choose the interview because it gives high-quality information that can be probed in detail in a face-to-face relationship with the respondent. If several means of collecting data are to be used in the audit, my advice is still to *start with the interview*.

ADVANTAGES OF INTERVIEWS

Collecting data through in-depth interviews has several advantages, which are reviewed in the following sections.

Familiarity. • In conducting interviews, the auditor develops a first-hand familiarity with the people and their work processes. In a real sense, one gets to know the organization in ways not possible through any written media. Furthermore, the interview often permits observations of the organization. For example, in a paper converting plant, a section manager once took me on a tour of his work area as we talked, and the tour enabled me to refine my appreciation of what he did and how he did it.

Fuller discussion. • The face-to-face interview allows a much more detailed discussion of topic areas. People just naturally will talk more than they will write, and the mark of a good interviewer is the ability to probe until a complete description is obtained and until the auditor really understands the interviewee's thinking. While there are time limitations for interviews, a large amount of material can be probed in a short time so that the auditor gains more in-depth knowledge than through other techniques.

Serendipity of topics. • Every auditor should have a basic interview guide to follow; nevertheless, we have found that good open questions often secure answers about areas that could never have been anticipated in designing a questionnaire. It is often wise to conclude an interview with the question, "Is there anything that we should have talked about that I have not asked?" I get some of my best information about unanticipated idiosyncracies of the organization that way.

Interviewee reward. • Generally, face-to-face interactions are rated as being more pleasing than written questionnaires, so the interview contains an intrinsic motivator. People like to talk about the things that are important to them, and frequently the organization does not provide a regular opportunity for this. Recently, a manager told me about a very significant problem in his unit. When asked about it, he said that he had never discussed the problem with anyone at the company. Yet, he felt comfortable having someone listen as he thought the problem through aloud.

Less time-bound. • One major advantage of interviews over written formats is the fact that they can grow, be refined, and change in light of new information. This is not to suggest that the same questions or topic areas should not be asked of everyone; initially, they should. However, we often get information from one source that needs to be checked out with other people. Furthermore, interviews give less of a snapshot view of an organization, because they can be scheduled over a longer period of time.

LIMITATIONS OF INTERVIEWS

No data-gathering instrument is perfect, and interviews are only as good as the interviewers make them. Furthermore, interviews have three inherent disadvantages.

Time. • Interviews are time consuming, and this makes them expensive. Not only is there the cost of the interviewer's time, but it is also expensive to take employees away from their jobs to be interviewed. In fact, in an audit of a university, cost considerations precluded the interviewing of most employees in food services. They were paid on an hourly basis, and the administration was unwilling to pay them to come in early or stay late just to be interviewed.

Analysis. • Information from interviews is more difficult to code, analyze, and interpret. Our society is so keyed to numerical data that we sometimes doubt the validity of anything that cannot be put into some numerical scale. How many people have to mention the same problem or strength for it to be considered significant? The interpretive skills of the auditor are tested here. Sometimes a person in an important position may present a good overview of a problem that others have not even mentioned, and it would be foolhardy to disregard it simply on the basis of numbers.

Limited to perceptual data. • Interview data basically comprise perceptual reports of how the interviewee sees the organization, and these perceptions often need to be verified. As was pointed out in Chapter 1, Odiorne's research (Filley, 1978, p. 74) has demonstrated that when a manager and a subordinate were each asked to describe the subordinate's job, they disagreed on an average of 25 percent of the things they mentioned. Is it any wonder that there are many different reactions to, and impressions of, the communication in an organization? Also, people's perceptions are sometimes inaccurate. For example, we had a number of people in an airline complain that they had not had an appraisal within the last year. We checked this complaint and found signed statements by several of the employees that indicated that they had indeed had appraisals. We did not know what had happened in those appraisals, but there was evidence that the complainers were apparently incorrect with respect to the time frame.

SCHEDULE TWO ROUNDS OF INTERVIEWS

Since one advantage of collecting data by interviews is that they are less time-bound, auditors can maximize this feature by scheduling two different rounds of interviews. These rounds are separate entities that may occur days or even weeks apart in order to tap developments in the organization. This schedule gives a perspective *over time.* Since changes often occur rapidly during an audit, it is useful to avoid a one-time snapshot based on one group of interviews or one group of questionnaires. One may also learn of some newly developed programs introduced after the first data were collected. It must be remembered that the audit itself is an intervention that focuses attention and perhaps motivates changes in the organization. In addition, having two rounds of interviews is particularly useful if multiple data collection methods are used in the audit. Data from the other instruments can be checked in the second round.

The preparation for each round culminates in the preparation of an *interview guide,* that is, a list of questions to be asked of all respondents. The purpose of the guide is to achieve consistency across interviews. Since there are two separate rounds of interviews, different guides are illustrated here in

Exhibits 4.1, 4.2, and 4.3. In the following discussion, each round of interviews and each interview guide is analyzed in terms of purpose, agenda, questions, and structure.

EXHIBIT 4.1   Exploratory Interview Guide

---

1. [Auditor: Introduce yourself and explain the purpose of the interview.]
2. Identify name and position of the interviewee.
3. Describe your position in the organization.
   a. What are your chief responsibilities and duties?
   b. With whom or with what positions do you regularly communicate?
   c. What factors tend to facilitate your effectiveness on the job? Please give me an example.
   d. What inhibits your effectiveness?
4. Describe the way decisions are made in your organization.
   a. What decisions do you normally make?
   b. What information do you need to make these decisions?
   c. Are these formal or informal policies that determine how you get the information?
5. Describe the organization's/unit's primary objectives for this year.
   a. How does the organization know when it has done a good or bad job? What are the criteria for success?
   b. What are your own personal objectives?
   c. What communication strategies do you use to achieve them?
6. What kinds of communication are necessary for you to have with other work units? How well does this inter-unit communication work?
7. Describe the formal channels through which you typically receive information. What kinds of information do you tend to receive? How often?
8. Describe the informal channels through which you typically receive information.
   a. What kind of information do you hear?
   b. How active are informal channels?
9. What are the major communication strengths of the organization? Be specific.
10. What are the major communication weaknesses of the organization?
11. What do you see as the greatest unresolved problem of this organization?
12. What would you like to see done to improve communication here?
   a. Why hasn't it been done already?
   b. What are the major obstacles?
   c. If you had a suggestion to improve communication, how would you make it?
13. When conflict occurs, how is it resolved? What normally causes conflict here? Give examples.
14. Describe the communication relationship you have with
   a. your immediate supervisor.
   b. top management.

    c. coworkers.

    d. subordinates, if applicable.

15. How do most people react to their managers?
16. How would you evaluate your manager in terms of:
    a. openness to new ideas?
    b. willingness to share information?
    c. ability to clarify expectations?
    d. ability to coordinate the work in the unit?
17. How do you get ideas about how your superiors feel about your work?
18. How would you evaluate the communication from top management?
19. How would you describe the general communication climate here?
20. How often do you receive information of little value? Give an example.
    a. How often are you overloaded with information?
    b. How often do you feel you get too little information?
21. How does your physical work setting here affect your communication?
22. How does communication here affect your job satisfaction? Is this typical for others?
23. How does communication here affect your productivity? Is this typical for others?
24. If you were to advise me as to what to look for to get the greatest insight into this organization, what would that be?
25. Describe the chain of command in this organization and how it operates.
26. What criteria for effective communication are used in this organization? How do these compare with the way people talk about communication?
27. Is there anything that I have left out that I should have included?

EXHIBIT 4.2   Management Level Follow-Up Interview Guide

1. Generally when we do an analysis of an organization, we find that people can identify some strengths and some weaknesses for the organization.
   a. What do you see as the strengths of ACME?
   b. What do you see as the weaknesses of communication here?
   c. What strengths do you think the employees will mention?
   d. What weaknesses will they mention?
   e. How accurate do you think their assessment is? Why?
2. A number of our questions deal with perceptions of upper management. What perceptions do you think the employees have of upper management? Why?
3. What is the communication role of the supervisors? How are they trained? Evaluated? What particular communication problems do they have? How do you think they are perceived by the employees?
4. In other organizations, we have found that employees desire increased opportunities to communicate upward on such matters as suggestions for improvement. Do you think that we will find this here? Why? How do you feel about this?

5. How timely is the information exchanged between units and departments within? What, if anything, could be done to alleviate any particular problems in this regard?
6. Generally, how do employees get information that affects them personally? For example, how do they find out about new policies?
7. Many employees often indicate a desire for more evaluative and informative feedback through face-to-face communication. What keeps this from being given? How does this affect productivity? Job satisfaction?
8. One suggestion we have encountered is that new policies should be programmed into the computers immediately. Is there any reason why this cannot be done?
9. The ratings for communication in ACME vary greatly among employees. The average rating, however, is not as high as it might be. Why do you think this is?
10. Have there been any significant changes in the communication patterns in this organization recently?
11. If you could make any changes you wanted in ACME's communication, what would you change?
12. Are there additional areas that we ought to cover?
13. What do you think will happen as a result of this audit?

EXHIBIT 4.3   Follow-Up Interview Guide

I. For the write-ups, please group your answers not only according to the question (1, 2, 3, etc.), but also according to the following classifications: Administration, Supervisory Classified, and Nonsupervisory Classified.
II. The introduction is very important because many people want to know how they were selected for the interview. I recommend that you take care of this in the introduction by explaining the following:
   A. Purpose: follow-up to check earlier perceptions and ask more pointed questions, to explore more about strengths and weaknesses. Selection of interviewees was determined by a desire to interview some of the same people in order to check earlier information and to interview others that would give a broader base than was had before; that is, to make certain all areas of the organization are represented.
   B. How information will be used: guarantee anonymity but state that data will help to explain some of the results.
III. The following questions are designed as a broad guide. In some cases, the respondents' answers will make you want to use them in a different sequence. You can also make whatever adaptions in the guide that you believe are needed after the initial interviews.
   1. Have there been any significant changes in your organization's communication patterns recently?

2. In our survey we found very positive reactions to some questions and identified areas that needed improving. The ratings of your organization's overall communication efforts were not as high as they might have been. Why do you think this occurred? How would you explain this?

3. What is motivating people in the organization now? What are their principal concerns? How is the communication here relating to and perhaps satisfying these concerns and needs?

4. Let's look at you as the receiver of information. We'd like to ask you questions about five areas of information that you might receive.
   a. Questions:
      (1) What information in these areas would you like to receive?
      (2) How would you get it? From whom?
      (3) Why aren't you getting it now?
   b. Areas:
      (1) Progress in job and how you are being judged.
      (2) Organizational policies.
      (3) How organization's decisions are made that affect you.
      (4) Promotion and advancement opportunities.
      (5) Important new service or program development.

5. Now, let's discuss you as the sender of information.
   a. How do you know what you need to send to others? How do you make the decision to initiate communication? Do you receive many requests for information?
   b. Do you find yourself requesting information to do your job? What kind? Why is this not sent routinely?
   c. Is there any way in which you do not get to participate in an evaluation of superiors or supervisors? Would you find this useful? How high up would you like to evaluate? What would happen if you could?

6. In terms of upward and downward flow of communication, what kinds of filtering are planned in the system? Relate this to the identification of the chief loci of responsibility in the organization.

7. What happens when you send upward communication to your
   a. immediate supervisor?
   b. middle management?
   c. top management?
   d. Where is the greatest lag or block? Why?

8. When there are blocks to communication, what kinds of formal techniques do you use to get around them? What kinds of informal techniques get the best results for you?

9. How much do you use the informal channels? How are they structured? How do people tap them if they want to?

10. Let's turn to your evaluation of other communication sources. What should top management be communicating that they are not?

11. How would you evaluate your immediate supervisor as a communicator?
12. How would you evaluate your departmental meetings in terms of
    a. information?
    b. decisions?
    c. frequency?
13. Are there important differences for you between communicating with employees in unit x and communicating with employees from unit y?
14. How do you get the information needed to do your job? What kinds of information do you need to know is available but do not necessarily need to receive all the time? How should it be made available?
15. What channels are best at keeping you abreast of the day-to-day operations and happenings in the organization?
16. How does the organization reward excellence in
    a. productivity?
    b. service?
    c. research?
17. Some people have said that there is a need for greater coordination within the organization. How do you feel about this? Are there some examples that you can share?
18. What do you think we are going to find as a result of conducting the audit? What is going to happen as a result of our report?
19. Are there questions that we have not asked that should be expected?

Purpose

The first round of interviews familiarizes the auditors with the organization, its people, and its communication as a task process. Exploratory in nature, these interviews help accomplish two basic things. First, they provide a general orientation to the organization that lays a foundation for everything else done in the audit. From this beginning, the auditors begin to sense what the communication problems might be. Second, they identify areas that need to be probed further, either on a questionnaire or in a second round of interviews. In other words, the results of the first round stimulate the desire for more information. In general, these findings cannot be as accurate in analyzing the organization as the later ones.

Whereas the first round of interviews are exploratory, the second round can be more issue-oriented. For that reason, several weeks should elapse before the second round is scheduled. In fact, the explanatory potential of the second round of interviews is so great that I recommend waiting until all other information collected from questionnaires and networks or other techniques has been processed. New discoveries prompt new questions, and the interview guide need not be static: let it grow with the understanding of the organization. For example, answers given on questionnaires often tell *how* people react but not *why* they react that way. I may be able to say from questionnaire data that 44 percent of the respondents do not think their meetings are productive, and a second round of interviews can help me enrich my understanding by probing why people are dissatisfied with meetings. In one audit the following question was asked:

> In our survey we found some very positive reactions to some questions and identified some areas that need improving. The general ratings of your organization's overall communication efforts were not as high as they might have been. Why do you think this occurred?

Note that the initial statement was complimentary enough to allay any defensive reactions. It also gave a rather general expression of findings without really breaking any news to the interviewee. But it did set the stage for probing the rationale behind a fact discovered among the answers to the questionnaire. Such revelations must be done carefully. At all costs, you should avoid revealing any information whose source could be identified. In an audit of a public utility, I used an example to get a better understanding of the operation. The manager responded, "Oh yes, and I know exactly who told you that." He happened to be right, but there would have been no justification for my acknowledging it.

Another audit team typified the interview development process perfectly. When they finished the first round of interviews in a chemical plant, they wrote a summary of their findings, which suggested new areas to probe. They concluded:

> In the next round of interviews we want to probe: (1) how jobs really are advertised here, (2) whether the rates of suggestions have actually increased or decreased, and (3) the communication impact of putting in a new plant. Another point of interest concerns vocabulary. In several interviews the phrases *efficient* and *mature operation* occurred with an unusual frequency. We should explore their origins.

Agenda

Differences in purpose between the two rounds of interviews are reflected in some agenda differences. The questions to be asked depend on the audit's objectives or the issues uncovered.

In the first round, target the most useful information for a general orientation. In doing this, the guidelines for focusing an audit discussed in

Chapter 3 are particularly useful. Preparing the first round is relatively easy, because there are some communication areas that usually need to be explored: the people with whom one communicates, the ways one gets the information needed to do the job, communication relationships, reactions to various informal and formal channels, perceived strengths and weaknesses of the unit, the relationship of communication to organizational goals, decision processes, resolution of conflict, and suggestions for improvement. The topics may vary somewhat, but Exhibit 4.1 presents the questions that were used in an audit of an airline and a university.

The number of possible questions is too great for one interview guide, but these suggestions can be tailored to any given organization. Notice that the questions are largely open-ended, explore all levels and aspects of the organization, are oriented to both the past and the future, ask for behavioral examples as well as general perceptions, and ask the respondent to propose solutions for some of the problems.

In the second round, target specific areas that will fill voids in understanding the organization. For illustrative topics, look at the follow-up interview guides in Exhibits 4.2 and 4.3. In the audit reported in Exhibit 4.3, a different guide was prepared for managers and nonmanagers. The one reported here is for the managers.

Note the references in the guides to such topics as perceptions of upper management, evaluative feedback, and organizational rewards. These were areas that had already been pinpointed as problematic in the first round of interviews and on a questionnaire. It was therefore important to get additional information to help interpret the results already obtained. Another especially important question in Exhibit 4.2 was question 12, "What do you think is going to happen as a result of this audit?" Conducting this audit caused employees to talk about the whole process, and it was instructive to discover how the managers viewed it. It was also useful to discover what obstacles managers perceived to be in the way of the auditors. In other words, this question probed an actual case study—the communication associated with an audit.

Developing an interview guide is not difficult, but it is very important. Three additional points should be considered when using the final product.

First, *the questions should be well thought out so that, of all the questions possible, these are the ones that will give the kind of information needed.* The interview guide identifies the target areas to be discussed. Just like in questionnaires, the questions in the interview need to be refined to assure that they are asking for useful information.

Second, the guide is a means of achieving consistency in the interviews. In each round of interviews, respondents should be asked the same basic questions. Since many audits involve multiple interviewers, the guide allows them to ask the same questions in the same way of all respondents.

Third, since interviews in an audit often turn into enjoyable conversations, the order in which the questions are asked need not be important. It is important, however, that all the questions are asked.

These guidelines do not imply that interviewers are at all restricted. In fact, a good interviewer is always attuned to the possibility of unsought relevant information. Furthermore, some real differences in the questions for managers and nonmanagers are likely. Although the basic guide is designed to let auditors obtain comparative information, it is possible to adapt the guides so that new information is supplementary as well as comparative. Exhibit 4.4 contains part of a guide that was particularly adapted to different types of managers. The questions are grouped under certain headings to direct the interviewer's attention.

EXHIBIT 4.4   Partial Guide for Second-Round Interviews

Preliminary Information to Double-Check
1. Some subordinates mentioned a supervisor-employer committee that originated ideas and presented them to a top manager. This is very ambiguous. Check it.
2. Someone was fired, so several people expressed concern over their jobs. How general is this concern?
3. The information about an upcoming move seems to change hourly. How is this circulated?
4. There seems to be wide differences in the company usage of performance appraisals.

INTERVIEW GUIDE
TO: Two Specific Top Managers: X and Y
1. When you have to make strategic decisions, what managers do you typically bring in?
2. For what type of decisions do you need information from _____ in order to decide?
3. What type of information do you need from _____ in order to make these decisions?
4. How much weight or value do you attach to their input?
5. What is the role of the marketing committee? How do you think the rest of the committee perceives it?
6. Who is on the marketing committee?

To All Managers:
1. How much input do you have in decisions made by upper management?
2. In what type of situation(s) is your input necessary or important?
3. What information is needed from you in order to make organizational decisions?
4. How much weight does your input carry?

5. How important are managerial meetings? Why?
6. How important should they be?
7. How many managerial meetings are there now?
8. How many should there be? Is that enough?

To All Managers: FEEDBACK AND PERFORMANCE
9. What do you say or do when you're not satisfied with your subordinates' day-to-day performance?
   Can you give me an example?
   How often do you do this?
10. What do you say or do when you're satisfied with your subordinates' day-to-day performance?
11. Do you use definite criteria in judging their levels of performance?
12. Are your employees aware of these criteria?
    How are they aware? (feedback, job descriptions, "work" contracts)
13. Do you conduct an annual performance review with your subordinates?
    What criteria are used?
    Describe it.
    (Probe for an example.)
14. Does the criteria used in the annual performance review match the criteria that you use on a day-to-day basis?

Questions

Just as the interview's agenda reflects the purpose, the questions should reflect the agenda. Therefore, there may be some important differences between the exploratory and follow-up interviews. Nevertheless, some general guidelines apply to both.

1. *Ask open questions primarily.* Open questions put few restrictions on how the interviewee answers. They are designed to get people to talk at length so that they will give in-depth information concerning what and how they think about the organization. Two examples are, "Tell me about your job" and "What are the communication strengths of the organization?" Neither question restricts the range of response. By contrast, closed quetsions restrict the respondents in terms of length of response as well as the topics covered by the answer. Typically, any question that calls for a yes–no or agree–disagree response is closed. So are all multiple-choice questions. Although closed questions are useful for classifying people's answers on questionnaries so that they are easy to analyze, they are less useful in interviews, where the objective is to get as much information as possible and to identify the range of responses for the organization.

In a sense, the first round of interviews is like a fishing expedition, since the auditor casts about for whatever preliminary information can be "caught." Open questions are well suited to this purpose because they help discover the employee's priorities, frame of reference, depth of knowledge, and unstructured perceptions of the situation. Furthermore, they give respondents a degree of freedom in structuring an answer and often permit a catharsis to take place as the employees get some things off their chests. Of particular importance here is the fact that open questions permit respondents to identify the areas most important to them. For example, if you were interviewing workers about how organizational communication affects their productivity, there may be five or six specific areas you would want to pinpoint. Rather than beginning with specific questions about each area, you could first ask the general question, "How does communication affect your productivity?" The answers may target important areas not on your list and give you a better insight to the respondents' thinking than you could have achieved had you asked specific questions.

Closed questions, on the other hand, do have a place in the interviews. When asking for very specific answers in prescribed formats, they save time, are easy to tabulate, and secure answers that can be classified without necessitating explanation. One effective technique is to get the interviewer to commit to an opinion and then to ask open questions as follow-up so that he or she will have to explain this commitment. For example, in a recent audit I asked, "Would you say the communication climate in this organization is better, the same, or worse compared to the climate in your previous work organizations?" Once the respondent had answered, I asked, "Why?" The short answer to the closed question led to a general discussion of the criteria used to make the comparison.

2. *Draw the interviewee out; probe skillfully.* Sometimes possible probes can be included on the interviewee guide. Knowing how exhaustive the answers should be is a problem, for you could spend much longer than you do for the entire interview on just one question. Therefore, the degree of probing is a matter of judgment. It is important to remember, however, that this interview is a new experience for most people. They have never dissected their jobs in the way the auditor has asked them to do. Therefore, it takes time and prompting to secure a good overview.

3. *Avoid focusing on the negative.* Many auditors fall into the trap of wanting to hear only about the problems since the reason for an audit may be to improve the organization in some way. It is vitally important to develop the positive points as well. These areas should be probed in as much detail as the negative ones, because the auditors needs to understand in detail how the communication system works.

4. *Adapt questions to specific levels or even to specific people.* I often modify the guides for managers, so I search for different information from nonmanagers. Or I may have a special guide adapted for a key source in the organization. This is particularly important in the follow-up interviews.

5. *Do not reveal what you are finding out about the organization.* Sometimes people will ask what the audit team is finding, but a response that "employees' answers vary a lot" will be sufficient.

Many times respondents intentionally or unintentionally try to make the interventionist violate some of his basic rules of professional conduct. Respondents may try to induce the interventionist to tell them what others have said in previous interviews. Some do this quite directly. For example, "Tell me, before I begin, what sorts of things the boys have been telling you." Still others are more indirect: "I bet you have found the boys quite helpful, heh, Doc? They tell you everything?" In both cases, the researcher may respond, "The people are most cooperative, and I am learning quite a bit; however, as I promised you, I cannot discuss what others have said any more than I will tell others what you say." When one woman said, "I bet a lot of people have been complaining about wages," the researcher answered, "People have certainly been cooperative in expressing their feelings." In this way, the interventionist prevents himself from being induced to quote other people (Argyris, 1970, p. 301).

6. *Let the guide grow; do not let it become static.* An audit is not a scientific study in which everything must be standardized. Although the basic guide should be followed, there are certainly reasons for exploring new information as it is uncovered. It may also be important to add new questions or to modify those that are not yielding much information.

Structure

Arranging the questions as an interview guide develops a structure for the interview. Several guidelines for accomplishing this follow.

1. *Begin each interview with an orientation.* Respondents' reactions to being interviewed may vary considerably, with some welcoming the opportunity and others being suspicious of the whole endeavor. Nevertheless, all will appreciate an overview explaining what you are trying to accomplish, and a good orientation can be a strong motivator to participation. Basically, the interview orientation should include each of the following.

First, introduce yourself. You are a stranger asking people to divulge information that affects their livelihood. Do your best to establish your credibility from the outset. Without overwhelming people with details, allude to your expertise and perhaps indicate who has contracted you to conduct the audit. This should be done even if the audit process has been well publicized.

Second, describe the general purpose of the audit. It is here that you can explain to the interviewees just how much of an impact they can have and how important their participation is.

Third, assure them of confidentiality. Be sensitive to any nervousness on the respondents' part, because some people require more assurance than others. Reluctance to say much or, in particular, to offer any criticisms is often a sign of nervousness, fear, or a lack of trust.

Fourth, state briefly how the interviewees were selected. One need not go into great detail; a general comment is usually sufficient to let them know they were not singled out for any negative reason.

Fifth, explain briefly how you would like to conduct the interview. Setting time constraints or emphasizing that you wish to focus on communication can be useful in letting participants know what your expectations are.

Sixth, suggest ways in which the information may ultimately be used. Many employees "hate exercises that are fruitless and that waste time and have made many complaints about either never hearing the results of surveys or never seeing anything occur as a result of them" (Downs, Smeyak, and Martin, 1980). It is helpful if you can promise them some kind of report.

Here is a sample orientation, following the six guidelines described previously.

Hello, I'm Cal Downs. I'm President of Communication Management, Inc., and you may have already heard that we are here to conduct a communication audit of ACME. Have you already filled out a questionnaire or heard about others being interviewed?

From the beginning, we have planned two rounds of interviews, and the purpose of the second round of interviews is to clarify and to probe some of the information already obtained in the first group of interviews and the questionnaire. We like to double-check our information to make sure that we detect as much as possible about the organization.

In order to do this, we don't need to talk to everyone. We simply select people to interview who represent all the diverse units and activities in the organizations. We chose to interview you because we felt that you were in a good position to give us some additional insight into the organizational communication, and, although we have questions about several areas, that you'll volunteer as much information as possible to give us the best picture possible of the organization. As was the case with the other interviewees, anything that we discuss will be strictly confidential. We'll give a final report to management, but we never identify individuals. Now, before I ask my questions, do you have any questions about the general audit process?

2. *Start with the job.* People find it easy and enjoyable to talk about their jobs, so opening the interview with a discussion of the job motivates conversation. This is also the most logical place to begin for the interviewer who needs to know how a particular employee fits into the total system. Finding this out at the beginning of the interview permits one to judge how much information is needed from this individual and how to interpret the answers.

3. *Probe more general areas before getting to specific ones.* Such a funnel system allows you to get a better idea of the respondent's frame of reference. For example, it is useful to say, "Tell me about the communication on the job" before asking specific questions about interdepartmental linkages or performance appraisals. A more general, somewhat ambiguous question such as this one does not structure the respondents' thought processes, and it may give you relevant information that would not be obtained through more specific questions.

4. *Do not permit the guide to restrict the interview.* The purpose of the guide is to ensure consistent coverage of topic areas. Sometimes there are strategies behind the order in which the questions are asked. For example, it is believed that asking questions about strengths first may make talking about weaknesses later seem less threatening. If a respondent starts talking about weaknesses first, however, it may be useful to pursue it. Or if a respondent starts the interview talking about a topic covered in question 8, there is nothing wrong in varying the order of the questions.

INTERVIEWEE SELECTION

Every employee is a potentially good source of information about the organization. Unless the organization is very small, however, auditors will not need to interview everyone to get an accurate picture. Since interviews are costly in terms of time and money, the selection of interviewees is a very important step in the audit. And there is an "art" to making these decisions, for there are no formulas that tell one exactly how many people or exactly who should be interviewed. The general guideline is to interview enough people from enough areas of the organization to give a comprehensive view of the communication. Nevertheless, the following considerations may be helpful in making these decisions.

In small organizations, it is both posssible and desirable to interview everyone. This prevents anyone from feeling left out. Furthermore, members of small organizations may occupy one-of-a-kind roles, making their individual contributions unique. Examples of organizations in which we have interviewed everyone include a Pontiac dealership of twenty-four, an alumni association administration office of forty-five people, a university department of twenty-five, a savings and loan institution of sixty-seven, and a government office of twenty-four people. The size of these organizations made interviewing everyone easy.

When there are more than fifty employees, you may normally elect to use a sample. Sampling is a scientific method of selecting people to participate in your audit. The actual size of the sample may be influenced by whether the interview is the only audit tool or whether it is being supplemented by some other means of data collection. To make generalizations about the total organization on the basis of a sample, it helps to make the sample (1) representative, (2) random, and (3) stratified.

Make representative sample of organization

A *representative* sample is one in which the respondents were selected so carefully that whatever you would have found out by interviewing everyone can be found out from the sample; that is, no significant new information would be learned if you interviewed people other than those in the sample. You need enough people to confirm trends, but most interviewers are able to recognize that point at which they are merely hearing the same thing over again from different interviewees.

To be representative, there must be a sufficient number of people interviewed, and the size of the percentages will vary with the size of the organization. It is common practice to select 10 to 20 percent of an organization that employs 150 to 200 people. If there are 1,000 employees, you might be content with 100 or less. Consulting the sampling table in Chapter 2 may offer some guidelines. If the interview is being used to supplement the use of questionnaires, however, you may not need to have as many participants as you would if the interview were your only data-collecting tool.

Randomize the sample

Some randomization of the sample is usually desirable. Randomness means that every employee has an equal chance of being included in the sample. The purpose of randomizing the sample is to eliminate potential bias that might occur if you were to select people on any other basis. Randomization can be achieved by putting all the names in a hat and drawing out the desired number or by picking from a list of employees using a Table of Random Numbers, found at the back of any statistics book.

Sometimes managers in the organization can be helpful in selecting a sample, but be careful that they do not led you to one group or one type of individual. A vice-president once tried to pick my interviewees by saying, "Interview Hatfield, Penley, and Brown, but don't interview Williams or Barge because they won't tell you the truth anyway." The vice-president probably thought he was being helpful, but had we taken his advice the results might have been skewed toward his point of view.

Include representatives from all units

There are limits to the wisdom of choosing only random samples. For example, a graduate student was auditing an organization that had four divisions. He took all the names and tried to take a random sample. When he finished, he noticed that one of the divisions had been badly slighted, and three of the four managers were not included. Somehow these oversights had to be corrected. An audit is a time for all sides and all segments to be represented, and one way of doing this is to choose a *stratified* sample.

The stratified sample ensures that every segment of the organization is included, and this is one of the most important points to remember. The number from any segment is less significant; it may or may not be proportional to its size in the organization. Consider the following examples:

1. Survey on a College Campus. The interviewers selected 50 freshmen, 50 sophomores, 50 juniors, and 50 seniors. The proportions were not based on percentage in each class, but rather on how many might give equal weight to each classification. The sample, however, was made proportional on the basis of sex. Since the enrollment was 40 percent female, 40 percent of the sample was female.

2. Audit in an Airline. There were three main divisions of unequal size in this unit. The total unit included 125 people, and the divisions included 60, 42, and 18 people. Because it was convenient, 40 people were interviewed. Interviewees were selected randomly from each division, but the numbers were not proportional to the size of the unit. The unit of 18 people probably was overrepresented because the manager wanted to make certain that enough of his people were included.

3. Audit in an Equipment Plant. All the people were members of the same unit but the job classification fell into four categories: engineers, designers, technicians, staff. There was initial evidence of some communication difficulty across these jobs, so people were

selected from each job; 26 of the 67 people were interviewed. I tried to interview a third of each category, but the fact that I accepted volunteers skewed the relative percentages a bit.

4. Audit in a Food Processing Plant. Employees were divided into three shifts. While most workers are employed on the first shift, it is still very important to interview people on other shifts. In this case, it was discovered that the style of organization, its problems, and its communication changed from shift to shift.

Stratification is an important way of gathering a sample that represents the whole organization, but it is not necessary to balance *all* the characteristics of a population, as the pollsters do. There are many different kinds of characteristics, and auditors have to choose among them. The most obvious characteristic for stratification is the unit in which one works. However, if I had a sense that male–female communication was a problem, I would stratify according to gender; or if I believed engineers and designers were having a problem, I would stratify according to job description. Ultimately, there is no substitute for your own sensitivity in choosing the sample. As was indicated earlier in this chapter, it is often necessary to explain how you selected your sample, and you may need to explain the need for stratifying the interviewees.

Interview key people

Generally, managers have more communicative contacts by nature of their roles in the organization. Therefore, it is highly desirable to interview all people in key positions. In fact, top management is a good place to begin to get a good overview; these managers have a lot to tell and can often pin-point problem areas.

Another reason for interviewing key people is that they normally want to participate and feel slighted if they are not included. I learned this quickly in an audit of a public utility. Since the president had hired me to conduct the audit, I thought of him as a person to whom I was to give the report and not as a person who wanted to contribute to the report. My perception of him was wrong, as a subordinate manager wisely counselled in the middle of the audit.

Do not overlook any key people. Interview as many heads of units as you can, and do not worry whether this part of the sample is random or not.

Invite volunteers

Many employees will jump at the chance to "make a contribution," tell you "the way it really is," or get "something off their chests." Obviously, volunteers think that they have valuable information to share, and frequently they are pleased that someone will take the time to listen.

In some cases, volunteers are a special breed who have an ax to grind, but this is not always true. At any rate, special consideration should be given to determine how widespread their concerns are. One always needs to be aware that there are some individual misfits in the organization whose perceptions are not shared by others. In an audit of a university, for example, we discovered that several volunteers came from a special clique in the faculty and their views did not reflect the opinions of most of the other faculty members.

Volunteers are useful, but how does one get them? There are a number of ways. In the audit of an engineering plant, the manager of each unit sent around a sign-up sheet explaining the reason for the interviews and asking people to sign up if they were interested. A secretary then made out a schedule. In another instance, employees were given a phone number to call if they wanted to volunteer. In an audit of an airline, respondents were given a space on the questionnaire to check if they wished to be interviewed. Finally, many contacts have come through other people. We have asked interviewees to name other workers that might want to be interviewed. It is not the most direct method, but it is sometimes beneficial.

Allow for contingencies

Accessibility is a key factor in selecting interviewees. Not everyone is equally available because of vacations, shifts, special work assignments, or crises. Some problems can be overcome if interviewers will make themselves accessible at 1 A.M. for the third shift, or after work, or on a day during another week. Do what you can.

On the other hand, it may not always be possible to include some of the people that you would like. Some people have refused for personal reasons. Others could not be interviewed because of a work schedule. In one audit the people who worked in the dining room could not be interviewed during mealtimes, and the organization would not pay them for an addditional hour for an interview. Therefore, they simply were not included in the audit.

SCHEDULE TIME AND PLACE

Whenever possible, it is wise to have a liaison in the organization to set up schedules and contact people. Whoever takes this assignment, however, should develop a complete timetable well in advance so that interviewees will know exactly when they are scheduled and how much time the interviews will take. This allows them to plan their schedules.

The length of the interview can vary widely, depending on the individual. However, in setting up the schedule, thirty minutes to an hour is appropriate for nonmanagers, and two hours is not too long for managers. Furthermore, it is wise to schedule breaks, as this time can give some elasticity to the schedule. Since one cannot forecast the length of each interview, it is better to allow too much time than to cut an interview short because you ran over on another or to play "catch-up" in the scheduling. Sometimes, for people who have flexible schedules, it is possible to have the liaison let the employees know that they are going to be interviewed on a certain day without setting formal appointments.

Work flow is another consideration in scheduling. Arrange optimal times when people can be most receptive to your interviews. For example, this may preclude Monday morning appointments for many managers because they typically have meetings to arrange the week. Similarly, the end of a shift is not a particularly good time for shift workers, because since they often are tired and eager to get home, they may try to shorten the interview.

Where the interview takes place is negotiable. In general, the location should be selected to assure privacy, to stimulate free communication, and to be convenient for the interviewee. Rather than dictating the location, it is wise to give the employee an option. For example, a manager may simply be asked, "Where would you like to have the interview?" Most employees probably will prefer their own offices, but I have interviewed some managers who arranged off-site locations to avoid interruptions.

One option is to set up a permanent office and have the interviewees come there. This arrangement saves the auditors some travel time while taking the respondents out of their immediate work environments to a place where they can relax and talk. When this option is used, it is particularly crucial to stay on schedule. People are reluctant to stand and wait when they could be working.

CONDUCT THE INTERVIEWS

Good planning is necessary for collecting accurate, useful information about the organization. However, the test of the planning comes when the interviews actually begin. The following sections discuss some of the most important considerations for conducting the interviews.

1. *Select competent interviewers who can be trusted.* Interview time is a precious commodity, and the interviewers need to use it wisely. You also need to be able to trust that the interviewers actually conduct the prescribed interviews. This is not often a problem, but a friend did have trouble when an interviewer reported interviews that never actually took place. Thus it is useful to validate that the interview did indeed occur.

2. *Train interviewers to use the interview guide.* Win acceptance for the interview questions by explaining the relevance of each. It is also important that interviewers are so familiar with the guide that they can ensure all questions will be asked even if the order is not followed. In fact, I encourage interviewers to let the interaction flow like a conversation without requiring a definite order to be followed. This maximizes flexibility and prevents the interview from becoming too stilted.

3. *Set a nonthreatening climate.* There is healthy tension between keeping the interview businesslike and on target and allowing it to be an enjoyable experience. Set the tone by explaining the purpose behind the interview but raising questions in a conversational way.

4. *Probe thoroughly.* Since one of the inherent advantages of the interview is the opportunity to probe for in-depth information, skill in probing is the interviewer's ultimate art. Although the interview must not become an interrogation, most answers do need some time to be developed. Therefore, interviewers should be trained to ask both directive and nondirective probes.

Directive probes ask pointed questions. Elaboration is needed when the answer is incomplete. Clarification is useful when terms or concepts are unclear. Repetition is needed when interviewees give a verbal response that does not really address the question. Confrontation in a nonaggressive way may be necessary when people seem to contradict themselves. Sometimes when the inconsistency is pointed out, they can clarify their positions quite well.

Nondirective probes, on the other hand, are merely designed to keep the employee talking. They include a number of nonverbal behaviors such as maintaining eye contact, nodding one's head, or leaning forward with a look of interest. They also include verbal expression such as "I see" and "uh-huh." One of my favorites, however, is the internal summary, in which you summarize for the person what you think you have covered and what conclusions you think have been drawn. This technique gives the respondent the opportunity to agree or disagree with you, providing valuable reactions to your summary.

5. *Motivate the interviewees.* A motivating introduction to the interview is absolutely necessary, and you must establish your credibility from the start. Normally, this can be accomplished by introducing yourself and explaining what your objectives are and how the information will be used. Assuring the respondent of confidentiality usually is necessary. I have had a few people walk in and announce "I came in here not to communicate" or "I asked not to be here." Whereas such people present a challenge, the reaction should whet your appetite, because these people usually have a reason for being defen-

sive that might be important. Getting their unique information can enrich the auditor's picture of the organization.

6. *Anticipate problems.* Interviewers can also be prepared to meet certain occasional problems. One common issue is whether or not to explain a question or word. An explanation can sometimes "lead" interviewees into certain areas; at other times, it may be perfectly safe to give examples or explanations. For example, recently I asked people in an audit how involved they were in their jobs. This was a very abstract question, and several people asked what I meant by "involved." In this particular company, I politely explained that I did not want to influence their answers by defining the term and that they could define it as they wished. They would be telling me a lot about the plant if they discussed their definitions. As this example demonstrates, it is sometimes wise to turn the question back to the person who asked it; however, one should make certain that this does not become a game.

Another problem is coping with the silent or overly talkative employee. In some ways the latter presents the greatest problem. Although many employees are delighted to talk about their jobs, you may ruin your entire interview schedule if you listen too long. Be polite, but never lose control over the process.

A third problem is the difficulty of remaining objective. Interviewers, being human, often find it easy to take sides and may find themselves expressing an evaluative reaction to what the respondent is saying. In general, the interviewer needs to remember that the interview is basically an information-gathering process, and neutrality and objectivity should guide their responses.

Finally, interviewers are faced with the problem of their own boredom. By following an interview guide, even loosely, you are going to hear the same information over and over. It is a challenge to keep responding with interest, but you must. The employee ought to leave the interview feeling appreciated.

RECORD INFORMATION QUICKLY AND SYSTEMATICALLY

Because interviews are spread over several days or weeks, it is imperative that you register the information you have obtainted as quickly as possible. Memory is simply not trustworthy when you are interviewing many people.

There are rules prescribing how one should take notes Some people write notes during the interview itself. Others leave a time for writing general reactions after the interview. Both procedures are useful. A technique that I have found to have merit is to ask an assistant to take notes while I ask the questions in the interview. This frees me to concentrate on the interaction while providing copious notes. Having the assistant "process" the interview after it is finished provides a different point of view about the employee, which can be provocative and can lead to better write-ups of the interviews.

After each interview, a written summary should be formalized. It should include at a minimum the following:

1. name of interviewee
2. date
3. name and position of employee
4. answer to each individual question
5. subjective reactions or observations
6. questions or areas that should be explored further in subsequent interviews.

An example of such a summary is presented in Exhibit 4.5.

EXHIBIT 4.5   Individual Interview Write-up
                Second Round Interview

NAME: Jane Doe
POSITION: Supervisor; Sales Support
INTERVIEWER: Carl Smith
DATE: June 10, 1986

1. *COMMUNICATION ROLE OF SUPERVISORS:* to communicate changes that take place and the *why's* behind them—"the people have a right to know"; to make yourself available to the employees on a personal level as well as job level. *HOW WELL DO THEY FUNCTION?* Supervisors communicate "only as good as the people that work with them do"; There must be an equal exchange between supervisor and employee. She expresses that there should be an equal give-and-take in communication with employees and supervisors for the sake of getting the job done and providing a good interpersonal atmosphere. *ANY PROBLEMS WITH SUPERVISORS IN THEIR COMMUNICATION?* MAKING THEMSELVES AVAILABLE TO THE AGENTS FOR THIS NEEDED AMOUNT OF GIVE-AND-TAKE COMMUNICATION.
   *Note: She took an overall defensive attitude to the first two questions by saying she felt as if they're "hounding" her to tell how she personally has been performing as supervisor.

2. *HOW MUCH INFORMATION DO EMPLOYEES RECEIVE ABOUT BEING JUDGED?* DAILY: not much individual judgment or recognition, but a comment on the overall unit's daily work is made. She doesn't like to evaluate agents that much verbally or informally because she says she doesn't want to seem to be "hounding" the agents about their work. No comment was made on possible informal *positive* evaluations though. *PERSONAL FEELINGS AND SUGGESTIONS FOR IMPROVEMENT:* Per-

sonally, she says it's hard to evaluate people, i.e., in terms of effort or in comparison to others. She didn't like the written evaluation in use. The previous form had "no middle ground," i.e., an employee was rated either excellent or fair to unacceptable. The old form also judged an employee on areas not related to CDP and left important areas such as *punctuality* and *attendance* out. The new form is more tailored to the organization.

3. *PERCEPTIONS WE'LL FIND ABOUT UPPER MANAGEMENT:* Dissatisfaction; that they're stupid, BUT she interjects by saying that upper management is not always responsible for the mix-ups and neither are supervisors because corporate headquarters interferes too much and upper management must answer to them.

4. *PERCEPTIONS WE'LL FIND ABOUT SUPERVISORS:* She says most complaints occur because many supervisors will further mess up mix-ups by not properly following through with communication about them (e.g., communication and feedback they get from management about mix-ups). Also, perceptions will include that supervisors don't respond enough to personal needs, which she feels greatly affects job performance. "Employees want attention." *SUPERVISOR SELECTION AND TRAINING:* Big problem with training—it's on-the-job training. She feels training programs would help.

5. *FAVORITISM:* She avoids it by having certain rules for herself to follow. She says most of what is labelled favoritism is just grumbling by employees who "sit on their butts all day and talk instead of work." She says the promotions that have been called favoritism she sees from a supervisory position as valid promotions based on *job performance* and not favoritism.

6. *JOB SATISFACTION:* Obtained through merit increases, through cross-utilization of employees. This is letting employees learn what they want and can learn in other departments as well as within the division, so they can be used elsewhere (therefore beneficial to the company) *and* so they can always have hopes of promotion (thus giving them individual incentive and motivation and keeping them happy). *JOB DISSATISFACTION: "People create their own dissatisfaction."* Anyone can do what they want in their job if they had the incentive. Those that are dissatisfied are the ones who don't do anything to improve their situation. They think something is going to be handed to them.

7. *GRAPEVINE:* Detrimental to her because sometimes overrides or arrives before supervision does, then subordinates ignore supervision and make supervisor look dumb because they already know.

8. *PTPs:* Good because chance for employees to tell management directly. Management really is concerned and she expresses that she doesn't think agents know or feel this. Management can't always do anything about the problem (here she again points out corporate headquarters), but they really want to know and help.

SYNTHESIZE THE INTERVIEW DATA

What does all this information mean? While it is fun to talk to people about the organization, ultimately it can be quite frustrating to try to make sense out of the various perceptions so that the conclusions really describe the organization. Some of the following procedures might be helpful in synthesizing the data.

1. *Set aside time for the interviewers to discuss what they are discovering about the organization.* Such group sessions need not be delayed until the end of the round; they can take place at the end of each day of interviews. In an audit of a university, six auditors debriefed each other this way for a week. There is something quite exciting and invigorating about interviewers sharing information that leads to new discoveries about the organization. Furthermore, such processing is a useful tool for checking and refining perceptions.

2. *Develop a summary sheet for each question.* It is not necessary to code each response separately, but the auditors should begin to analyze the answers' content in categories. Then they should look at the range of responses in each category. At the end of this process, the interviewing team should try to write generalizations that can be made from these answers.

3. *Keep the first analysis descriptive.* Do not go beyond the data. For example, watch the tendency to make inferences about why things happen as they do or to provide a rationale for a given behavior. Ultimately you will want to develop explanations and theories; however, at this point, limit yourself to what can be described from the direct statements from the interviews.

4. *Analyze the data from each round of interviews separately.* It is important that some tentative descriptive conclusions be drawn after the first round of interviews. These conclusions will provide targets to be checked by the collection of additional data. Since they are the first data on the organization, the conclusions must be tentative, and the auditors should look for evidence to confuse or reject them.

5. *Look for qualitative interpretations.* We are only somewhat interested in numerical data gathered from the interviews, so it is not necessarily appropriate to report frequency counts of how many people gave what response. Nevertheless, one cannot hide the fact that frequency of mention may indicate how widespread or intense a problem is. For example, in a small survey within an academic unit, every graduate student answered the question "What is the chief weakness of the organization?" with the same answer. This frequency was significant. On the other hand, none of the undergraduates or the faculty members mentioned it as a problem. In the total scheme the particular

weakness might not have shown up as significant, but in communicating with graduate students, it was the most important communication phenomenon.

6. *Draw conclusions across questions.* Communication operates in the organization as a system with many subsystems. The goal is to obtain a good view of the entire system, and this cannot be achieved by looking at answers to individual questions. Therefore, one must examine data intuitively across all dimensions to see how things are related. Exhibit 4.6 demonstrates how this was done in an industrial plant.

EXHIBIT 4.6   Sample Summary of Interviews, Industrial Plant

OVERALL:

CDP appears to be a fairly pleasant place to work whether you are management, supervisory staff, or production worker. The *attitude* coming through in interviews was generally positive with a few exceptions. Upper management was most positive, and satisfaction seemed to diminish as the management hierarchy was descended. The most negative interviews were of workers who had no subordinates and handled production, maintenance, or production support work. Even though some negative attitudes showed through, no one complained of not having someone to complain to or offer suggestions. At the same time, some workers mentioned that the flow of complaints and suggestions upwards was often blocked somewhere so that many received no response. This was mentioned at the third tier, as well as at the bottom.

The chain of command *hierarchy* was viewed as certain and for the most part rigid. Lower level employees suggested that they could communicate with upper management and that to do so they would send the message through proper channels. Communication among department heads, general management staff, and the resident manager seemed more informal, yet the hierarchy remained clear in everyone's understanding. Not all communication funnels neatly through the system. That which does not comes from outside the local plant. The division office of CDP communicates directly to plant personnel at various levels of the hierarchy. The information is technical or directly related to raw materials shipments, production plans and changes, research and development of products, and manufacturing techniques, as well as marketing and shipping. Such messages come from across the hierarchical strata within the division office.

Formal channels at CDP include monthly department reports, a monthly plant report (derived from department reports), an in-house local newspaper, a corporation and a division magazine and newsletter, the bulletin board on which all information for employees is posted, safety meetings, and department or communication meetings. In addition, the resident manager holds a weekly staff meeting attended by his immediate subordinates, and the general superintendent holds a weekly staff meeting of his subordinates, the department heads. Brief written reports of operations every twenty-four hours are prepared and sent to the general superintendent as well as other interested managers and superintendents. Work plans are sent from shift to shift via log books, which indicate the production plan, progress toward it, and other vital operations information.

Evaluating these channels, interviewees were generally positive toward each one. The monthly reports were criticized lightly as excessive but only insofar as the government required the reporting of things that seem to be unimportant to production. The paper received split reviews with most negative comments coming from line workers and some supervisors. Those who criticized it thought of it as a waste of paper, a gossip sheet, or both. The bulletin board was also seen as being both positive and negative. The majority of comments about it stated that it was read regularly by all employees and that important information was put on it such as job notices and employee benefit information. Most of the negative comments came from line workers and some supervisors. They complained of the job listings (referring to openings within the plant and in the plant being built) being incomplete or late. Department or communications meetings were seen as positive by some and negative by others. The negative comments were more evenly spread across the authority strata. Often the meetings were criticized for being a waste of time and unimportant. The meetings are intended in part to air employee questions and grievances, but those that are sent in seem to seldom make the agenda. Safety meetings, which in many cases precede the department meetings, are generally seen as important and useful. The resident manager's weekly staff meeting is not loudly applauded. It was seen as too long and as a gathering where each staff member was expected to contribute something no matter how trivial. The "result" then was supposedly an informed staff knowledgeable of the goings on in each unit. One critic felt that the result came from informal contacts and seldom from the meeting. Other channels are perceived as positive.

One strikingly positive aspect of the CDP operation is *decision making* in general. Although a few negative comments about insufficient subordinate input or involvement are noted, on the whole those who wanted to contribute knew of a channel through which to express views. Others considered to have necessary information were accessible and were contacted. The bulk of the decisions have to do with production. Others deal with employee issues. All or most seem to follow the same format. Decisions are made very close to where they will have an effect. Line workers make decisions, although few in number aside from following established procedures. They are trusted to do their job and be reasonably autonomous in that effort. The same is generally true on up the hierarchy. At each level, the job holder has a range of decisions for which she is responsible and information necessary to make the decisions is easily accessible by talking with whoever should know, face to face or on the phone. Another feature of decision making that was fairly clear was that an individual usually has final responsibility for any particular decision. He may solicit any and all the information he feels is necessary and consider all the points which to him seem significant, yet one person makes or takes responsibility for the decision.

Workers in the *lower strata* did *complain* some of not being heard on up the line. This decision-making system may stifle or weed out some of their remarks. Some claim that for all the emphasis on safety, employees in fact do unsafe things at management request and an injury or two has been glossed over to maintain a good record. Suggestions about safety and production efficiency seem to get lost sometimes. The industrial relations unit has a reward system for such suggestions. Workers are selected to go out to dinner, to a ball game, or to an amusement park at company expense in exchange for the best suggestions of the month. Evidently the system is lax, not serving rewards on time, and it is charged with pulling unimportant and repeated suggestions. On balance, though, the safety emphasis was seen as management interest in employee welfare and safety meetings were viewed positively.

Upper level managers complained of a lack of interdepartmental coordination. The meetings being held by the general superintendent may correct this. Another issue at this level is the use of MBO. The system is seen as ineffective. Departments get their objectives in order and send them up for approval. The approval comes usually after management has revised and sent back the objectives to be resubmitted in the revised form. It was suggested that a meeting time be established to hash out an agreement on objectives. This could eliminate some frustration, at least, if not the contradiction of the intent of the system.

Workers at the lower levels wanted two things in particular. They want a cleaning crew for the plant. They want this so that operators don't have to clean their own areas. Secondly, they want a more responsive and effective maintenance operation. Complaints about maintenance were only general and directed at slowness and unsatisfactory work.

In the *next round of interviews,* we want to probe the areas of advertising of jobs, the impact of putting in the new plant (some hints of an issue, although a necessarily short-term one, come through in this round), and whether the rate of suggestions has increased or decreased. Another point of interest is one of vocabulary. In several of the interviews the word "efficient" came up often, as did the phrase "mature operation." The occurrence of these seemed unusually frequent and we're curious about where they came from.

Examples from previous audits

The following conclusions were drawn from several audits to suggest the kinds of observations that are obtainable.

Manufacturing plant. • People here think that this is a good place to work. In fact, this is the most pervasive perception encountered in the interviews. When anyone compares this company with a previous job, this one was always rated as the best.

Motivation has been affected by a perceived change in hiring only college-educated managers. Workers resent the fact that internal promotions are now blocked. This is a communication problem, because actually 50 percent of the promotions are still from within.

Teamwork is lacking across the board, that is, among shifts, among departments, and among management levels. One person said "lack of coordination" is the culprit.

The communication climate has changed dramatically in the last two years. Productivity is up 50 percent, but the pressure leads people to believe they are uninformed.

Major decision making seems to be mostly downward, even though management talks of looking for ways to increase participation. Meetings are not seen as being the best avenue for securing participation.

Airline. • Ratings of supervisors differ remarkably and run the gamut from excellent to poor. When there is a negative rating, the reason is usually noted as lack of experience or technical expertise. Interestingly, there seems to be a high degree of empathy for a supervisor's job demands.

All supervisors mention *overload* and the fact that everyone one in unit ABC is spred very thin. Some supervisors think that ABC is overcommitted and that people are often trying to handle more than they can be responsible for.

There seems to be a uniform desire for information to be communicated through multiple channels. Many supervisors expressed the desire for written notification of all information that affects overall operations, rather than so much reliance on oral messages. Twilight shift supervisors specifically mentioned the need to put more information in writing.

Most managers contend that communication among them is very good and that they keep each other informed. Supervisors and agents share this perception of the managers. One notable exception seems to be the communication to and from *(person)*.

Public utility. • The least effective means of communication tends to be the informal channel. In Unit A, it is almost nonexistent. Unit B has an active grapevine, but most people seemed to doubt its reliability.

Of all the communication areas considered, the greatest dissatisfaction was expressed over an apparent lack of information about job vacancies and advancement. Some workers were not even certain that a system existed. They seem to rely on word-of-mouth almost as much as published information. Those employees who desire mobility want an updated, more effective system.

Group managers saw very little conflict either within their units or between units. Isolated incidents were not thought to be important. Nevertheless, there is a kind of competitiveness communicated between the offices at B and C.

Training generally gets high marks as a communication vehicle. As new policies are developed, employees are advised by their managers, at meetings, by booklets, and through special quizzes. The employees generally thought these procedures were both adequate and satisfactory.

CONCLUSION

The skillful interviewing of employees is one of the richest means of diagnosing the communication dynamics of an organization. In addition to learning about people's perceptions, you are able to gauge the people giving you information, which lets you assess the value of what particular individuals tell you. The data are not as easily packageble as with quantitative methods, but some insights could never be obtained any other way. Therefore, a round of interviews should be the first diagnostic tool used in a communication audit.

Face-to-face interviews offer a perfect opportunity to establish and sustain the auditor-client relationships. Although you are at first a stranger, soon the audit becomes a fixture for a while in the organization. People grow accustomed to your presence at work, and the informal channels often discuss you. A new relationship develops, and the wise auditor will nurture it. Alderfer (1968) reports ways of doing this. First, "be as visible and as approachable as possible." Look for special opportunities to interact with employees informally while eating or visiting their work stations. Next, "preserve the confidentiality of the data without damaging the self-esteem of the people who seek information." Finally, "be accessible to key members of the organization, even if it means altering a research design." These points suggest that collecting useful information is not limited to formal interviews or other data-generating methods.

REFERENCES

Alderfer, C. "Organizational Diagnosis from Initial Client Reactions to a Researcher." *Human Organization* 27 (1968): 260–265.

Argyris, C. *Intervention Theory and Method.* Reading, Mass.: Addison-Wesley, 1970.

Downs, C.; Smeyak, G.; and Martin, E. *Professional Interviewing.* New York: Harper and Row, 1980.

Filley, Alan C. *The Compleat Manager.* Middleton, Wis.: Green Briar Press, 1978.

Goldhaber, Gerald, and Rogers, Don. *Auditing Organizational Communication Systems.* Dubuque, Iowa: Kendall-Hunt, 1979.

5

Diagnosis Through Questionnaires

The mainstay of most audits is some type of questionnaire, because questionnaires have advantages over other methods of data collection. The primary advantage is *sample size*. Whereas one can interview only a limited number of employees in sizable organizations, a questionnaire can be given to all employees, if that is desired. Furthermore, it can be given to all in the same time frame, so it is a *faster* means of getting information. The questionnaire is also one of the *cheapest* audit procedures. Not only is it inexpensive to reproduce and circulate, but it avoids the expenses incurred from paying interviewers or taking people away from their jobs. Generally, a questionnaire can be filled out during slack periods when it does not compete with work time. A major advantage to a questionnaire is that a certain amount of *anonymity* can be assured, so sensitive information can be obtained from people who might not risk disclosing it in another way. A questionnaire provides a *permanent written record,* so it can be restudied during the analysis time, and it can be designed so that tabulating standardized answers is easy. Finally, a questionnaire has the advantage of comprising *more topics* than is normally covered in other ways of data collection.

These advantages are suggested under the assumption that one has a good questionnaire to administer. Basically, two options are available: designing your own questionnaire or using a standardized one. I shall explore each of these options in depth. The rest of this chapter will describe the process of designing your own questionnaire. Chapters 6 and 7 examine standardized questionnaires.

DESIGNING A QUESTIONNAIRE

Designing a good questionnaire sounds easier than it actually is, but it is profitable when done well. Therefore, considerable time ought to be spent planning the questionnaire. Some of us can easily think of questions to ask, but it is important to design them so that you always know in advance how you plan to use the information you will obtain in the answers. Some of the following considerations may help in designing a questionnaire.

Develop a focus

Decide what information is most crucial to the audit. Chapter 3 described the variety of communication information that it is possible to collect, but because so much is available, one must decide whether to sample numerous topics with a few questions each or to probe a few topics in depth with many questions. There is often pressure to cover as many of the communication processes and systems as possible. Remember that the preliminary interviews may be very helpful in identifying areas to be investigated. As was described in Chapter 3, some of the most important potential topic areas are as follows:

1. Kinds of information needed and sent
2. Reactions to sources of information
3. Adequacy of channels used
4. Relationships among people
5. How communication network or structure affect the work processes
6. Directions of communication: upward, downward, and horizontal
7. Communication outcomes such as satisfaction and productivity
8. Feedback mechanisms and performance
9. Communication problem areas
10. Interdepartmental communication.

Choose questions for each topic area

Generally, it is useful to start off with more questions than you need and to evaluate which ones are most important for your purposes. Ask whether a question is necessary and how an answer to it can be used. There is a kind of science about question development, and some of the major considerations are identified in the following sections.

Scope. • The wider the scope of any one question, the more difficult it may be to obtain comparable answers across respondents and to interpret each one's responses. Sometimes several questions are needed to tap the multidimensionality of the topic area. A good example is the superior-subordinate relationship. There are too many aspects to this relationship to be covered in one question. One can explore the superior's receptivity to upward communication, the adequacy of downward communication, the communication climate between the two, and so on. Therefore, this relationship may need to be explored through several questions, each of which pinpoints a different aspect. The choice seems to be whether to ask general, open questions or to explore specific issues.

Specificity. • Here the auditor is in a bind. The more specific the question, the more questions that are necessary to probe an area. On the other hand, the more abstract or confusing the terms in the question, the less certain you can be about understanding what the answers really mean. For example, in one audit we asked employees to react to "how organizational decisions are made that affect your position." The employees indicated that they wanted a great deal more information than they were receiving on this topic. Although this was one of our most significant findings, we did not know from the question exactly what decisions interested the respondents. Furthermore, it would be rather tedious to list on a questionnaire all the major kinds of decisions that could be subsumed under that question. This case demonstrates how follow-up interviews can be helpful.

Wording. • It is important to anticipate how the respondents may interpret the questions. If a question can be misunderstood, it will be. That is why it is better to ask yourself the question "How can this be misunderstood?" rather than "Can it be understood?" The frame of reference is never exactly the same for everyone, but you can reduce the likelihood of some problems occurring by considering several points. Is the wording biased toward an expected answer? Couching a question in terms of a "problem" may be biasing, because some people try to avoid problems. Are there unstated assumptions in the questions? For example, asking "how does your job satisfaction affect your productivity?" implies a connection between satisfaction and productivity that has not been supported by research. Finally, avoid evaluative words like "bad," "good," or "fair" because the criteria used will not be known unless they are probed specifically.

Relevance. • Questions should be relevant to the goals of the audit, but they should also be relevant to the individual respondent's experience. Novice auditors often become enamored of asking as many questions as they can, and the answers to many of them are never used. In other words, questions need to be focused on meaningful areas with an intended use in mind. For example, there is a tendency to ask for much demographic data that are never used in the analysis.

Choose appropriate response format

Choosing whether a question should be open or closed is one of the most important decisions that you will make. Each type has some particular strengths, and I recommend that your questionnaire should have a mixture of both.

An *open question* does not restrict the answer in any way. A good example is, "What improvements would you like to see in communication in your job?" The respondent can answer any number of ways. The advantages of this type of question are many. Since it does not structure the respondent's thinking, you may discover both the individual's priorities and his or her frame of reference. Also, the responses are likely to be longer and more detailed, providing more information. Open questions are particularly useful when the subject is complex or when the list of alternatives is either too long or unknown. For example, asking the question about improvements mentioned previously will probably generate a list of things that the auditor could not have anticipated and, therefore, that could not have been framed in a closed question.

It is also important to be aware of open questions' limitations. Because answers to them are not standardized, tabulation may be more difficult. Some answers will include irrelevant information, and others will be too sketchy to be of real value. Another problem we have encountered is that a majority of respondents will not take the time or effort to fill them out.

Closed questions typically restrict the answers in specific ways. They take the forms of rating scales, ranking, dichotomous alternatives, inventories, checklists, or grids. This makes them easier and faster to answer, to code, to compare, and to sample many different topics quickly. Multiple choice test questions are good examples of closed questions. On the other hand, closed questions are limited in some ways, too. Some respondents are frustrated when they cannot elaborate, clarify, or qualify responses. Furthermore, variations among responses are artificially removed through forced choice, and differences in interpretation go undetected. The auditor cannot be certain whether the respondent is guessing or taking the responses seriously. Finally, closed questions do not provide nearly as much information as well-answered questions.

Example:

1. (Open) Describe your relationship with your supervisor.

versus

2. (Closed) To what extent do you trust your supervisor?

    Little   1   2   3   4   5   Great

One can readily see that the answer to the open question could reveal a great deal. But if the respondents did not talk about the same things, tabulation and thus generalization may be difficult. The closed question may ask everyone to pick a number, so you can easily see how many people do not trust their supervisors. However, the only aspect of the relationship that you can comment on is "trust," and in the absence of the respondents' comments and elaborations, you may not even know what they meant by the term. Therefore, it is useful to use closed and open questions in supplemental fashion. In the case of the trust question, you could use the scale to get people to commit themselves, and then follow with an open question such as "Why?" or "What could be done to make this relationship better?"

Because there are so many aspects of communication to cover in an audit, well-designed closed questions are very helpful. This means that the choice of a rating scale is very important. Contemporary research would urge you to be consistent throughout the questionnaire, because changing rating scales form section to section may throw respondents off. There is no particular pattern that ought to be followed, so several possibilities will be mentioned.

Agree–disagree statements. • A full statement is made, and the person is asked to indicate how strongly she or he agrees or disagrees.

Example:

Your supervisor gives you personal feedback about the progress in your job.

Strong Agreement • *Agreement* • *Disagreement* • *Strong Disagreement*

This scale forces the respondent to make a choice and also assesses the intensity of feelings. A particular problem to avoid is the framing of questions around a confusing double negative. Suppose the statement had said that "the supervisor does not give you personal feedback." Some people would be confused about how to respond. One has to mark "disagree" in order to make a positive statement about the supervisor. In other words, one has to select a negative to counter the negative phrasing of the question.

Our society seems to be fascinated with numbers, and the rating scales used most often are numerical. Generally, an item is mentioned and the respondent indicates the strength of the response by a number. It is common practice to use odd numbers so that there is a middle ground. Also, the longer the continuum, the more sensitive it is; for example, scales of 1 to 5 give more variation than scales of 1 to 3. However, there is a point of diminishing returns so that extensions from 1 to 11 may render the difference between a 7 and an 8 meaningless. The most common scales are either five or seven choices long.

Example:

How satisfied are you with the amount of personal feedback you get
from your supervisors?

| Little | 1 | 2 | 3 | 4 | 5 | 6 | 7 | Great |

Semantic differential. • This is also a popular scale for getting a
large amount of information quickly. Basically, the individual is given a concept followed by a series of bipolar adjectives that describe the concept (Osgood,
Suci, and Tannenbaum, 1967). The respondent is asked to check one of the
spaces between each adjective pair.

Example:

Communication with Supervisor

Adequate	____	____	____	____	____	Inadequate
Cold	____	____	____	____	____	Friendly
Trusting	____	____	____	____	____	Distrusting
Timely	____	____	____	____	____	Late

When such a technique is used, one must choose the adjectives carefully and
vary the list so that not all of the positive attributes are listed on the same
side. This variation may help to prevent a response bias resulting from a
tendency to answer everything on the same side. This technique can test whether
or not people are filling out the questionnaires carefully. Again, in analyzing
the responses, each blank is coded with a number. In the example here, the
range would be 1 to 5.

Rank order. • If a respondent is asked to rank order, care must be
taken not to allow the original order of listing to influence the response. Some
auditors vary the listing on various questionnaires to randomize any error that
comes from order.

Whatever the rating scale, a good question allows for a complete range
of responses. Sometimes forcing a choice can be useful, but it still is forced.
That is why the agree--disagree scale may contain an undecided component
or an indication of the degree of strength, and the satisfied–dissatisfied continuum will let a respondent choose among a range of responses so that different
degrees of satisfaction are evident. An answer's degree of strength may be
very important. For example, if you ask me merely to indicate whether I agree
or disagree with a series of statements about communication, I could agree
with them all, but your question format would not allow you to discover my
highest priorities or the things about which I feel most strongly.

Use companion responses

Ask for similar information in more than one question. For example, one questionnaire asked both "Do you like the kind of work you do?" and "Are you satisfied with your job?" Although both questions contain an element of satisfaction, there are some subtle differences in what they are asking. Furthermore, companion responses may allow you to check the reliability of the answers.

Prepare simple instructions and cover letter

The purpose of this is similar to the introduction in an interview — to motivate people to take the time and energy to fill out the questionnaire and to explain to them how to complete it. Motivation is extremely important, because many employees have filled out other questionnaires without ever having received any follow-up. Therefore, you must explain why it is useful for them to complete the questionnaire and, if possible, suggest how the information is going to be used. Assuring them of confidentiality also has a motivational quality.

In addition, I like to have a top manager send a cover letter with the questionnaire to lend credibility to the project as well as to encourage employees to complete it.

Order the questions

Experience has taught me that the following suggestions about order have merit.

Ask easy-to-answer questions first. This "hooks" the respondent.

Ask interest-arousing questions first.

Intersperse some open questions among the closed ones so that you may tap the respondents' frames of reference before they are completely structured by the closed questions.

Look for natural ways of grouping questions by topics. In some cases they may be grouped under headings, such as channels or outcomes. There are circumstances, however, when one may also wish to mix up the topic areas. For example, in an audit designed to explore reactions to communication climate and supervisor-subordinate relations, questions were distributed throughout the questionnaire to investigate either topic. The idea was to circumvent the possibility that the answer to one question might influence another or that having all questions about a certain topic together might condition respondents to answer them in the same way.

Watch for possibilities that answers are conditioned undesirably by answers to preceding questions.

Leave demographics until last. Some respondents become suspicious that you may try to identify them; therefore, personal information at the beginning deters them. Ask for only the demographic data that you plan to use.

Balance positive and negative questions. If you ask about weaknesses, ask about strengths first so that it does not appear that you are merely interested in the negative side of the organization.

Pretest the questions

Such a test requires that a number of people similar to those in the organization complete the questionnaire. Also, show pretest questionnaires to representatives of the organization to get their reactions. Such pretests are invaluable in detecting variations in interpretation and range of response. Auditors cannot anticipate all the ways that people might interpret a question. What seems so obvious as you labor over the questionnaire may be lost to the respondent who is viewing it for the first time. Finally, the pretest is also valuable in determining whether or not the answers can be analyzed as you had expected.

Be realistic about response time

Lengthy questionnaires are not only intimidating at the outset, but they can generate fatigue. As people become discouraged, they may skip questions or not complete them. Although circumstances may vary, fifteen to forty-five minutes is a good time range for completing the questionnaire, and this should be forecast in the introduction. Keep in mind that filling out a questionnaire is an unusual (and undesirable) activity for many employees.

Present an attractive product

Remember that the design affects people's impressions. Therefore, attractive margins and sufficient space between items is necessary. Distinguish carefully between instructions and questions, and use good quality paper and printing. The more professional the questionnaire looks, the more incentive people have to respond to it.

ADMINISTERING THE QUESTIONNAIRE

Administering a questionnaire involves the distribution and collection of the completed questionnaires. These two processes are quite separate in terms of the mechanics involved, and each is important to the success of the audit.

Distribution

Two things need to be accomplished during distribution. First, the questionnaires should reach all employees at about the same time. Second, the process should motivate the employees to respond. Some of the following procedures have been found to be useful.

1. *Publicize the process.* As a part of the publicity, an officer of the company should write a memo backing the audit. This is frequently attached to the questionnaire.

2. *Include a cover letter with the questionnaire.* A sample letter is included in Exhibit 5.1. The letter should explain the purpose of the audit, assure confidentiality, forecast how long it might take to answer, and attempt to motivate employees to make a contribution.

3. *Give each individual a personal copy of the questionnaire.* Whenever possible, an auditor should actually hand them out and let the employees fill them out according to their own schedules. The advantages of this system are that (1) employees can complete the questionnaire when they want, (2) anonymity is assured, and (3) costs are minimized since it does not interfere with work. The disadvantages are that (1) some people forget to return the questionnaires and anonymity prevents you from knowing who did not return them, (2) several respondents may discuss the questions, so the answers are not completely uncontaminated, and (3) there is no opportunity for the auditor to answer questions about the questionnaire.

Although individual distribution by an auditor is the ideal, circumstances sometimes requires an adaptation, and we have used three alternatives. First, members of the organization have distributed the questionnaires. For example, in one audit the questionnaires were given to the managers of each unit, who in turn passed them out individually. In this case, a 90 percent return rate indicated that the process worked well, and it seemed to demonstrate management's backing of the survey. Second, the questionnaires have been mailed or put in mail boxes. This is much less personal, and the response rates tend to drop. Nevertheless, this may be the only viable alternative. In the audit of a public seminar organization, the speakers

EXHIBIT 5.1   Cover Letter

Dear ACME Employee,

For the next two weeks, representatives of Communication Management, Inc., will be conducting a Communication Survey of ACME. The enclosed questionnaire is one part of that survey. The results of the survey will be analyzed and a complete report will be given to ACME. This is an important survey that *gives you an opportunity to give information that might improve the operation of ACME.* Therefore, we hope that you will fill it out.

There are several things that we want to emphasize.

1. Your COMPLETE ANONYMITY is GUARANTEED. NO PERSON FROM ACME WILL SEE THE COMPLETED QUESTIONNAIRES.

2. ONCE ALL THE QUESTIONNAIRES ARE COLLECTED, A GENERAL REPORT WILL BE GIVEN TO ACME, AND A SUMMARY REPORT WILL BE GIVEN TO YOU.

3. PLEASE MARK YOUR ANSWERS DIRECTLY ON THE QUESTION-NAIRE, AND PLEASE ANSWER EACH QUESTION, AS EACH HAS SOME SPECIAL MEANING.

4. For the purpose of this survey, certain terms require the use of common definitions.
   Immediate supervisor: The most direct management person of the unit to which you are assigned.
   Middle management: This category represents the managers to whom your supervisor reports.
   Top management: This term refers to the Manager of ACME, Manager of Passenger Systems Development, and Director of Reservation Services.

5. When you have completed the questionnaire—which should take you 15 to 20 minutes—PLACE IT IN THE BROWN DISPATCH ENVELOPE, AND PUT IT IN THE BOX LOCATED NEXT TO THE EXTRA LIFT CLERK NO LATER THAN 12:00 P.M. WEDNESDAY, (DATE).

6. PLEASE COMPLETE THEM BY:

Thank you for your cooperation,

Cal W. Downs, Director

---

travelled constantly, and the only way to obtain their responses was to mail them a questionnaire.

A third alternative to individual administration is to have people assemble in groups to fill out the questionnaire. Such groupings suffer from the fact that time away from work is expensive and that people do not work at the same rate, thus wasting some employees' time. Nevertheless, this group method has three big advantages: (1) The rate of return is high. Given an opportunity to explain the purpose and answer questions, I have rarely had someone refuse to answer the questionnaire. (2) It is fast because the answers are collected immediately. (3) The interaction between the auditor and respondent allows for instructions, questions, and the development of trust. I have used the group process in both university and commercial settings.

4. *Set a reasonable response time for the questionnaires to be returned.* Three days is generally adequate. If you permit respondents to take longer, there is a likelihood of their putting the questionnaire on the "back burner," and it loses its urgency. The time frame should never exceed a week.

Collection

Privacy and anonymity must be ensured; this eliminates individually picking up the completed questionnaires. However, we have found two systems to be effective. The first is to put a box clearly labeled "audit" in an area of the organization easily accessible to most—that is, a coffee room or receptionist area—and to let respondents seal their questionnaires in envelopes and drop them in the box. In this case, provisions should be made to pick up the envelopes at the end of each day. The second method came at the insistence of an organization who wanted to avoid any possibility of invasion of privacy. Each employee mailed his or her responses directly to our office, using the U.S. Postal Service.

ANALYZING THE QUESTIONNAIRE

Questionnaires have all the advantages mentioned earlier, but you should never lose sight of their limitations. Basically, they report what people think or feel at a particular time. These self-reports do not represent actual behaviors; the auditor simply infers behavior from the reports. You should always be mindful of the possibilities for lying, distortion, and simple misinformed responses caused by a reader misunderstanding a question.

The questionnaires can be analyzed in the following ways.

Frequency distribution

The first task is to prepare a frequency distribution for every question. If we look at the data in Exhibit 5.2, we note immediately how varied the responses are. There is little consensus on many questions, and this is important to remember. Even though responses may show there is a problem in a particular area, there may still be people who feel very good about this area.

Means and ranks

Once the means are completed, they can be rank ordered in descending order to determine what kinds of information people are receiving most successfully or least successfully. This is also illustrated in Exhibit 5.2. In this example, information about pay and benefits is ranked the highest, but "how decisons are made" and "how I am being judged" is ranked the lowest. In these cases a majority of respondents indicated that they receive little information.

Once the process of rank ordering is complete, it is useful to compare the means for each item on "amount of information received now" with the "amount I want to receive." For example, "how I am being judged" ranked thirteenth in terms of information the plant employees now receive, but it ranked fifth in terms of what they wanted to receive. This difference indicates that there may be a problem. It is also possible to discover some areas where more information is given than is needed. In this organization, company policies ranked second in amount of information received, but ranked ninth in terms of what information was wanted. Discrepancies in the rank orders of more than four or five points may point out areas to beginning looking for problems.

At this time it is perhaps useful to look at some artifacts of this particular scale. Notice that very few people indicated that they want little information on any topic. Furthermore, in every case they said that they want more information than they are getting. Because people generally feel a need for more information, regardless of how much they receive, we may be measuring a "curiosity index" here rather than a true information need.

Differences between actual means

Difference scores can be found by subtracting one mean from another. For example, the score for the amount of information received can be subtracted from the score for the amount that people want to receive.

EXHIBIT 5.2 Receiving Information from Others

Topic area	I. This is the amount of information I receive now							II. This is the amount of information I want to receive						
	Very little	Little	Some	Great	Very great	Mean	Rank	Very little	Little	Some	Great	Very great	Mean	Rank
Progress in your job	17	22	37	16	5	2.57	8	1	1	39	36	16	3.74	8
Your job requirements	5	21	35	23	5	3.02	4	2	1	22	43	21	3.93	2
The company policies	7	6	45	24	9	3.24	2	2	3	32	39	14	3.67	9
Pay and benefits	2	2	31	42	11	3.66	1	4	1	17	46	24	4.06	1
How technological changes affect your job	16	18	30	17	9	2.83	6	4	4	35	32	14	3.54	12
Mistakes and failures of the company	31	26	25	6	4	2.20	11	6	5	45	25	9	3.29	13
How you are being judged	35	26	17	11	1	2.08	13	2	2	29	31	26	3.86	5
How your job-related problems are being handled	23	22	33	8	4	2.42	9	1	2	25	38	23	3.90	4
How organization decisions are made that affect your position	34	22	21	10	4	2.20	12	3	3	22	39	22	3.83	6
Promotion and advancement opportunities in the company	22	17	30	19	4	2.63	7	2	2	22	39	26	3.93	3
Important new service of program developments in the company	11	8	45	24	4	3.02	3	2	2	34	40	13	3.66	11
How your job relates to the total operation of the company	12	14	35	21	9	3.01	5	1	3	28	41	17	3.78	7
Specific problems management faces in the company	28	23	27	9	5	2.35	10	2	3	37	30	19	3.67	10

The assumption is that the greater the differences, the more likely it is that a problem exists, because the discrepancy represents a dissatisfaction on that item. These differences can then be rank ordered to determine the greatest problem areas. An example from the manufacturing plant is given in Exhibit 5.2. The greatest difference occurred for "how I am being judged," $(3.86 - 2.08 = 1.78)$, and the auditors concluded that more information needed to be circulated in this regard. Later, the company implemented a positive discipline approach that spelled out exactly what procedures and standards would be used for infractions, and one of the managers praised it for eliminating the ambiguities of judgments.

Such differences in means provide a useful way to assess the strengths and weaknesses of each category, but the categories must also be examined in terms of other data. For example, on "sources of information" in the manufacturing plant example, the greatest discrepancy between what employees wanted and what they were receiving was on a certain item. Nevertheless, when we examined the rank orders of the means on the frequency distribution, we found that the item ranked 7 out of 9 on what the workers wanted and 9 out of 9 on what they received. This finding indicates that the difference may not be really important after all.

Correlations

One of the most popular ways of analyzing data is to select one important item on the questionnaire and determine what other items correlate with it. Actually, correlations identify how answers to questions vary together. A high correlation between two questions, for example, simply means that fluctuations in one answer co-vary with fluctuations in another answer. Therefore, correlations are often used to explain how communication phenomena coexist. Although correlations do identify positive or negative relationships between items, they do not necessarily explain cause-and-effect relations. When we find that satisfaction with personal feedback has a high correlation with job satisfaction, we cannot say necessarily that one *causes* the other.

Statistical comparisons among demographic groups

Most of the information presented so far has been at the organizational level, with data from all employees combined to represent the total organization. This is useful as a beginning point. However, to make some data more meaningful, it is often wise to analyze the data across certain demographic parameters. Normally, these comparisons involve some analysis of variance (ANOVA) of the data.[1]

[1]For an explanation of analysis of variance, consult a standard text on statistical analysis.

Work Units. • There are many ways to divide a company into work units, but four examples will illustrate the point. In a telephone company, management wanted the audit to compare two groups of operators, because they thought there was some friction between the groups. The audit revealed none. In an audit of an equipment engineering group, answers were compared between engineers and non-engineers. These people had to work together, and some important differences were discovered in their reactions to communication in meetings. In an audit of an airline, the units of three different managers in a department were compared. Finally, in auditing a university, analyses were made for each school within the university.

In addition to revealing information about the individual work units, these comparisons help develop comparative standards.

Productive or less productive units. • If the auditor has access to data concerning different levels of productivity for units, these data can help determine whether the units differ significantly in terms of communication. Discovering the relationship between communication and productivity is one of the chief aims of any audit.

Sex. • It is sometimes popular to compare the responses of males and females. However, in the audits that I have conducted, I have never found significant impact on internal communication on the basis of sex.

Satisfied versus dissatisfied groupings. • Many audits have a measure to report job satisfaction, and it is important to find out what communication phenomena really differentiates the satisfied employees from the dissatisfied ones. This analysis can be helpful in identifying what communication problems seem to coexist with the dissatisfaction, and it is a very useful way of determining what problems are most significant.

Managers versus nonmanagers. • Because communication patterns often differ widely between managers and nonmanagers, this is an important comparison to make. Managers generally occupy more central roles in the communication networks, and their view of communication adequacy is likely to differ from nonmanagers.

Tenure. • Length of time on the job sometimes can be a factor in surprising ways. We have found both strengths and dissatisfactions when we had not anticipated them. For example, in a manufacturing plant, we used seniority to judge the reaction to the company's overall communication efforts on a 1 to 5 scale. The findings were as follows:

Years	Mean
−1	4.01
1 to 5	3.23
6 to 10	3.22
11 to 15	2.77
15+	3.60

All tenure groups were fairly satisfied with communication except for the 11 to 15 year group. Therefore, we began to probe what was operating within this group, and it seemed to be related to both age and to career stage.

Additional demographics. • You may wish to make other comparisons suitable to the organization, the audit, or any research questions. Some additional ones include: whether or not the respondent has had communication training; age; work status (full-time versus part-time); length of time in the job; pay categories such as salary, hourly, exempt or nonexempt from overtime pay; salary earnings; or mobility (number of previous jobs).

ANOTHER OPTION

As desirable as it is to use one's own questionnaire, another possibility is to use a standardized questionnaire that has been refined through research, has been used extensively, and has produced practical information of immediate use to managers. Three such questionnaires that analyze communication will be reviewed in depth in subsequent chapters: (1) the International Communication Association Survey, (2) the Downs-Hazen Communication Satisfaction Questionnaire, and (3) ECCO Analysis by Keith Davis.

REFERENCES

Downs, C.; Smeyak, G.; and Martin, E. *Professional Interviewing.* New York: Harper and Row, 1980.
Osgood, Charles; Suci, George; and Tannenbaum, Percy. *The Measurement of Meaning.* Urbana: University of Illinois Press, 1967.

6
The International Communication Association Survey

Under the leadership of Dr. Gerald M. Goldhaber, members of the International Communication Association (ICA) worked together from 1971 to 1979 to develop and refine a method to diagnose communication in organizations. The total assessment package included a standardized survey questionnaire, interviews, observations, network analyses, critical incidents, and a communication diary. Although all of these techniques were incorporated into the ICA audit process, only the survey was truly unique, because the other methods had been derived independently by others. Therefore, this chapter provides an overview of the ICA survey and offers it as an alternative resource that is readily available and very practical. It should be remembered that the survey is generally used in conjunction with other methods, but it can stand alone and still give practical information.

AN OVERVIEW OF THE SURVEY

One of the outstanding advantages of the survey is its comprehensiveness. Its 122+ questions are divided into eight major sections, designed to cover the most important aspects of organizational communication. Some sections are divided into subsections, as follows:

1. Amount of Information Actively Received About Topics.
   Amount of Information Desired About These Topics.

2. Amount of Information Actually Sent About Topics.
   Amount of Information Desired to Be Sent About These Topics.
3. Amount of Follow-up by People Now.
   Amount of Follow-up Needed.
4. Amount of Information Received from Sources.
   Amount of Information Desired from These Sources.
5. Timeliness of Information Received from Key Sources.
6. Organizational Communication Relationships.
7. Satisfaction with Organizational Outcomes.
8. Amount of Information Received from Channels Now.
   Amount of Information Desired from Channels Now.

Because questions under the various sections are grouped together, it is possible to use some sections while not using others and to get a quick overview of what is actually covered in each individual section. Each section is described separately in this chapter.

Information received

In selecting the questions presented in Exhibit 6.1, it was important to decide which kinds of information were most crucial to one's job. A quick review indicates that the two general areas are information useful in doing the job (items 1, 3, 5, 9, 13, and 15) and information useful in keeping informed about the organization (items 11, 17, 19, 21, and 25). While the latter may not be necessary to do the job, this type of information possesses a motivational quality that helps workers identify with their organization.

Sending information to others

Because most people seem to be concerned with information they do or do not receive, that area was listed in the first section of the survey. However, workers also need to send information, and the questions in Exhibit 6.2 concern the amount they send. Question 37, "Evaluating the performance of my immediate supervisor," may be problematic, because not every organization permits the sending of this type of information.

Note that all of these questions are oriented toward *upward* communication in the form of reports, complaints, or requests for more information. It would be possible to phrase additional questions about sending information *horizontally* to colleagues and *downward* to subordinates. An example may validate such additions. When I conducted a teamwork seminar for a division of an organization, one of the workers' most frequent complaints

EXHIBIT 6.1   Receiving Information from Others

Topic Area		This is the amount of information I receive now					This is the amount of information I need to receive				
		Very Little	Little	Some	Great	Very Great		Very Little	Little	Some	Great	Very Great
How well I am doing in my job	1.	1	2	3	4	5	2.	1	2	3	4	5
My job duties	3.	1	2	3	4	5	4.	1	2	3	4	5
Organizational policies	5.	1	2	3	4	5	6.	1	2	3	4	5
Pay and benefits	7.	1	2	3	4	5	8.	1	2	3	4	5
How technological changes affect my job	9.	1	2	3	4	5	10.	1	2	3	4	5
Mistakes and failures of my organization	11.	1	2	3	4	5	12.	1	2	3	4	5
How I am being judged	13.	1	2	3	4	5	14.	1	2	3	4	5
How my job-related problems are being handled	15.	1	2	3	4	5	16.	1	2	3	4	5
How organization decisions are made that affect my job	17.	1	2	3	4	5	18.	1	2	3	4	5
Promotion and advancement opportunities in my organization	19.	1	2	3	4	5	20.	1	2	3	4	5
Important new product, service or program developments in my organization	21.	1	2	3	4	5	22.	1	2	3	4	5
How my job relates to the total operation of my organization	23.	1	2	3	4	5	24.	1	2	3	4	5
Specific problems faced by management	25.	1	2	3	4	5	26.	1	2	3	4	5

was that they did not get enough recognition for their efforts. The employees thought that it was management's responsibility to do the recognizing. Of course, this is management's responsibility—but not management's alone. Positive feedback exchanged horizontally becomes a kind of glue that holds

EXHIBIT 6.2   Sending Information to Others

Instructions for Questions 27 through 40

For each topic listed on the following pages, mark your responses on the answer sheet that best indicates: (1) the amount of information you are sending on that topic and (2) the amount of information you need to send on that topic in order to do your job.

Topic Area	This is the amount of information I send now						This is the amount of information I need to send now					
		Very Little	Little	Some	Great	Very Great		Very Little	Little	Some	Great	Very Great
Reporting what I am doing in my job	27.	1	2	3	4	5	28.	1	2	3	4	5
Reporting what I think my job requires me to do	29.	1	2	3	4	5	30.	1	2	3	4	5
Reporting job-related problems	31.	1	2	3	4	5	32.	1	2	3	4	5
Complaining about my job and/or working conditions	33.	1	2	3	4	5	34.	1	2	3	4	5
Requesting information necessary to do my job	35.	1	2	3	4	5	36.	1	2	3	4	5
Evaluating the performance of my immediate supervisor	37.	1	2	3	4	5	38.	1	2	3	4	5
Asking for clearer work	39.	1	2	3	4	5	40.	1	2	3	4	5

groups together, and each member of a group has a responsibility to send such information. An audit can remind one of the⁺

Follow-up on information sent

    The key to understanding this section is the word *follow-up*. When we send messages to people, we expect them to be open to those messages and then to acknowledge or use that information in some way. The questions in Exhibit 6.3 attempt to get an impression of how well the major groups of people with whom one works respond to messages.

EXHIBIT 6.3   Follow-Up on Information Sent

Instructions for Questions 41 through 50.

Indicate the amount of action or follow-up that is and needs to be taken on information you send to the following:

Topic Area		This is the amount of follow-up now						This is the amount of follow-up needed					
		Very Little	Little	Some	Great	Very Great		Very Little	Little	Some	Great	Very Great	
Subordinates	41.	1	2	3	4	5	42.	1	2	3	4	5
Co-workers	43.	1	2	3	4	5	44.	1	2	3	4	5
Immediate supervisor	45.	1	2	3	4	5	46.	1	2	3	4	5
Middle management	47.	1	2	3	4	5	48.	1	2	3	4	5
Top management	49.	1	2	3	4	5	50.	1	2	3	4	5

Sources of information

One of the earlier sections focused on the types of information received by employees, and this section lists the various sources from which that information can come. It gives each employee an opportunity to indicate how much information he or she receives from each source and how much he or she needs to receive from that source. The list generated in Exhibit 6.4 includes normal classifications for organizations and can be adapted to the unique sources in the organization under study.

Four observations should be made about the interpretation of the data generated from this section.

First, these questions involve only general reactions to the sources. They do not, for example, tell the auditor specifically what information is needed but is not being passed on.

Second, top management is the one thing that everyone in the organization has in common. Therefore, most audits pinpoint problems with the communication from management. Of course, top management *is* responsible for the general nature of communication, and "the buck stops here." Nevertheless, one needs to recognize that part of the result is often an artifact of the audit.

EXHIBIT 6.4   Sources of Information

Instructions for Questions 51 through 68.

You not only receive various kinds of information, but can receive such information from various sources within the organization. For each source listed below, mark your response on the answer sheet that indicates: (1) the amount of information you are receiving from that source and (2) the amount of information you need to receive from that source in order to do your job.

Sources of Information:		This is the amount of information I receive now						This is the amount of information I need to receive				
		Very Little	Little	Some	Great	Very Great		Very Little	Little	Some	Great	Very Great
Subordinates (if applicable)	51.	1	2	3	4	5	52.	1	2	3	4	5
Co-workers in my own unit or department	53.	1	2	3	4	5	54.	1	2	3	4	5
Individuals in other units, departments in my organization	55.	1	2	3	4	5	56.	1	2	3	4	5
Immediate supervisor	57.	1	2	3	4	5	58.	1	2	3	4	5
Department meetings	59.	1	2	3	4	5	60.	1	2	3	4	5
Middle management	61.	1	2	3	4	5	62.	1	2	3	4	5
Formal management presentations	63.	1	2	3	4	5	64.	1	2	3	4	5
Top management	65.	1	2	3	4	5	66.	1	2	3	4	5
The "grapevine"	67.	1	2	3	4	5	68.	1	2	3	4	5

Top management is the only category on the questionnaire that is the same for everybody. Employees are not responding to the same co-workers, department meetings, or immediate supervisors.

Third, because of the differences just mentioned, the responses must be compared by units or departments to make this information really meaningful. What good is it, for example, to know that 50 out of 250 people rate immediate supervisors low in communicating information? It makes a big difference in the usefulness of the information to know whether those 50 complaints are spread across all departments or whether they are concentrated in one or two departments. If it is the latter, specific individuals can be counseled.

Fourth, all but one question refers to formal sources. The grapevine, on the other hand, refers to the informal channels so pervasive in most organizations. An interesting tendency we have found is that employees often want less information to come to them through informal channels. It is the only case in which "less is better." For some reason, employees tend to think that information necessary to them should come through formal channels.

Timeliness of information

There can be no doubt about the importance of timing in the processing of communication. People want information exactly when they need it. If it comes too early, they are temporarily overloaded; if it comes too late, there is an underload. Therefore, timing is a crucial area to investigate in an audit. Exhibit 6.5 presents the questions concerning timeliness.

The focus in this section is again on key sources. Although information derived from these questions contributes to an overall impression of the adequacy of the sources, it does not precisely measure the kinds of information not being received on time. To identify specific needs, one could easily formulate additional questions that ask about the *kinds* of information needed to be communicated more quickly or one could check it out in follow-up interviews. Some information we have found to be communicated late in organizations include availability of jobs (chemical plant), ticket price changes (airline), summer schedules (university), management changes (manufacturing plant),

---

EXHIBIT 6.5   Timeliness of Information Received from Key Sources

Instructions for Questions 69 to 74.

Indicate the extent to which information from the following sources is *usually timely* (you get information when you need it—not too early, not too late).

Sources of Information:		Very Little Untimely	Little	Some	Great	Very Timely
Subordinates (if applicable)	69.	1	2	3	4	5
Co-workers	70.	1	2	3	4	5
Immediate supervisor	71.	1	2	3	4	5
Middle management	72.	1	2	3	4	5
Top management	73.	1	2	3	4	5
"Grapevine"	74.	1	2	3	4	5

and benefit changes (public utility). These examples suggest areas where an auditor might develop meaningful categories. Timeliness is an example of an area where a questionnaire can identify problems that need probing in a second round of interviews.

Organizational communication relationships

Every time two people communicate, they are not only exchanging information but they are also building, maintaining, or destroying a relationship between them. Therefore, communication relationships are among the most important areas to be examined in any communication audit. The questions in Exhibit 6.6 are oriented toward relationships with co-workers, the immediate supervisor, and top management, and they also consider the employee's general relationship to the organization. There are more questions about the relationship with the immediate supervisor than any other relationship because of this relationship's extreme importance in communication. In a number of audits the supervisors have been identified as the most important communication link between the employees and the organization.

Organizational outcomes

Organizational communication accomplishes a specific purpose. At a basic level, that purpose is to exchange information, but the exchange is supposed to result in something that we call *outcomes*. On the ICA audit, the outcome measured is one's *satisfaction* with the organization. In fact, many items in this section are the same ones that other writers use to measure communication climate. It is important to measure the level of one's satisfaction with the organization, the job, and the pay associated with it. Thirteen outcome questions are presented in Exhibit 6.7.

The questions in this section do not address level of performance or productivity, and the auditor must not necessarily assume that low satisfaction results in low productivity. Research does not support such a conclusion. On the other hand, high levels of dissatisfaction do generate problems, and dissatisfied workers often leave the organization. Therefore, do not minimize the importance of knowing something about people's levels of satisfaction.

Channels of communication

Every organization communicates through channels, which need to be evaluated periodically. To make this section really valuable, each of the organization's individual channels must be listed. Because the channels will

EXHIBIT 6.6   Organizational Communication Relationships

Instructions for Questions 75 to 93.

A variety of communicative relationships exist in organizations such as your own. Employees exchange messages regularly with supervisors, subordinates, co-workers, etc. Considering your relationships with others in your organization, please mark your response on the answer sheet that best describes the relationship in question.

Relationship:		Very Untimely	Little	Some	Great	Very Timely
I trust my co-workers	75.	1	2	3	4	5
My co-workers get along with each other	76.	1	2	3	4	5
My relationship with my co-workers is satisfying	77.	1	2	3	4	5
I trust my immediate supervisor	78.	1	2	3	4	5
My immediate supervisor is honest with me	79.	1	2	3	4	5
My immediate supervisor listens to me	80.	1	2	3	4	5
I am free to disagree with my immediate supervisor	81.	1	2	3	4	5
I can tell my immediate supervisor when things are going wrong	82.	1	2	3	4	5
My immediate supervisor praises me for a good job	83.	1	2	3	4	5
My immediate supervisor is friendly with his/her subordinates	84.	1	2	3	4	5
My immediate supervisor understands my job needs	85.	1	2	3	4	5
My relationship with my immediate supervisor is satisfying	86.	1	2	3	4	5
I trust top management	87.	1	2	3	4	5
Top management is sincere in its efforts to communicate with employees	88.	1	2	3	4	5
My relationship with top management is satisfying	89.	1	2	3	4	5
My organization encourages differences of opinion	90.	1	2	3	4	5
I have a say in decisions that affect my job	91.	1	2	3	4	5
I influence operations in my unit or department	92.	1	2	3	4	5
I have a part in accomplishing my organization's goals	93.	1	2	3	4	5

EXHIBIT 6.7   Organizational Outcomes

Instructions for Questions 94 to 106.

One of the most important outcomes of working in an organization is the satisfaction one gets or fails to receive through working there. Such satisfaction can relate to the job, one's immediate supervisor, or the organization as a whole. Please mark your response on the answer sheet to indicate the extent to which you are satisfied with:

Outcome:		Very Little	Little	Some	Great	Very Great
My job	94.	1	2	3	4	5
My pay	95.	1	2	3	4	5
My progress in my organization up to this point in time	96.	1	2	3	4	5
My chances for getting ahead in my organization	97.	1	2	3	4	5
My opportunity to "make a difference"—to contribute to the overall success of my organization	98.	1	2	3	4	5
My organization's system for recognizing and rewarding outstanding performance	99.	1	2	3	4	5
My organization's concern for its members' welfare	100.	1	2	3	4	5
My organization's overall communicative efforts	101.	1	2	3	4	5
Working in my organization	102.	1	2	3	4	5
My organization, as compared to other such organizations	103.	1	2	3	4	5
My organization's overall efficiency of operation	104.	1	2	3	4	5
The overall quality of my organization's product or service	105.	1	2	3	4	5
My organization's achievement of its goals and objectives	106.	1	2	3	4	5

differ among organizations, there is not a standard list. Nevertheless, the ICA survey always contains this section, but the items on the list must be adapted to the specific organization. For illustrative purposes, the comprehensive list

EXHIBIT 6.8   Channels of Information

Listed below are a variety of channels through which messages are transmitted. Please indicate on the answer sheet (1) the amount of information you now receive through that channel, and (2) the amount you need to receive through that channel.

		This is the amount of information I receive now (Very Little / Little / Some / Great / Very Great)						This is the amount of information I need to receive (Very Little / Little / Some / Great / Very Great)				
Face to face	107.	1	2	3	4	5	108.	1	2	3	4	5
Telephone	109.	1	2	3	4	5	110.	1	2	3	4	5
Written memos, letters, and notices	111.	1	2	3	4	5	112.	1	2	3	4	5
Bulletin boards	113.	1	2	3	4	5	114.	1	2	3	4	5
Corporate newsletter	115.	1	2	3	4	5	116.	1	2	3	4	5
Plant newsletter	117.	1	2	3	4	5	118.	1	2	3	4	5
Procedural manual	119.	1	2	3	4	5	120.	1	2	3	4	5
Home mailings	121.	1	2	3	4	5	122.	1	2	3	4	5
Pay envelope stuffers	123.	1	2	3	4	5	124	1	2	3	4	5
Communication committee minutes	125.	1	2	3	4	5	126	1	2	3	4	5
Safety steering committee minutes	127.	1	2	3	4	5	128.	1	2	3	4	5
Shift briefings	129.	1	2	3	4	5	130.	1	2	3	4	5
Meeting with supervisor	131.	1	2	3	4	5	132.	1	2	3	4	5
Meeting with divisional management	133.	1	2	3	4	5	134.	1	2	3	4	5
Meeting with plant management	135.	1	2	3	4	5	136.	1	2	3	4	5
Departmental safety meetings	137.	1	2	3	4	5	138.	1	2	3	4	5

shown in Exhibit 6.8 was developed for an audit of a manufacturing plant. The items were generated in conferences with management.

Rank ordering the discrepancy scores is a quick way to see the general reactions to each of these channels. One can also evaluate effectiveness of the media in terms of cost or effort.

ANALYSIS AND INTERPRETATION

Some of the interpretive implications of the survey have already been explored. This section indicates traditional ways that the data from this questionnaire are analyzed.

Frequency counts and means

A basic approach to analyzing the data collected about an organization is to plot the frequencies with which each question is answered on each part of the scale and to compute a mean for all the responses to that question. The frequency count permits an auditor to examine how individual responses vary across the scale for each question. Such spectrum analysis allows one to determine the degree of agreement in the organization about strengths and weaknesses. The mean or average, on the other hand, allows comparisons among the items. A rank ordering of the means can indicate what the employees rate as being most effective about the organization and what items are rated as ineffective.

Difference scores

Questions 1 through 68 are designed to gather data about the amount of information being received currently versus the amount needed. Subtract the score of the amount received from the score of the amount wanted or needed, and the resulting difference score theoretically gives one a measure of satisfaction on that question:
Satisfaction = Amount Needed/Wanted − Amount Received Currently.
The assumption is that the wider the gap between "need" and "current amount received," the more a problem exists. Therefore, a rank ordering of all different scores will indicate where the major problems occur. This is a legitimate way to analyze the ICA Survey in its entirety or by individual sections.

Comparisons

Like other questionnaire data, the ICA Survey can be analyzed across all demographic data as was reviewed in Chapter 5. The results allow one to identify where groups are significantly different from one another, and this is important.

ADVANTAGES OF THE ICA SURVEY

The comprehensiveness of the survey has already been noted, but there are other positive aspects that should be mentioned.

Conceived by scholars and seasoned through years of pilot testing, the ICA Survey has probably received more scrutiny than any other single communication instrument. Although it has been somewhat controversial, many auditors have used it successfully. Furthermore, frequent usage has prompted people to refine it in significant ways, and the end product is a highly usable instrument.

The survey has been adaptable to many kinds of organizations: banks, colleges, military units, governmental organizations, hospitals, unions, manufacturing plants, airlines, utilities, volunteer organizations, and retail operations. Furthermore, the size of the organizations has varied widely.

The reliability and validity of the survey questions have been thoroughly researched and documented. Goldhaber and others have tested each section of this questionnaire extensively, and their reliability and validity scores are demonstrated in Exhibit 6.9. The reliability coefficients show the extent to which people answer the question the same way across time. Validity determines whether or not auditors are measuring what they think they are measuring. In this case, the coefficients measure the correlations between each scale and the organizational outcomes scale. Finally, the discrimination ability percentages indicate the number of items that significantly discriminated between the top 17 percent of the respondents and the bottom 17 percent (Goldhaber and Rogers, 1979, p. 34).

EXHIBIT 6.9

	Reliability	Validity	Discrimination Ability
Amount of Information Received	.88	.69	100%
Amount of Information Desired	.85	.07	100%
Amount of Information Sent	.83	.56	100%
Amount of Information Desired to Send	.79	.10	100%
Amount of Information Received from Sources	.70	.63	.78%
Amount of Information Desired from Sources	.76	.06	.89%
Relationships	.90	.70	n.a.*
Organizational Outcomes	.88	n.a.*	100%

*n.a. = not applicable.

The fact that a data bank is available gives this instrument an enormous advantage. From the beginning, the ICA scholars set out to build a data bank that might generate the compilation of norms for comparative purposes. In 1979, for example, Porter synthesized the results of 17 audits representing responses from 4,600 people. While the expectations of building truly national norms have never been fully realized, the data banks are available for comparative and research purposes. They are currently housed at SUNY-Buffalo, Ohio University, Purdue University, University of South Florida, and the University of Kansas. Access can be obtained by contacting members of the communication departments at these universities. Although it is exciting to be able to compare one organization with others, extreme caution must be used when comparing data from a local company with data from many different organizations throughout the country. For this reason, some auditors have begun to develop regional data banks. DeWine and her colleagues (1985) have done this at Ohio University, and they have found that the regional norms often differ from the national data.

The ultimate testimony to this instrument is that is has performed well as a practical analytic tool. DeWine, James, and Walence (1985) surveyed several organizations that had been audited, and they discovered "noticeable improvement" in most communication variables except load.

Despite the advantages, the survey is vulnerable in some significant ways, which are discussed in the next section.

VULNERABILITIES OF THE ICA SURVEY

With usage, some of the vulnerabilities of the instrument have been exposed. These are pointed out here not to attack the survey but to suggest that any potential user will encounter certain problems.

Many respondents have complained about the length and complexity of the survey. There have been reports that some people do not finish it, and some managers resent the "down time" at work because it takes so long to fill out. Because this liability is indeed inherent in the instrument, extra care must be taken in administering the survey to motivate respondents.

Originally, a five-point Likert scale was used, and this is what is described in this chapter. As auditors have become more sophisticated, they have looked for more refined scaling techniques. Today, some people have rejected the old Likert scale and have replaced it with different kinds of scales. The differences in scaling sometimes make it difficult to compare new and old audits.

Ambiguous terms also constitute a problem. The respondents are not certain what is being asked or the auditors are not certain how the question was interpreted. For example, in one section employees are asked to contrast the amount of information wanted and the amount currently received. The amount received is then subtracted from the amount wanted to compute a difference score. One question emerged as a significant difference score in two different audits; it was ranked as the number one difference score in one audit and as number two in the other. The topic area was "how organizational decisions are made that affect your position." Employees in both organizations wanted a great deal more information than they were receiving about this topic. It was one of our most significant findings, and we were at a loss to interpret how employees perceived the question. In which decisions were they interested? Did they want more performance appraisals? Did they want to know board decisions? Did they want more information about facilities and operations? Each of these explanations could be plausible; yet, they led to quite different recommendations. The ambiguous item thus stymied the interpretation.

Another significant result that was difficult to interpret was "the extent to which you have a say in decisions that affect you (your job)." Since the question did not ask the respondent to contrast the amount she or he wanted with the amount now exercised, the finding is problematic. Should we assume that low participation is necessarily a problem? This question may reflect a bias toward participatory decision making; but not all workers want to have more say than they have. *The problem with questions such as these is not that the analysts cannot generate possible interpretations, but rather that these interpretations may not be faithful to the meanings intended by respondents.*

The form of the comparison of the amount of information needed or wanted minus the amount received creates another difficulty in interpreting the questionnaire. Using the terms "want" or "need" apparently biases the respondent to indicate that high levels of information are desired, implying deficiencies in information in the organization. Perhaps the most telling proof for this conclusion is that in audits, every respondent, on every difference question pair except one (information from the grapevine), *always* indicated they needed more information than they received. Thus the scale may be more of a "curiosity index" than an information-needs inventory.

The ICA Survey is basically a self-report, perception-based instrument. Therefore, it is subject to questions about the congruence between the report and the actual communication realities. This, of course, is a legitimate objection. It can, however, be answered in two ways. First, discovery of perceptions is important because organizational members shape their behaviors on the basis of their perceptions. Second, the survey instrument is rarely used alone. The complete audit calls for it to be used with other methodologies that may overcome the reliance on mere self-report. In this regard, what the auditor observes about actual communication is important, but it may not be any more important than the members' beliefs about the "truth" of the matter.

Occasionally, auditors discover that this instrument, while comprehensive, still leaves out significant areas. In his description of networks in Chapter 10, for example, Porter states that he believes the structure of networks to be important. Since the survey does not analyze structure, it would not meet all of Porter's needs. For these kinds of objections, however, one should remember that the ICA Survey is merely one tool available for use in conjunction with other methodologies to build a comprehensive assessment of the organization.

CONCLUSION

The descriptions of the ICA Survey have been brief by necessity. A greater appreciation of its history, development, and significance can be obtained from Goldhaber and Rogers (1979), Goldhaber and Krivonos (1978), and Greenbaum, Hellwegg, and Falcione (1983). Since 1979 the pooled effort so instrumental in the survey's development has declined. Nevertheless, it continues to be a viable tool for individual auditors, and as such it merits our attention.

REFERENCES

DeWine, Sue; James, Anita; and Walence, William. "Validation of Organizational Communication Audit Instruments." Paper presented to the International Communication Association, Honolulu, May 1985.

Downs, Cal W.; Clampitt, Phillip; and Laird, Angela. "Critique of the ICA Communication Audit." Paper presented to the International Communication Association, Minneapolis, May 1981.

Goldhaber, G., and Krivonos, Paul. "The ICA Communication Audit: Process, Status, and Critique." *Journal of Business Communication Systems* 15 (1978): 41–55.

Goldhaber, G., and Rogers, Don. *Auditing Organizational Communication Systems*. Dubuque, Iowa: Kendall-Hunt, 1979.

Greenbaum, Howard; Hellwegg, Susan; and Falcione, Raymond. "Evaluation of Communication in Organizations: Rationale, History and Methodologies." Paper presented to the International Communication Association, Dallas, May 1983.

Porter, Thomas. "The ICA Communication Audit: Norms and Instrument Documentation." Unpublished paper, 1979.

7

Downs/Hazen Communication Satisfaction Questionnaire[1]

The Communication Satisfaction Questionnaire offers both an efficient and a comprehensive approach to auditing the communication practices of organizations. Composed of only sixty items, the questionnaire has proved to be easy and quick to administer while being remarkably thorough in covering a variety of communication practices that range from personal feedback to corporate-wide communications. During the past decade it has been used in several foreign countries as well as the United States. It has also been used in a number of different kinds of organizations, including manufacturing plants, television stations, school districts, consulting firms, banks, hotels, and a mental health center. In short, this instrument has proved to be exceptionally useful in a variety of organizations. This chapter discusses how to utilize it in a communication audit.

HISTORICAL DEVELOPMENT

Traditionally, communication satisfaction was thought of as a unidimensional construct. Thayer (1968) defined communication satisfaction as "the personal satisfaction inherent in successfully communicating to someone or in successfully being communicated with. . ." (p. 144). Redding (1972) reviewed some of the literature about communication satisfaction and asked

[1]This chapter was written by Phillip G. Clampitt, Ph.D.

whether communication satisfaction may indeed be a multidimensional concept. Such questions often spur theoretical and empirical investigations.

Indeed, two research efforts have suggested that communication satisfaction is multidimensional. Osmo Wiio's (1976) work suggested four dimensions of communication satisfaction: job satisfaction, message content, improvements in communication, and channel efficiency. His methods involved conducting twenty-two organizational communication audits in Finland and factor analyzing the results.

Downs and Hazen (1977) used similar procedures to investigate the communication satisfaction question. They developed a questionnaire and administered it to 225 employees from many kinds of organizations, including a military unit, a hospital, professional organizations, various businesses, and universities. The results were factor analyzed, and a new questionnaire was refined and administered to four different organizations. Factor analysis was again conducted, and the result was eight stable dimensions of communication satisfaction.

1. *Satisfaction with Communication Climate* reflects communication on both the organizational and personal level. On one hand, it includes items such as the extent to which communication in the organization motivates and stimulates workers to meet organizational goals and the extent to which it makes them identify with the organization. On the other, it includes estimates of whether or not people's attitudes toward communicating are healthy in this organization. There is some indication that climate is the strongest dimension and that workers tend to think of it when they respond to general questions about communication.

2. *Satisfaction with Superiors* includes both upward and downward aspects of communicating with superiors. Three of the principal items deal with the extent to which they are open to ideas, the extent to which they listen and pay attention, and the extent to which they offer guidance for solving job-related problems.

3. *Satisfaction with Organizational Integration* revolves around the degree to which individuals receive information about the immediate work environment. Workers want to know about departmental plans, the requirements of their jobs, and some personnel news. Such information makes them feel a part of the organization.

4. *Satisfaction with Media Quality* obtains reactions to several important communication channels. Of particular concern here is the extent to which meetings are well organized, written directives are short and clear, and the amount of communication in the organization is about right.

5. *Satisfaction with Horizontal and Informal Communication* concerns the degree to which the grapevine is active and the extent to

which horizontal and informal communication is accurate and free flowing.

6. *Satisfaction with Organizational Perspective* concerns the broadest kind of information about the organization as a whole. It includes the notification about changes, the organization's financial standing, and the overall policies and goals of the organization.

7. *Satisfaction with Subordinates* focuses on upward and downward communication with subordinates, who are expected to be responsive to downward communication and also to anticipate the supervisor's needs and initiate upward communication that will be helpful.

8. *Satisfaction with Personal Feedback* is one of the strongest dimensions because workers in general have a need to know how they are being judged and how their performance is being appraised.

Downs and Hazen conclude that "it is possible that the various dimensions of communication satisfaction can provide a barometer of organizational functioning, and the concept of communication satisfaction can be a useful tool in an audit or organizational communication" (p. 72). Hecht (1978) reviewed various instruments used to assess communication satisfaction. Generally he was quite critical of most approaches used to measure communication satisfaction, but, in contrast, his remarks on the Communication Satisfaction Questionnaire were basically positive.

The thoroughness of the construction of this satisfaction measure is apparent. While one could comment on the fatigue factor in requiring respondents to complete 264 scales (88 items multiplied by three scaling styles), the strategies employed in this study are exemplary. Input into initial item construction was obtained from a wide variety of sources and items were tested and factor analyzed for variety of scaling styles. Internal consistency reliability for each dimension and validity information as a whole are lacking (p. 363).

Recently, Crino and White (1981) reported a study that answered most of Hecht's concerns. The subjects were 137 first-line supervisors from five textile mills. After data collection, the researchers sought to determine the dimensional stability and intrascale internal consistency of the measure. Their results show that the eight factor solution is reasonable. While the intrascale internal consistency is not as strong as it could be, the scales are still useful. They conclude that "although still in a somewhat embryonic stage of development, the construct, communication satisfaction, appears to possess few of the problems which have plagued the construct, organizational climate" (p. 832). Thus, the communication satisfaction questionnaire provides a uniquely theoretical and empirically sound method of gathering information about organizational communication.

OVERVIEW OF THE QUESTIONNAIRE

Of particular importance to the auditor is the actual layout of the survey. Exhibit 7.1 contains the basic questionnaire used in numerous organizational audits.

EXHIBIT 7.1   Communication Satisfaction Questionnaire

Cal W. Downs and Michael D. Hazen
Copyright, 1973

INTRODUCTION. Most of us assume that the quality and amount of communication in our jobs contribute to both our job satisfaction and our productivity. Through this study we hope to find out how satisfactory our communication practices are and what suggestions you have for improving them.

We appreciate your taking the time to complete the questionnaire. Hopefully, you should be able to complete it in 10–15 minutes.

Your answers are completely confidential, so be as frank as you wish. This is not a test—your opinion is the only right answer. Do not sign your name; we do not wish to know who you are. The answers will be combined into groups for reporting purposes.

1. How satisfied are you with your job? (Check 1)

   ____ 1. Very dissatisfied   ____ 5. Somewhat satisfied
   ____ 2. Dissatisfied   ____ 6. Satisfied
   ____ 3. Somewhat dissatisfied   ____ 7. Very satisfied
   ____ 4. Indifferent

2. In the past 6 months, what has happened to your level of satisfaction? (Check 1)

   ____ 1. Stayed the same   ____ 2. Gone up   ____ 3. Gone down

3. If the communication associated with your job could be changed in any way to make you more satisfied, please indicate how.

A. Listed below are several kinds of information often associated with a person's job. Please indicate how satisfied you are with the amount and/or quality of each kind of information by circling the appropriate number at the right.

	Very Satisfied	Satisfied	Slightly Satisfied	Indifferent	Slightly Dissatisfied	Dissatisfied	Very Dissatisfied
4. Information about my progress in my job.	1	2	3	4	5	6	7
5. Personnel news.	1	2	3	4	5	6	7
6. Information about company policies and goals.	1	2	3	4	5	6	7
7. Information about how my job compares with others.	1	2	3	4	5	6	7
8. Information about how I am being judged.	1	2	3	4	5	6	7
9. Recognition of my efforts.	1	2	3	4	5	6	7
10. Information about departmental policies and goals.	1	2	3	4	5	6	7

	Very Satisfied	Satisfied	Slightly Satisfied	Indifferent	Slightly Dissatisfied	Dissatisfied	Very Dissatisfied
11. Information about the requirements of my job.	1	2	3	4	5	6	7
12. Information about government action affecting my company.	1	2	3	4	5	6	7
13. Information about relations with unions.	1	2	3	4	5	6	7
14. Reports on how problems in my job are being handled.	1	2	3	4	5	6	7
15. Information about employee benefits and pay.	1	2	3	4	5	6	7
16. Information about company profits and financial standing.	1	2	3	4	5	6	7
17. Information about accomplishments and/or failures of the company.	1	2	3	4	5	6	7 •

B. Please indicate how satisfied you are with the following. (Circle the appropriate number at the right.)

	Very Satisfied	Satisfied	Slightly Satisfied	Indifferent	Slightly Dissatisfied	Dissatisfied	Very Dissatisfied
18. Extent to which my superiors know and understand the problems faced by subordinates	1	2	3	4	5	6	7
19. Extent to which company communication motivates and stimulates an enthusiasm for meeting its goals.	1	2	3	4	5	6	7
20. Extent to which my supervisor listens and pays attention to me.	1	2	3	4	5	6	7
21. Extent to which the people in my organization have great ability as communicators.	1	2	3	4	5	6	7
22. Extent to which my supervisor offers guidance for solving job related problems.	1	2	3	4	5	6	7
23. Extent to which the company's communication makes me identify with it or feel a vital part of it.	1	2	3	4	5	6	7
24. Extent to which the company's publications are interesting and helpful.	1	2	3	4	5	6	7
25. Extent to which my supervisor trusts me.	1	2	3	4	5	6	7
26. Extent to which I receive on time the information needed to do my job.	1	2	3	4	5	6	7

	Very Satisfied	Satisfied	Slightly Satisfied	Indifferent	Slightly Dissatisfied	Dissatisfied	Very Dissatisfied
27. Extent to which conflicts are handled appropriately through proper communication channels.	1	2	3	4	5	6	7
28. Extent to which the grapevine is active in our organization.	1	2	3	4	5	6	7
29. Extent to which my supervisor is open to ideas.	1	2	3	4	5	6	7
30. Extent to which horizontal communication with other employees is accurate and free-flowing.	1	2	3	4	5	6	7
31. Extent to which communication practices are adaptable to emergencies.	1	2	3	4	5	6	7
32. Extent to which my work group is compatible.	1	2	3	4	5	6	7
33. Extent to which our meetings are well organized.	1	2	3	4	5	6	7
34. Extent to which the amount of supervision given me is about right.	1	2	3	4	5	6	7
35. Extent to which written directives and reports are clear and concise.	1	2	3	4	5	6	7
36. Extent to which the attitudes toward communication in the company are basically healthy.	1	2	3	4	5	6	7
37. Extent to which informal communication is active and accurate.	1	2	3	4	5	6	7
38. Extent to which the amount of communication in the company is about right.	1	2	3	4	5	6	7

C. *Please tell how you feel about your productivity on your job by answering the three questions below.*

39. How would you rate your productivity in your job? (Check 1)

___ 1. Very low   ___ 5. Slightly higher than most
___ 2. Low   ___ 6. High
___ 3. Slightly lower than most   ___ 7. Very high
___ 4. Average

40. In the last 6 months, what has happened to your productivity? (Check 1)

___ 1. Stayed the same   ___ 2. Gone up   ___ 3. Gone down

41. If the communication associated with your job could be changed in any way to make you more productive, please tell how. _____

D. Answer the following only if you are a manager or supervisor. Then indicate your satisfaction with the following.	Very Satisfied	Satisfied	Slightly Satisfied	Indifferent	Slightly Dissatisfied	Dissatisfied	Very Dissatisfied
42. Extent to which my subordinates are responsive to downward directive communication.	1	2	3	4	5	6	7
43. Extent to which my subordinates anticipate my needs for information.	1	2	3	4	5	6	7
44. Extent to which I *do not* have a communication overload.	1	2	3	4	5	6	7
45. Extent to which my subordinates are receptive to evaluation, suggestions, and criticisms.	1	2	3	4	5	6	7
46. Extent to which my subordinates feel responsible for initiating accurate upward communication.	1	2	3	4	5	6	7

Two questions are open-ended and seek to determine what types of communication changes could be made that would increase employee satisfaction and productivity. The responses to these open-ended questions provide a useful check on the statistical data generated from the other questions. Frequently the problems highlighted in the open-ended responses serve to confirm the results of the other parts of the survey. In addition, when reporting the results to a company, a well-turned phrase can sometimes be more persuasive than statistical data.

Four survey items are reflective of end-product variables. Two of these questions ask employees to indicate their degree of job satisfaction and whether their level of job satisfaction has decreased, increased, or stayed the same during the past six months. Similar questions are used to assess employee productivity. As a group these four questions are often the focus of much discussion in feedback sessions with management. Through the use of correlational statistics, the auditor can frequently "explain" the productivity and satisfaction levels by relating these variables to the communication satisfaction factors.

Forty items ask about employee satisfaction with various types of communication that correspond to the eight factors discussed previously. Each factor consists of five items as designated in Exhibit 7.2. Various scaling devices have been used. Originally it contained a 1 to 7 scale, ranging from "satisfied" to "dissatisfied," but I prefer the 0 to 10 scale because it offers greater choice to respondents. When describing this kind of scale on the survey, it is important to use the language "by placing a 0–1–2–3–4–5–6–7–8–9–10 in the blank provided" instead of "by placing a number from 0–10." Using the latter can result in respondents only utilizing zeros, fives, and tens on the surveys. Hence, the full value of the scaling device is not realized, rather like using only three gears on a ten-speed bicycle.

Companies frequently wish to add other questions to the survey. I encourage this for two reasons. First, it allows the company to develop some ownership of the survey, which hopefull may induce commitment to the auditing process and ensure a higher return rate. The aim is to move the discussion from "the auditor's questionnaire" to "our company survey." Secondly, adding questions can help ease pressure to change the wording of questions in the heart of the survey. Any changes in the wording of the forty key items would hinder the reliability of the survey. While encouraging additional questions is useful, it is important to avoid an overly enthusiastic response. Part of the charm of this instrument is its brevity.

ANALYSIS

Quantitative and qualitative data can be used to arrive at conclusions. The related data analysis techniques that have special significance for this instrument are reviewed next.

Quantitative data

Few research activities are more routine than entering data in a computer and utilizing statistical packages to calculate means, standard deviations, and frequency counts. Assuming that this step has been completed, there are several approaches that can be used at this juncture: (1) categorize items into groups; (2) rank order items; (3) utilize factors scores; and (4) make data bank comparisons.

EXHIBIT 7.2   Communication Satisfaction Factor Key

Factor	Items				
Corporate Perspective	6	12	13	16	17
Personal Feedback	7	8	9	14	18
Organizational Integration	4	5	10	11	15
Relation with Supervisor	20	22	25	29	34
Communication Climate	19	21	23	26	27
Horizontal Communication	28	30	31	32	37
Media Quality	24	33	35	36	38
Relations with Subordinates	42	43	44	45	46

Categorize items. • A thorough examination of the means and standard deviations for each survey items can prove revealing. In a very rough and tentative fashion, those mean scores that fall well below the conceptual midpoint (a 5.0 on a 0 to 10 scale) can be thought of as weaknesses. Those scores that are well above the conceptual midpoint can be seen as strengths, while scores falling around the mean are areas of average satisfaction.

For instance, if a company had the following responses to question 9, the auditor would be safe in tentatively concluding that the feedback area was an area of concern for many employees.

Question 9: Recognition of my efforts.

Satisfaction

Low				High	Mean
0–2	3–4	5–6	7–8	9–10	
24.4%	10.3%	34.6%	17.9%	12.8%	3.94

More specifically, the auditors would want to explore the issue of praise and how individuals are recognized for good work within the organization. On the other hand, should the results reveal that the mean for question 25 is 8.64, it would be reasonable to conclude that supervisory communication is an area of strength. However, that may be a hasty conclusion if other questions about the supervisory relationship are not rated equally high. Hence, the auditor must use a great deal of discernment in coming to these conclusions.

Question 25: Extent to which my supervisor trusts me.

Satisfaction

Low				High	Mean
0–2	3–4	5–6	7–8	9–10	
9%	6%	19%	34%	32%	8.64

The difficulty with this approach is that sometimes no items fall in the dissatisfied area. Is it proper to assume that this company has no communication difficulties? Conversely, there are companies that have been audited in which no items fall in the satisfied area. Can the auditor then assume the organization has no communication strengths? Or, more to the point, can the argument be made that *all* companies have at least some communication strengths and weaknesses? No doubt that proposition could be debated in some depth. Yet, making such an assumption is a sound strategy in actually reporting the results. To ineffective organizations, designating certain strengths can be motivating, whereas for the effective organizations, designating weaknesses can stimulate even better performance. If this assumption can be made, some

[2]All of the data used in this chapter come from actual audits.

other method is needed to arrive at conclusions, which leads us to the next method.

   The rank-order method. • Each of the forty communication satisfaction items can be rank ordered on the basis of the means from 1 to 40. Statistical tests can be used to determine which items are significantly different from one another. Hence, a group of relatively high, moderate, and low means emerge. These groupings can be examined to determine conceptual patterns within each group. Based on the auditor's knowledge of the organization, certain items will appear to naturally cluster together, pointing to certain areas of strength and weakness.

   For instance, in one audit the following items clustered at the top of the ranking:

Sample Rank Order

Rank	Mean	Question
1	6.88*	Extent to which my work group is compatible.
2	6.87	Extent to which the grapevine is active in our organization
3	6.68	Extent to which my supervisor trusts me.
4	6.66	Extent to which the amount of supervision given me is about right.
5	6.35	Extent to which my supervisor is open to ideas.
6	6.31	Extent to which written directives and reports are clear and concise.
7	6.29	Information about employee benefits and pay.
8	6.15	Extent to which my supervisor listens and pays attention to me.
9	6.04	Extent to which horizontal communication with other employees is accurate and free flowing.
10	5.55	Extent to which my supervisor offers guidance for solving job-related problems.

*Note: These means are based on a 0 to 10 scale.

   Clearly, a number of the questions cluster together around supervisory communication and coworker communication, suggesting that these are areas of *relative* strength in this organization. Formal communication practices such as written directions and information about pay/benefits also seem to be relatively theoretical dimensions of communication satisfaction. In this case the auditors, using other supporting data as well as the survey items, concluded that the area of "formal communication" was a unique strength of this particular company. Hence, an item-by-item ranking of the questions, used in conjunction with other methods, can suggest conclusions other than those designated by the eight communication satisfaction factors.

The obvious difficulty with the rank order method is that communication strengths and weaknesses are always discovered. In the context of the rank-order method, a strength could actually be an item of average satisfaction if the absolute standard method suggested previously is used. In the last example, some of the items may be thought of as strengths but may actually fall in the "average satisfaction" area. Hence, the auditor should always temper this type of conclusion by underscoring the fact that these are *relative* strengths or weaknesses.

Factor scores. • Another method of arriving at conclusions is to calculate the factor scores for each of the eight communication satisfaction dimensions. The factor scores could be compared to the conceptual midpoint. With the 0 to 10 scale this midpoint would be 25 for each factor, because there are five items per dimensions. Rank ordering the factor scores and testing for statistical significance could also prove to be useful.

Theoretically, utilizing the factor scores should prove revealing because each of the five items that make up an individual factor are measuring the "same thing." Yet using only the factor scores may obscure subtle differences unique to a particular company. Hence, auditors should examine individual survey items in addition to the factor scores. Note that, in addition to factor analysis, statistical analyses such as principal component analysis can be used to explore the unique groupings for each organization.

Data bank comparisons. • One of the more exciting alternatives now available is the comparison of one organization's results to those of other companies. Such an opportunity is enthusiastically embraced by most organizations, because most want to know "how they stack up."

To date, the communication audit data bank at the University of Wisconsin–Green Bay's Communication Research Center has responses from more than fourteen hundred individuals in eighteen companies. The data base collected during a four-year period includes a wide range of organizations, including banks, TV stations, and manufacturing companies. Furthermore, the response rate from the various organizations surveyed is relatively high at over 84 percent. Hence, a reasonable cross-section of individuals and organizations is represented in the data. One of the problems of the data base is that it has been generated in only one section of the country. Yet, the firms are representative of the types of organizations found in other locales. In spite of this minor difficulty, the data bank provides a useful research base.

There are two formats of output, as seen in Exhibits 7.3 and 7.4. One form displays the mean scores with standard deviations whereas the other suppresses the standard deviations. The one that the auditor should use depends on the client's sophistication.

EXHIBIT 7.3   Communication Satisfaction Data Bank Comparison
(Standard Deviations Suppressed)

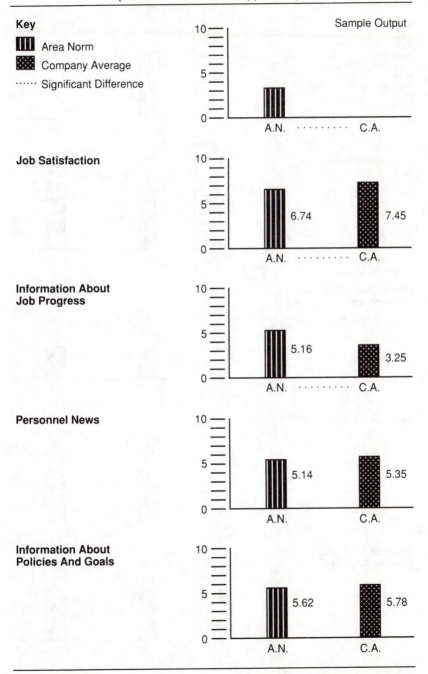

EXHIBIT 7.4   Communication Satisfaction Data Bank Comparison with
               Standard Deviations

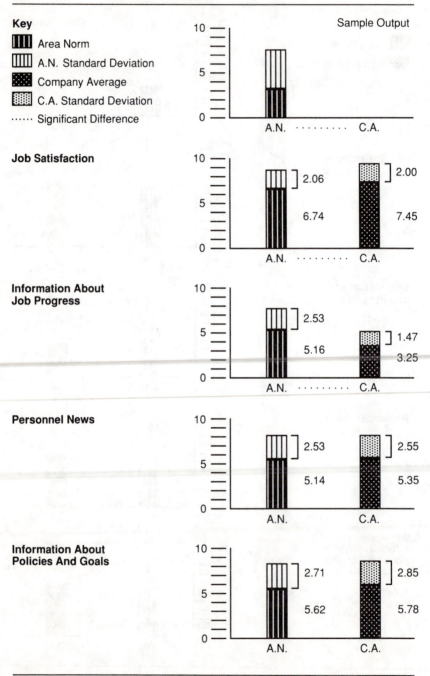

Significant differences between the data bank norm and the organization's norm are displayed with an asterisk in Exhibit 7.3. Standard statistical tests can be used to determine if the differences are significant.

Since companies differ in terms of functions, procedures, competitive environment, and goals, it may not always be appropriate to compare some organizations to the data bank. However, there is the capability of evaluating the target organization against similar types of organizations. For example, the auditor could compare a savings and loan to other financial institutions in the data bank.

A more perplexing problem can occur when this technique is used in conjunction with the other approaches detailed in previous sections. In the first three methods, the basis of comparison is internal. The organization is examined essentially in isolation, which is similar to asking the question, "What are the strengths and weaknesses of the Green Bay Packers compared to the other teams in the NFL?" This situation can set up some interesting dilemmas. An item or factor that emerges as a weakness using the rank order method may turn out to be a strength when the data bank analysis is conducted. The situation would be like the Packers rating their linebackers as the weakness of *their team* when they look internally, but when compared to *other NFL teams* the Packer linebackers look fairly impressive. Resolution of this dilemma can only occur when the auditor and the client agree on adopting a given perspective in light of the objectives of the audit.

Qualitative data

One of the most enlightening aspects of the audit is reading through the responses to the open-ended questions. It can also be the most misleading. One particularly insightful or impressive comment may become overly persuasive in weighing the actual evidence. To avoid these difficulties, a rigorous system of analysis, known as content analysis, is needed. The process has been reviewed in considerable depth elsewhere (Krippendorff, 1980), but basically the following six steps are involved.

Step 1. Read through the entire list of responses and try to discern central concerns that are common to many of these respondents. After a thorough review of all the responses, a series of nonoverlapping categories should emerge for each of the open-ended questions. For example, assume that the following comments were made to the question about communication changes needed to improve job satisfaction.
A. "More listening by managers."
B. "Would like more responsiveness to upward communication."
C. "More meetings."
D. "More coverage of our department in the newsletter."
E. "There are not enough meetings."
F. "The newsletter is frivolous."

The categories that emerge would be as follows:
1. Improvement of upward communication (Responses A and B)
2. More meetings (Responses C and E)
3. Changes in newsletter (Responses D and F)

Step 2. Another researcher should read through the same list of responses and, without discussion between the auditors, determine a list of categories.

Step 3. The two auditors should reconcile the differences between their category lists. A working list of categories should be agreed upon for each open-ended question.

Step 4. Both auditors should separately categorize each response according to their working list.

Step 5. The reliability of the coding procedure should be determined by comparing the number of coding agreements between the judges. The following formula should be used to calculate the reliability (Holsti, 1969, p. 40).

$$\text{Reliability} = \frac{2(M)}{N_1 - N_2}$$

M = Number of coding decisions on which there was agreement.
N_1 = Total number of coding decisions by person 1.
N_2 = Total number of coding decisions by person 2.

The reliability should be 90 percent or better. If this level of reliability is not achieved, the category system should be reevaluated.

INSTRUMENT EVALUATION

All research instruments have biases. In a decade of experience with the instrument, I have encountered relatively few difficulties. However, there are two areas of concern. First, most of the questions have a conceptual bent toward the communication behaviors of others. However, the relatively few items that ask for self-evaluation of communication tend to have an upward bias. For example, the items for the subordinate communication factor all ask supervisors to evaluate their own communication with their subordinates. Even the question about the "extent to which the supervisor trusts me" may be interpreted in terms of the respondents' trustworthiness rather than an evaluation of the supervisor's behavior. Having a data bank available for comparison can to some extent alleviate this difficulty.

Second, the survey does not contain any specific items about interdepartmental communication. Analyses of the open-ended questions has revealed this to be a prevalent problem in many organizations. It would be convenient to have quantitative data in this area.

Nevertheless, the instrument has proved useful in a variety of organizational settings and cultures. Exhibit 7.5 reviews some of the theses and dissertations that have used the instrument to date. These studies have yielded a

EXHIBIT 7.5   Communication Satisfaction Research

Researcher	Organizations	Subjects	Sample Size	Country
Avery (1977)	Government Agency	Government Employees	135	U.S.A.
Thiry (1977)	Hospitals and Clinics	Registered Nurses	1,069	U.S.A.
Gordon (1979)	University	Administrators	41	U.S.A.
Kio (1979)	Government and Business	Administrators and Line Workers	134	Nigeria
Nicholson (1980)	Urban School	Administrators and Teachers	290	U.S.A.
Jones (1981)	Rural School System	Administrators and Teachers	142	U.S.A.
Duke (1981)	Urban School System	Business Education Teachers	309	U.S.A.
Alum (1982)	Social Service	Managers and Line Workers	274	Mexico
Wippich, B. J. (1983) and Wippich, M. L. (1983)	School District	Teachers	150	U.S.A.
Pincus (1984)	Teaching Hospital	Nurses	327	U.S.A.
Lee (1983)	Church-Related Schools	Teachers	224	U.S.A.

number of insights. Across various audits, the subordinate communication and supervisory communication factors tend to be deemed the most satisfactory areas of communication, while the feedback and climate dimensions are considered to be areas of less satisfaction. (See Exhibit 7.6.) The University of Wisconsin–Green Bay (UWGB) data bank, alluded to previously, shows a more precise picture. Exhibit 7.7 presents those findings. Note that the supervisory communication and subordinate communication factors cluster at the top, just as found in previous research (Clampitt and Downs, 1983). The personal feedback dimension, as before, settles at the bottom. Such findings are particularly useful to practitioners seeking to deal with typical organizational difficulties. To the auditor these findings can provide a yardstick of comparison for the particular organization being investigated and may suggest a context for interpreting the data.

RESEARCH TRENDS

Numerous investigators have uncovered a series of trends. Reviewing all of these studies in depth would prove too lengthy an endeavor for the present purpose. Of particular interest to auditors is the relationship of com-

EXHIBIT 7.6 Summary Rankings of Communication Satisfaction Factors

Overall Rank	Communication Dimension	Avery (1977) Rank	Thiry (1977) Rank	Gordon (1979) Rank	Kio (1979) Rank	Nicholson (1980) Rank	Jones (1981) Rank	Duke (1981) Rank	Alum (1982) Rank	Wippich (1983) Rank
1	Subordinate Communication	1	1	4	1	1	1	—	2	—
2	Supervisor Communication	2	2	1	1	2	4	3	1	1
3	Organizational Integration	4	3	2	4	3	3	6	6	2
4	Horizontal Communication	5	4	5	8	4	2	1	3	3
5	Media Quality	3	5	7	3	5	8	4	5	4
6	Corporate Perspective	8	6	3	6	8	5	2	8	5
7	Communication Climate	6	8	8	5	7	6	7	4	6
8	Personal Feedback	7	7	6	7	6	7	5	7	7

EXHIBIT 7.7 UWGB Data Bank Norms

Rank	Dimension	Mean	SD	N*
1	Supervisor Communication	34.18	10.50	1370
2	Subordinate Communication	33.43	8.62	323
3	Horizontal Communication	31.81	7.84	1345
4	Organizational Integration	29.62	9.54	1371
5	Media Quality	29.17	9.14	1344
6	Communication Climate	26.56	10.23	1358
7	Corporate Information	26.35	11.12	1360
8	Personal Feedback	23.99	10.68	1366

*Note that all results are based on a 0 to 50 scale, with 50 designating the maximum degree of satisfaction. Only complete cases can be used for analysis, so the size of N varies from factor to factor.

munication to end-product variables. Hence, this section examines the relationship communication has to job satisfaction and the relationship of communication to productivity.

Communication and job satisfaction

Most of the studies that have used the Communication Satisfaction Questionnaire have sought in one way or another to relate communication to job satisfaction. Different techniques have been used, but almost every study shows some relationship between job satisfaction and the communication satisfaction variables. Based on a thorough review of the theses and dissertations in Exhibit 7.5, three communication factors seem strongly related to job satisfaction: personal feedback, communication climate, and supervisory communication. The results of the University of Wisconsin–Green Bay data bank show similar trends. The correlations between the factors and a simple job satisfaction measure are shown in Exhibit 7.8. All the factors show significant relationships at the .01 level of significance. In short, results from numerous sources show that the communication satisfaction factors are related to job satisfaction.

EXHIBIT 7.8   Communication Satisfaction and Job Satisfaction Correlations

Factor	Job Satisfaction (r)	N
Personal Feedback	.5316	1328
Communication Climate	.5207	1321
Supervisory Communication	.5028	1332
Organizational Integration	.5023	1332
Media Quality	.4966	1307
Corporate Perspective	.3916	1321
Horizontal Communication	.3888	1307
Subordinate Communication	.3833	311

Communication and productivity

The relationship between communication and productivity seems self-evident, yet surprisingly little research has been conducted to verify this assumption. The strong relationship of individual communication satisfaction factors to job satisfaction does raise some question about this assumption. Other research has suggested that increasing job satisfaction does not always ensure a related increase in productivity, and in some cases productivity can actually decrease. What has the research shown?

One study was initiated that explored how employees thought the eight communication satisfaction dimensions affected their productivity, with supervisors rating employee productivity. In the study employees were asked to rate the impact of the factors on their productivity and the productivity of their department (Clampitt and Downs, 1983). One-hundred point scales were used in which 0 represented no impact on productivity, 50 designated an average impact, and 100 represented a maximum impact. Employees from two different companies were interviewed and their opinions solicited on why and how each factor affected productivity.

  The results seen in Exhibit 7.9 detail the effect of the various dimensions on productivity. Each of the communication satisfaction factors were perceived to have an "above average" impact on productivity, but certain factors appeared to have greater impact than others. The personal feedback dimension had a significant affect in both companies, while horizontal communication, media quality, and corporate information had a relatively lower impact on productivity. In sum, the interview data seem to suggest that the perceived relationship between communication and productivity is strong and concrete.

  The implication of the research trends is fairly clear. Auditors must realize that the various communication satisfaction dimensions are related to job satisfaction and productivity in different ways. Like manipulating a Rubik's cube, a strategy designed to increase employee satisfaction may have no impact on perceived productivity. Another twist of the communication variables meant to align productivity may throw out of kilter an array of job satisfaction variables. For instance, the data bank shows a fairly strong relationship between the communication climate dimension and job satisfaction, but not between communication climate and the self-productivity estimates. Hence, when auditors make suggestions to an organization based on the use of the Communication Satisfaction Questionnaire, they must carefully consider which end-product variables the organization is most concerned with.

EXHIBIT 7.9   Communication Satisfaction and Productivity Correlations

Factor	Self-Estimate of Productivity (r)	N
Subordinate Communication	.1747	322
Organizational Integration	.1635	1368
Supervisor Communication	.1592	1368
Personal Feedback	.1116	1363
Corporate Information	.1075	1358
Horizontal Communication	.1006	1343
Media Quality	.0979	1342
Communication Climate	.0688	1356

CONCLUSION

  The Communication Satisfaction Questionnaire has a noteworthy heritage. Grounded in a firm developmental process, possessing a rich theoretical orientation, and utilized in a variety of organizational settings, it has proved to be a useful, flexible, and efficient means to audit organizational communication. The well-established analytical techniques have yielded many research findings that are useful to practitioners and theorists alike. The research trends have underscored the importance of auditors thinking carefully and deeply about how planned changes in communication affect key end-product variables. Indeed, these very ponderings may prove to be the greatest challenge of all for the auditor.

REFERENCES

Alum, Carlos Vidal. "A Case Study of Communication Satisfaction in Nova De Monterrey." Master's thesis, University of Kansas, 1982.

Avery, Brad E. "The Relationship Between Communication and Job Satisfaction in A Government Organization." Master's thesis, University of Kansas, 1977.

Clampitt, Phillip, and Downs, Cal W. "Communication and Productivity." Unpublished paper, 1983.

Crino, M. D., and White, M. "Satisfaction in Communication: An Examination of the Downs-Hazen Measure." *Psychological Reports* 49 (1981): 831–838.

Downs, C., and Hazen, M. "A Factor Analysis of Communication Satisfaction." *Journal of Business Communication* 14 (Spring 1977): 63–74.

Duke, Peggy. "Communication Satisfaction of Business Education Teachers in an Urban School System," Ph.D. diss., Vanderbilt University, 1981.

Hecht, M. L. "Measure of Communication Satisfaction." *Human Communication Research* 4 (1978): 350–368.

Holsti, O. R. *Content Analysis for the Social Sciences and Humanities.* Reading, Mass: Addison-Wesley, 1969.

Jones, Jean. "Analysis of Communication Satisfaction in Four Rural School Systems." Ph.D. diss., Vanderbilt University, 1981.

Kio, James. "A Descriptive Study of Communication Satisfaction, Need Satisfaction, and Need Importance Index Among Nigerian Workers." Ph.D. diss., University of Kansas, 1979.

Krippendorff, Klaus. *Content Analysis.* Beverly Hills, Calif.: Sage, 1980.

Lee, Kerbe B. "Communication Satisfaction in Private Church-Related Schools." Ed. D. diss., University of Tulsa, 1983.

Nicholson, Jean H. "Analysis of Communication Satisfaction in an Urban School System." Ph.D. diss., Vanderbilt University, 1980.

Pincus, J. David. "The Impact of Communication Satisfaction on Job Satisfaction and Job Performance." Ph.D. diss., University of Maryland, 1984.

Redding, W. C. *Communication Within the Organization.* New York: Industrial Communication Council, 1972.

Thayer, Lee. *Communication and Communication System.* Homewood, Ill.: Richard D. Irwin, 1968.

Thiry, Robert Vankirk. "Relationship of Communication Satisfaction to Need Fulfillment Among Nurses." Ph.D. diss., University of Kansas, 1977.

Wiio, Osmo. "Organizational Communication: Interfacing Systems in Different Contingencies." Paper presented to the International Communication Association, May 1976.

Wippich, Barbara J. "An Analysis of Communication and Job Satisfaction in an Educational Setting." Ph.D. diss., University of Kansas, 1983.

Wippich, Marvin L. "Communication Satisfaction, Communication Style, and Perceived Organizational Effectiveness in an Educational Setting." Ph.D. diss., University of Kansas, 1983.

8

Critical Communication Experience

When the Air Force was looking for a better procedure for selecting air crews during World War II, it created the Aviation Psychology Program under the direction of John C. Flanagan. This program developed various studies to discover why some pilots were eliminated from flight school, why some bombing missions failed, why some pilots became disoriented during flight, and how cockpit design could be improved. In their studies, the psychologists developed a systematic method for collecting descriptions of behavior, which later became known as the *critical incident method*. The basic objective was to focus on concrete behaviors while eliminating statements of opinion, gross generalizations, imprecise evaluations, and stereotypes.

The critical incident technique was so successful that after the war the psychologists continued to use and to perfect it. In 1949, for example, Thomas Gordon determined the critical requirements for airline pilots. Use of the technique spread, and by 1972 Fivars compiled a list of 600 studies using this technique. Focal groups have included public school administrators, teachers, judges, college administrators, extension agents, military police, salespeople, and industrial foremen.

The technique is well respected, and it can be a valuable audit tool. However, we have changed the name for political reasons. In 1971 I used the technique on a questionnaire in auditing a public utility. When I showed the president the preliminary draft, he balked at the word "critical," because to him it implied that we were asking the respondents to provide only negative information. Even though the word "critical" is intended to mean "vital" in this instance, we changed the name to "communication experience." The goal is still the same: to determine the most critical communication behavior on which success or failure depends.

ADVANTAGES OF THE METHOD

The technique itself is guided by some basic principles but is not governed by rigid rules. This gives it several advantages.

1. *The technique focuses on specific behaviors.* The purpose is to collect representative samples of observed behavior, which Flanagan (1949) asserts is the "only source" of data regarding critical requirements of a job.

It should be emphasized at this point that observations of the behavior of the individual, or of the effectiveness of this behavior in accomplishing the desired results in a satisfactory manner, constitute not just one source of data but the only source of primary data regarding the critical requirements of the job in terms of behavior (p. 32).

2. *The technique focuses on behaviors that have been directly observed* — but not necessarily by the auditors. The observations are made by those people who actually experience the organization. It is true that they look at the experiences through their communication filters and that the data they provide are susceptible to all the subjectivity of self-report; however, people behave in objective ways in their organizations, and learning about their subjectivities can enhance the value of an audit. Auditors constantly battle the tension between subjectivity and objectivity, but David Smith (1972) has maintained that auditors may sometimes need to reject the concept of objectivity to gain a grasp on reality.

3. *The responses are unstructured by the auditor.* Questionnaires and interview guides are normally planned in detail so that the auditor gathers data about predetermined areas. Since the communication experience technique gives the respondent complete freedom in describing any experience, it stresses those incidents people assess to have high priority. Furthermore, such incidents are likely to deal with phenomena that have a strong impact on the success or failure of an operation.

4. *The technique can be adapted to any specific observable situation or context.* Furthermore, it can be left entirely open, or certain areas can be specified. For example, Downs and Conrad (1982) indicated that they wanted critical incidents about supervisor-subordinate relations. Mackintosh (1973) audited an organization of prison guards and specified that he wanted incidents involving communication among guard to inmates, guard to guard, and guard to other prison elements. In still another audit it was requested that critical incidents concern interdepartmental relations.

5. *The technique is both reliable and valid.* Anderson and Nilsson audited store managers in a Swedish grocery company and concluded:

> The material . . . seems to represent very well the behavior units that the method may be expected to provide. After a relatively small number of incidents had been classified, very few new behavior categories needed to be added. . . . it would appear justifiable to conclude that information collected by this method is both reliable and valid (1964, p. 402).

6. *The rich, qualitative data obtained from critical incidents is invaluable in interpreting the data from questionnaires.* For example, one may be able to report accurately from questionnaires how many people are satisfied or dissatisfied with their performance reviews, but the findings are not likely to explain what creates the satisfaction or dissatisfaction. Critical incidents can help fill that void. Focusing on specific behaviors, the technique asks the respondents to evaluate the behaviors as being either effective or ineffective and to explain what makes them so.

THE BASIC FORM

Exhibits 8.1 and 8.2 depict the basic form for recording the incident. Note that the forms are simple, having lots of open space for writing and very explicit directions. The amount of detail provided by respondents is not likely to be great unless there is some coaching from the auditor. The Mackintosh form was the primary means of auditing a prison facility, whereas the form in Exhibit 8.1 was integrated into a longer questionnaire.

EXHIBIT 8.1   Communicative Experience Form

Think of an experience in which communication was particularly effective
or ineffective, and describe that experience in as much detail as you can.
In doing so, please be certain that the following questions are answered.

1. With whom were you communicating? (position)
2. What happened?
3. Why did it happen?
4. Was it effective or ineffective?
5. Is this experience typical of the communication in this organization?

Describe the communicative experience, the circumstances leading up to
it, what the person did that made him/her an effective or ineffective communicator, and the results (outcome) of what the person did.
PLEASE PRINT. THANK YOU.

_____

_____

_____

_____

_____

_____

_____

_____

_____

_____

ADMINISTERING THE QUESTIONNAIRE

Specify need for both effective and ineffective experiences

Both forms presented in Exhibits 8.1 and 8.2 allow the respondent
to determine whether to report an effective or ineffective incident. This is a
strategic decision, for one would normally expect people to focus on what they

EXHIBIT 8.2   Mackintosh Form Used in Study of Prisons

BACKGROUND DATA:
1. My personnel grade is (write in your personnel grade) _____.
2. I have worked in a correctional facility for: _____ _____.
                                                 (years) (months)
3. The communication incident below was significantly **effective** or **ineffective** (circle one) in providing correctional treatment, care, and custodial supervision to inmates.

___ ___ ___ ___ ___ ___ ___ ___ ___ ___ ___ ___ ___ ___

SITUATION: Please write a short but complete description of the incident. Tell just what the people said or did. (Who, what, when, where, and with what effect.)

RESULTS: What was there about the communication behavior of the prison guard that made it significantly effective or ineffective?

YOUR ANSWERS ARE TO BE ANONYMOUS!!
PLEASE DO NOT RECORD THE NAMES OF THE PERSONS INVOLVED.

---

do not like; therefore, the data from the incidents would be overwhelmingly negative. One variation on the procedure is to give the respondents several forms, with some specifying effective incidents and others specifying ineffective incidents. This method attempts to get a more balanced view, because an audit should look at strengths as well as weaknesses.

Choose most appropriate means of collecting data

There are basically three ways of gathering information: individual interviews, questionnaires, and group administrations. These may be used alone or in combination.

If the communication experiences are integrated into questionnaires, coverge is increased. However, we have encountered a low response ratio for this method, and many of the questionnaires returned are likely to have insufficient details to be useful. For example, Page (1973) received a return rate of only 34 percent. It appears that many employees do not like to write or to take the time to do so. This is a basic problem with the critical incident methodology. On the other hand, both the interview and the group administration allow two important communications that increase the return and utility of incidents. First, the face-to-face interaction allows the auditor to be persuasive. Second, the respondents can be coached about how to complete the form, or questions can be asked that probe for more details.

ANALYZING THE DATA

Although the ratio of return is not great for communication experiences, they can still add unique insights to the audit report. Flanagan maintained that fifty to one hundred incidents might be enough to analyze a job (p. 343). And Anderson and Nilsson (1964) found that after a small number of incidents had been classified, not much new information appeared. To make the most of the findings dervied from incidents, the following guidelines are given.

Screen the experiences

Unfortunately, not all communication incidents are usable. Sometimes the descriptions are too vague, are too incomplete, or do not meet some other important criteria. It is important that the auditor decide at the beginning the criteria for accepting the incidents. Some important ones follow.

Observer. • Was the reporter the actual observer? If not, the incident is hearsay and may not be used.

Time frame. • Did the incident occur within the last six months or year? If the incident is not recent, the organization or person may have changed.

Evaluation. • Was the experience classified as either effective or ineffective? It is usually important for the auditor to know how the respondent viewed the behavior. For example, some employees respond to the same supervisory behavior in different ways. Whereas some classify a supervisor's asking questions about a project as "sincere interest" (effective), others view it as "supervising too closely" (ineffective).

Behavior. • Are actual behaviors reported in sufficient detail? In his study of trial judges, Page (1972) rejected the following incident because it did not describe actual behaviors and the details were insufficient.

> I watched two attorneys in action. I thought one had the evidence while the other seemed to be more persuasive. The one with the weaker evidence seemed to identify with the jury, and the jury voted

in favor of him. If I had been judging, I would have gone for the other person.

Focus. • Sometimes the auditor has specified that the incidents should be about a definite area, such as supervisory communication or interdepartmental communication. If they are not, they need to be rejected.

Identify incidents with specific person, position, or department

To interpret trends, it is useful to know exactly where the incident originated. Furthermore, the identification permits checking it against other questionnaires or against interview information from the respondent.

Divide into effective and ineffective groups

It is easy to put all the effective incidents together and all the ineffective ones together to look for trends. The two groups should be analyzed separately. This is illustrated in Exhibit 8.3, which contains the exact statements made by the respondents.

EXHIBIT 8.3   Summary by Categories

I. Effective Incidents
  A. Job-related Information
    1. Supervisor took the time to familiarize individual with job duties for new job.
    2. Supervisor gave detailed and basic explanations.
    3. Employee received praise, and errors were corrected in helpful way.
    4. Used visual aids in explanation.
    5. Co-worker gave information that helped with a work problem.
    6. Supervisor gave critical yet helpful evaluation.
    7. Praise and recognition received from superiors.
  B. Personal Situations
    1. Understanding with a personal situation.
    2. Understanding and development of procedures related to a health problem.
    3. Concern about an illness; no pressure to return.
  C. Job Transfer
    1. Help with a job transfer request.
II. Ineffective Incidents
  A. Poor Follow-up
    1. Request for supplies; had to ask again three months later.
    2. Suggestion made to improve efficiency; "never left the office."

3. Supervisor asked to talk to another operator (by several other operators) about a problem; not done.
4. Asked questions about service and equipment use; waited over two months for answer; had to ask again.
5. Question asked about criteria to be used for evaluation; went to immediate supervisor and then to _____; took over two weeks for an answer.
6. Question asked about mistake in calculation; after one week asked again and after three weeks gave up.
7. Attempted to make report to supervisor; tried three times, but no response from supervisor; supervisor got information from someone else.
8. Two incidents: rude customer reported, but no follow-up by supervisors involved.

B. Ineffective Feedback Given
1. No acknowledgment or praise for commendations received.
2. Supervisor reprimanded subordinate but did not explain reasons for procedure.
3. Feedback given to correct a judgment error from a supervisor to subordinate given in such a way to stifle initiative.
4. Feedback given to co-worker at wrong time and place.
5. Supervisor not listen or respond to question about an evaluation.

C. Job Transfer and Promotion
1. Asked Personnel about transfer; after a month asked again; no attempt made to help from Personnel or immediate supervisor.
2. Performance standards required are "artificial" barrier to promotion or transfer; jobs not advertised for bids as in other departments.
3. Supervisor refused to discuss transfer, so had to go to another level to obtain recommendation; still nothing has been done by supervisor.

D. Inappropriate Use of Channels
1. Supervisor listens to gossip via "grapevine" and draws conclusions from what she hears—very unbusinesslike.

E. Inadequate Guidance or Training
1. Not enough guidance with new job, so employee reprimanded for poor work.

F. Overall Dissatisfaction
1. Stress by management on speed; no concern for courtesy and accuracy; can't combine high speed and helpfulness to customers.
2. Two incidents: survey merely another reflection of ineffectiveness of communication in the office; survey vague, irrelevant, and no changes will occur.

Classify incidents into themes or categories

Sometimes categories can be identified in advance. Exhibit 8.4 contains a classification used in the audit of a large university. This system was developed in part because a quick analysis was needed. Respondents read the list and identified the areas about which they were going to write incidents. On a separate form, they indicated the person to whom the experience related, whether the incident was effective or ineffective, and the number of the item on this list to which the experience primarily related. They were then asked to write the incident.

Although this system has merit, it does impose a great deal of structure on the respondents' answers. Consequently, we prefer the use of ad hoc categories, that is, classification schemes that come to the auditors while they read them. This makes for more work in the short-run, but it does sometimes force the auditor into new ways of thinking. Exhibit 8.5 contains actual summaries of incidents obtained in a public utility.

EXHIBIT 8.4   Communication Experiences

Please read the following descriptions of communication experiences found in most organizations. Then, in the left margin, place a checkmark next to those descriptions that are **extremely important** to you in your organization. To simplify your task, check only five or six descriptions that **most critically** affect your performance on your daily job.

1. *ROLE*
____ 1.1 Clear or unclear, confused or not confused, informed or not informed about role in organization (e.g., job description is confusing).
____ 1.2 Differ or not on what your role should be (e.g., expectations differ).
____ 1.3 Did or did not perform role adequately (e.g., used or misused authority, did or didn't follow correct procedures).

2. *INFORMATION ADEQUACY*
____ 2.1 Presence or absence of information (e.g., was or wasn't informed).
____ 2.2 Amount of information adequate or inadequate (e.g., lack of sufficient verbal information or presence of redundant information).
____ 2.3 Timeliness of information adequate or not (e.g., message received too late to be used).
____ 2.4 Clarity of lack of clarity of information (e.g., message was understood or misunderstood).
____ 2.5 Usefulness or lack of utility of information (e.g., message was impractical).
____ 2.6 Accuracy or inaccuracy of information (e.g., message was or wasn't distorted or faulty or honest).

3. *PROPER USE OF LANGUAGE*
____ 3.1 Correct or incorrect use of words (e.g., correct or incorrect use of jargon or terminology).

4. *FEEDBACK*
____ 4.1 Presence or absence of feedback (e.g., did or didn't follow up).
____ 4.2 Amount of feedback adequate or inadequate (e.g., possible information overload).
____ 4.3 Timeliness of feedback adequate or inadequate (e.g., feedback not on time).
____ 4.4 Clarity or lack of clarity of feedback (e.g., feedback not understood).
____ 4.5 Usefulness of feedback (e.g., feedback was impractical).
____ 4.6 Accuracy or inaccuracy of feedback (e.g., feedback was distorted).

5. *CHANNEL*
____ 5.1 Presence or absence of channel (e.g., a needed channel was missing).
____ 5.2 Frequency of usage (e.g., sufficient or insufficient channel usage).
____ 5.3 Appropriateness of channel (e.g., the wrong channel was used).
____ 5.4 Quality of channel operation (e.g., the channel was not operating efficiently; the intercom was broken).

6. *PARTICIPATION IN DECISION MAKING OR PROBLEM SOLVING*
____ 6.1 Presence or absence of participation (e.g., did or didn't accept or give input to decision making).
____ 6.2 Amount of participation sufficient or not (e.g., token amounts of input allowed).
____ 6.3 Timeliness of participation adequate or not (e.g., participation was allowed before decision was made).
____ 6.4 Effectiveness of participation (e.g., decision was more effective and resulted in higher morale).

7. *PERCEPTION OF INTERPERSONAL RELATIONSHIPS*
____ 7.1 Liking or disliking each other (e.g., personality clash).
____ 7.2 Similarity or dissimilarity of backgrounds (e.g., perceptions differ due to cultural differences).
____ 7.3 Degree of supportiveness of relationship (e.g., boss was strongly supportive of position).
____ 7.4 Hostile or friendly to each other (e.g., petty conflicts or fights).
____ 7.5 Degree of blocking or encouraging message flow (e.g., blocking downward or upward flow).
____ 7.6 Cooperative or uncooperative with each other or others (e.g., having good rapport with each other).

8. *PERSONAL COMMUNICATION COMPETENCIES*
____ 8.1 Good/bad listening (e.g., did or didn't listen).
____ 8.2 Good/bad speaking (e.g., ineffective nonverbal facial and eye behaviors).

____ 8.3 Good/bad writing (e.g., spelling or typos in written memos).
____ 8.4 Good/bad reading (e.g., insufficient time to read required
documents).
9.   *OTHER (PLEASE SPECIFY)*
9.1 _____

9.2 _____

9.3 _____

9.4 _____

PROVIDE AN EXAMPLE OF AN EFFECTIVE OR INEFFECTIVE COM-
MUNICATION EXPERIENCE FOR EACH OF THE DESCRIPTIONS YOU
INDICATED WERE IMPORTANT TO YOU.

EXHIBIT 8.5   Sample Critical Incidents[1]

Effective

(5) Supervisors volunteered info that the Y employee had done an excellent job in catching up the back log of work on previous day.
Used a low keyed and sincere approach. Left no doubt that he was
genuinely grateful for everyone's effort.

(18) Another company called for information. 2) My immediate super took
the call—which required a call back after the info was obtained 3)
when the call back was made the person requesting the info was not
available so a message was left. 4) I was advised of the situation so
that I was able to intelligently and quickly handle the situation when
I got the call. WHY EFFECTIVE? 2) It saves time. 2) eliminates
duplicated efforts. 3) it allows a better impression to a third party be
they CRC or others. 4) also gave me info and/or knowledge for
future reference.

(20) About a month ago, top management came to our location to inform
all staff about the company and where we were going. We were told
good and bad points to expect during the next year. We were able
to ask questions and a member of top management would answer.
The questions were answered in a clear and knowledgeable manner.

(21) When—Jan 24, 1980, Who—An agent from the previous shift,
Why—the need to pass information not easily written, What
happened—specific facts passed-on by this individual enabled me to
perform my duties in a more efficient and expeditious manner,
What—this person gave a brief yet accurate summary of actions he

---

[1]The material in this exhibit represents verbatim responses to the questionnaire in one
organization.

had taken. This summary allowed me to complete this joint task with a minimum of waste in time and effort.

(23) When—14 Feb-lunch, Who—Immediate Supervisor and me, Why—we were alone at the lunch table, What happened—we just sat and talked about various things, totally informal. What person did—Listen-reply honestly-was sympathetic.

(24) Wednesday, Jan. 13, Bill, Regarded a meeting I held with our Y agents regarding our procedures. Y agents were upset by secrecy of our new manual. I couldn't tell them about new proposals per my supervisor. Felt trapped in situation. Told them some of our "secrets." I didn't care to be involved in this type of approach again. They wouldn't give constructive methods for working. I was upset. Bill talked to me about the situation by calling me into his office. Gave me encouragement and pointers for this type of situation.

(29) After the Holidays, a group of workers noticed an individual who was on vacation during Christmas. When he should not have been. It was presented to our immediate supervisor. He then said he would look into it, which he did. He gave us an answer within a couple of days. He has searched and talked with management and told them we were all concerned. He gave us the best possible answer he could in the position that he was in. It was all done in a very sincere and business like manner. We thanked him for looking into the matter and proceeded to go to the top management, not because of our supervisor, but because we wanted to hear from the horses mouth. We felt that our Supervisor could only do so much and get so much information-which he did-in fact more than usual. But we were not satisfied with that and wanted more. We greatly appreciate our Supervisors efforts and kindness and helpfulness. He really went beyond the call of duty.

Ineffective

(42) Received my paycheck which was for more money than usual. Inquired with immediate supervisor who advised me that I had received a merit raise. It would be more rewarding to be advised personally that your efforts are appreciated than to be advised only at the time you receive your pay check.

(48) Team coordinator has no tolerance for opposite viewpoint. To accomplish a procedural change is impossible. If difference of opinion is expressed, it must be shouted for the longest duration to even be acknowledged. When acknowledged, the Team Coordinator never changes his view point until ordered to do so by upper mgmt. Then it is done grudgingly and with lots of grumbling. Yet, this Team Coordinator is thought to be super smart by upper management.

(50) February 14, 1980. X was very ineffective when explaining a new procedure. It went into effect 4 days ago. No one told us. It makes a job harder and it takes longer to drive the tickets. X explained it

poorly admitted he had not checked it out himself yet. Yet he expected us to know all about it and be able to do it, when it was not
communicated to us in the first place. He is very ineffective as a
team coordinator.

(53)   Feb 3 - Brought to X's attention discrepancies on procedures regarding putting tickets in the problem file—very negative response from
X. I insisted he present the issue to B—He Never!! Feb 8—
Approached B with the issue, he agreed the procedure should be
changed and said a bulletin to that effect would be issued immediately. Today is Feb. 17—we have seen no bulletin regarding the
above procedure change!

(54)   I went in to talk to my manager about putting in for a new job so I
could go to a full time position because I am going to be married
soon. He kind of gave me the feeling that he was preoccupied with
other things. I guess at a time when I need some definite answers. I
get the same old excuses about waiting for the next quarters
budget, or we need to hear from the big guys, etc. I wish they would
just level with us and not play games. This same person has helped
me out at other times. But sometimes, I wish our organization would
get things together and level with all of its employees. The
employees would be happier thus creating a happier department and
a great company to work for. This would boost the company far
above if the morale of its employees were higher.

(70)   Our supervisor called a meeting to present his ideas for a new plan
for an ongoing program and to get feedback from his people on the
new plan. After lengthy discussion, it was obvious that the near-
unanimous opinion of the subordinates was that the new plan was
very inferior to the old plan, and that the program would suffer if the
new plan were implemented. The supervisor said, "Thank you for
your opinions, but I think we wil try the new plan anyway." He did,
the program suffered, and we were all bitter and frustrated.

Sometimes a single incident can be classified in several categories.
Mackintosh (1973) recalls such an incident in auditing the communication
behavior of prison guards. The description of the incident recounted how a
guard requested assistance in handling a belligerent inmate, and it also related
the subsequent communication behavior of another guard answering the call
for assistance. Therefore, the incident was classified in both the guard-to-inmate
category and the guard-to-guard category.

There is no established format for grouping the incidents, but an initial step may be to look for references to basic communication phenomena
(described in Chapter 3), such as relations among people, certain types of
messages, use of channels, or communication outcomes. These can be as
elaborate as the system warrants. Listed in Exhibit 8.5 are some of the actual

incidents reported in the analysis of one organization. The numbers on the left refer to a certain respondent's questionnaire.

INTERPRETING THE RESULTS

In a sense, dealing with critical incidents is both easy and interesting. It is inherently more satisfying to read detailed reports than it is to deal with statistical data revealing the fact that 55 percent of employees say they do not get enough information about X. However, the challenge of drawing meaningful conclusions from communication experiences is great. In fact, there are four obstacles to the effective use of communication experiences: (1) a low return rate, (2) difficulty in developing categories, (3) problems of insuring anonymity, and (4) difficulty in deriving generalizations.

Note the return rate

As was pointed out earlier, low response rate is the greatest liability of the communication experience format. It is not so much of a problem when the communication experience form is the only questionnaire used in the audit or when the experiences are obtained orally. However, when it is used in conjunction with other questionnaires, the response rate often drops below 50 percent. Many people fill out the rest of the questionnaire without answering the experience portion, leading us to conclude that people do not want to take the time to write. The low response rates makes generalization more difficult.

Develop categories

My preference is to read the incidents until ad hoc categories come to me, and this is a legitimate means of content analysis. It is, however, a slow process if many experiences are involved. Nevertheless, the extra time and effort are the prices to be paid for collecting very unstructured data. There are such numerous ways that a common theme can be expressed. As a way of expediting the process of developing categories, the list of themes in Exhibit 8.4 was used in the audit of a university, where hundreds of experiences were collected. This list is not meant to be an instrument in itself but merely to suggest some themes that may aid interpretation.

Maintain privacy

In all audits, individual anonymity is promised. Keeping that promise is sometimes difficult when reporting specific instances for interpretation. A great deal of care must be taken to disguise the individuals, and there is still the likelihood that someone will know who was involved in the incident. In reporting an audit to a utility president, I used a disguised incident to support a generalization I was making, and the president quickly retorted, "I know exactly who that was, and let me tell you why that happened." He was correct, too. This situation reinforced my belief that unless the experiences are totally innocuous, others are going to recognize them.

Derive generalizations

The three observations that follow were taken from the summary of an audit of a telephone company.

1. Most of the effective incidents involved job-related situations in which praise and recognition was given.

2. Almost half of the ineffective incidents involved the lack of, or slowness of, follow-up by supervisors.

3. Other ineffective incidents focused on the giving of feedback. Respondents indicated that workers were corrected for errors in inappropriate ways, supervisors refused to listen to worker concerns about evaluations, and good work was not acknowledged by supervisors. Most of these occurred in Department B.

These observations point out some of the problems of interpreting data from critical incidents. First is the problem of grouping the incidents under some overall umbrella concept that makes sense. Consider observation 3. Several different items were included under the general category of "feedback," even though they call attention to very different phenomena. Likewise, the term "follow-up" in observation 2 is rather vague. In addition, there is an apparent conflict between observations 1 and 3. Supervisors who give positive feedback are considered to be effective, whereas those who do not are ineffective. Or maybe some supervisors are being described in observation 1 whereas others are described in observation 3. Which of these conditions really characterize the organization? We cannot tell from this observation, so we may need to check these findings against some questionnaire or interview data.

There is also the tendency to report the data in quantifiable terms (i.e., "almost half") so that counting the number of times a category occurs becomes all important. This, however, is where a communication audit differs from the standard academic research project. Frequency of response can be very useful and should not be undervalued, but it is not always the standard by which the audit is to be judged. The number of incidents is not likely to come from a representative sample of the workers in the first place. Furthermore, one truly perceptive incident may illustrate a great deal about an organization's operations. For example, in an analysis of an engineering firm that involved three departments, only one supervisor reported an incident that showed how employees in Department C believed they were always last in receiving communication. This incident was so on-target that we later discovered this perception revealed a root problem for some teamwork inadequacies.

CONCLUSION

In the total audit process, communication experiences can enrich the auditors' understanding of the organization. (See Exhibit 8.6.) However, in numerous audits in which I have used this method in conjunction with interviews or questionnaires, I have found the communication experiences to be of less value than the other methodologies. Nevertheless, it is highly desirable to obtain descriptions of specific behaviors to balance out the perceptual data obtained from standardized questionnaires. Furthermore, communication experiences are particularly useful in pinpointing specific problem areas that cannot be picked up by looking at statistical means across all respondents. Localizing a problem can be of value in auditing the total organization.

EXHIBIT 8.6   Sample of Communication Experiences

Overview of Findings

Thirty-four employees provided us with a communication experience on the questionnaire in which they described an effective or ineffective communication situation. Twelve of these responses reported effective communication experiences, and twenty-two reported ineffective communication experiences.

Since only half of the sixty-seven questionnaire respondents provided a communication experience, it is difficult to generalize from this data. The experiences do, however, provide us with the following information:

1. The responses supported data from the interviews and clarified some areas on the questionnaire.

2. The majority of the responses were concerned with communication necessary or vital to doing the job.

3. The results of the effective experiences tended to indicate that an open, supportive atmosphere for communication exists at all levels.

4. The primary problems described in the ineffective communication experiences dealt with information sharing, dissemination, and timeliness.

Effective Experiences

Information gleaned from the communication experiences labeled "effective" tended to be best categorized as task-oriented. A breakdown of the responses is as follows:

A. Task-Oriented
1. A coworker accurately handled changes in personal schedule.
2. A telephone conversation with a coworker was accurate, purposeful, and cordial.
3. Upper management established policies and supported employees for abiding by policies.
4. Supervisor gave critical feedback to a subordinate that led to improved productivity.
5. Negotiations between speaker and management led to win-win situation.
6. (Two instances) Immediate supervisor gave supportive feedback and assignments.
7. A supervisor was open to suggestions or requests for help in getting job done.
8. An employee had an effective meeting with a supervisor.

Ineffective Experiences

The communication experiences that were labeled ineffective covered a wide range of problem areas. These areas included information sharing, timeliness of information, follow-up, promotion and transfer, evaluation/feedback, and general communication. Specific examples follow. Again, it is important to note that these are individual responses and may not represent general trends in the organization.

A. Information Sharing
1. A supervisor ignored a request for special information.
2. One person expressed a lack of understanding of what is going on throughout the organization.
3. One person believed upper management hoarded information from its meetings. This caused an uneasy feeling.
4. (Two instances) A worker withheld vital information from coworker.
5. (Two instances) Instructions from top management necessary to perform job were unclear.
6. Worker did not receive all necessary memos to do his/her job.

B. Timeliness of Information
1. Information was mailed late by subordinate.
2. Employee received information from upper management late. This has occurred before and is frustrating.

C. Follow-up
1. Person suggested to immediate supervisor that s/he create a memo index for easy future reference. Nothing has been done.
2. Employee gave specific instructions to supervisor of another department regarding a mailing being sent out. The supervisor was then to pass on information to his/her people. Supervisor did not complete task.

D. Promotion and Transfer
1. Immediate supervisor posted new job position opening, then the next day canceled the job—caused frustration.

E. Evaluation/Feedback
   1. Worker unsure of how upper/middle management is evaluating his/her work and whether or not the evaluation is impartial. Causes strained relations.
   2. Worker receives no recognition or appreciation of work done.
F. General Communication
   1. Coworker did not clearly identify to whom a memo was being sent.
   2. Immediate supervisor handled an employee meeting poorly.

REFERENCES

Anderson, Bengt-Erick, and Nilsson, Stig-Goran. "Studies in the Reliability and Validity of the Critical Incident Technique." *Journal of Applied Psychology* 48 (December 1964): 398–403.

Downs, Cal W., and Conrad, C. "Effective Subordinancy." *Journal of Business Communication* 14 (1982): 27–38.

Fivars, Grace. "The Critical Incident Technique, A Bibliography." Unpublished bibliography sponsored by American Institute for Research. Palo Alto, Calif., 1972.

Gordon, Thomas, "The Airline Pilot's Job." *Journal of Applied Psychology* 33 (April 1949): 122–131.

Mackintosh, H. B. *A Critical Incident Study of Communication Factors Utilized by Prison Guards.* Master's thesis, University of Kansas, 1973.

Page, Paul. *Critical Requirements for the Oral Communication of State Trial Judges.* Ph.D. diss., University of Kansas, 1973.

Smith, David. "Communication Research and the Idea of Process." *Speech Monographs* 39 (August 1972): 174–182.

9
ECCO Analysis

ECCO (Episodic Communication Channels in Organizations) analysis is a specialized questionnaire specifically oriented toward individual messages. In this sense, it is very different from the previously described questionnaires. Developed in 1952 by Keith Davis, it is a versatile instrument that traces a particular message through the organization. In doing so, judgments can be made about the length of time information takes to circulate, the media usage for this message, and the ways that different types of information are processed. Other questionnaires ask for a response, such as satisfaction with the way the informal channel or grapevine works in the organization, but ECCO analysis has been used by a number of auditors to plot the grapevine network and to see how it actually works. ECCO analysis's ability to reveal such information makes it very appealing as an audit instrument.

ECCO technology has been used with consistent success in organizational audits, and, therefore, it is an option worth considering. Whether or not it is the best instrument to use may depend on the auditors' purposes and plans for using other technologies.

DESIGNING THE ECCO QUESTIONNAIRE

There is a basic format for an ECCO log, but the actual questionnaire has to be tailored to the organization being audited. A simple instrument, it can be constructed easily and quickly, for it usually contains only four to five parts. These are illustrated by the examples in Exhibits 9.1 and 9.2, taken from actual audits.

EXHIBIT 9.1   Rudolph Survey of Information Flow

Survey No. 1   (Confidential)   _____

                                                            _____
                                                            Your Code No.

Prior to receiving this questionnaire, did you know the information in the
box **or any part of it?**
   a)
   b)
   c)   (Message is divided into four parts.)
   d)

Please check **one:** ___ Yes, I knew all of it.
                       ___ Yes, I knew part of it. If so please list the
                           numbers of the parts you knew ___ ___ ___ ___.
                       ___ No, I did not know any of it.

If your answer above was "Yes, I knew all of it" **or** "Yes, I knew part of it,"
please complete the questionnaire by providing the information requested
below.

If your answer above was "No, I did not know any of it," you have completed the questionnaire. Please return the questionnaire to me or drop it
in the Information box. Thank you very much for your cooperation.

If you had the information in the box **but** the facts you heard were different, please write the facts you heard next to the associated number.

   1.
   2.
   3.
   4.
   5.

Question #1.   From whom did you **first** receive the information in the
               box? Please place the source's code number (from your
               code sheet) on this line _____.
               Remember that by using the code number **you never iden-
               tify** the specific person who gave you the information
               because **each** code number is assigned to **several** persons.

Question #2.   Where were you when you first received the information in
               the box above? Please check one:
               (11) ___ At my desk or other location where I carry out my
                        job duties
               (12) ___ Elsewhere in the room where I work
               (13) ___ Outside this room but still working
               (14) ___ Away from my unit-department but still working
               (15) ___ Away from my unit-department but not while work-
                        ing (coffee break, etc.)

(16) ___ Away from the building and while not working for
the organization

Question #3. How long ago did you first receive the information in the
box? Please circle the approximate time:

Today   Yesterday   3   4   5   6   7   *days ago*
                        2   3   4   5   6   *weeks ago*

Question #4. By what method did you first receive the information in the
box above? Please **check only one** of the following
methods:

Written or Visual Methods	*Talking or Sound Methods*
(20) Personal letter from the Co.	(30) ___ Talking with one other person in his presence
(21) ___ Letter, memo, or service program.	(31) ___ Talking over the telephone
(22) ___ Annual report	(32) ___ Talking (and listening) in a small group of two or more
(23) ___ News	
(24) ___ Magazine	
(25) ___ Tempo-70	
(26) ___ Company film	
(27) ___ Public newspaper or magazine	(33) ___ Attending an organized meeting or conference
(28) ___ Company records	(34) ___ Overhearing what someone else said
	(35) ___ Radio or television

Miscellaneous:

(41) ___ I did it or I originated the information or decision.
(42) ___ Other. Please explain.

Thank you very much for your cooperation. Please return the questionnaire to me or drop it in the information box.

EXHIBIT 9.2   ECCO Log in a Church

A. Please check below the items of information you had by noon of the
day you received this ECCO Log (if you have received none, see Section B; if your information varies, see Section C):

___ 1. Another "Bert Nash Seminar" for parents
___ 2. wishing to improve child-raising skills
___ 3. is now being held at Plymouth Church
___ 4. on Monday evenings from 7:00 to 9:00 P.M.

B. I have received no information on the above subject.

C. If your information *differed* from that listed in Section A, please write next to the associated number the information you have:

1. _____
2. _____
3. _____
4. _____

D. Please check the source from which you first received the information:

1. ___ Church posters
2. ___ The "Plymouth Rock"
3. ___ Church bulletin board
4. ___ The 1973 "annual report"
5. ___ Announcement in worship
6. ___ "Coffee hour" conversation
7. ___ Sunday worship bulletin
8. ___ Local radio/TV
9. ___ The annual meeting
10. ___ Word of mouth
11. ___ Mail from the church
12. ___ "United Church News"
13. ___ Church group meeting
14. ___ Do not recall
15. ___ "Lawrence Journal World"
16. ___ Other _____

E. Please check the appropriate time period in which you first received information:

1. ___ Before January 1,
2. ___ January 1–15,
3. ___ January 16–31,
4. ___ February 1–14,
5. ___ February 15–28,
6. ___ After February 28.

The log breaks the message into several distinct parts and the respondents check off those parts that they know. It is then possible to determine how well a particular message is circulated. This is important to know, because people often hear only bits and pieces of messages. In the example of the church in Exhibit 9.2, some people had heard that a seminar was being offered, but many people did not know who was conducting it or its intended audience.

ECCO also tests the accuracy of the information being processed by asking respondents to indicate for each part whether or not they received information that differs in any way from the message stated on the log. These findings have great potential for checking inaccuracies in the informal channels. Our experience, however, suggests that the auditor is much more likely to discover incomplete messages than inaccuracies.

The following sections list the requirements for the effective use of ECCO methodology.

Choose the messages

Whereas other audit questionnaires examine more global reactions to general types of information such as "personal feedback" or "information to do the job," ECCO focuses on whether or not respondents know a *very specific message*. This distinction is important. ECCO does not assess satisfaction with, or reaction to, a message; its sole emphasis is on the process of circulating a specific message. Since the process may be different for different kinds of messages, auditors generally construct several different ECCO logs, each of which features a different kind of message. These are then administered serially through the organization. Bailey (1974), for example, circulated fifteen different ECCO logs to audit communication in a church. Some messages may be work-oriented, but ECCO has also been one of the primary ways of charting informal channels (the grapevine or rumor mill).

Some specific criteria for the messages include the following: (1) They should be typical of the ones circulated in the organization. (2) All parts of the messages should be true and accurate. (3) They should be simple and straightforward. In the most desirable instances, they can be phrased in single declarative sentences. For example, the following message would be appropriate: "Greg Kessler has resigned as the Director of Organizational Development and will become the Vice-President of Personnel at Corporate Headquarters." (4) Since the ECCO log is used for the total organization, messages should be of interest or applicable to the entire organization. (5) For measurement purposes, the messages will have been released through a specific channel and will not have been widely known before the specific time of release. (6) To trace networks, the serial administration of messages must reflect both the upward and downward flow of the messages. For example, in her investigation of the university administration, Sanders (1976) chose messages involving the resignation of a dean, a new requirement announced by the Office of Affirmative Action, and the movement of the Endowment Association to a new building.

Identify the media

This section of the questionnaire must be tailor-made for the organization, as all possible channels need to be listed. Written media can often be specified, but oral interactions may have to be classed more generally under headings such as "discussions during coffee breaks" or "interviews" or "meetings." Question 4 in Exhibit 9.1 and Section D in Exhibit 9.2 are good illustrations of how media can be arranged.

Set up categories for reception time

One of the most common complaints is that information moves too slowly in organizations. Of course, the speed is relative and is not equal for every employee. Therefore, plotting reception times allows the determination of how quickly information flows to each section and the comparison of the speed of different types of information. The exact scales can be modified to suit different needs; they can range from months to weeks to days. Keep in mind that respondents often have difficulty remembering exactly when they received messages; therefore, the categories need to allow plenty of leeway for differences. It is through the use of this technique that informal channels have been discovered to be faster than the formal ones.

List potential sources

Originally, ECCO analysis was designed to identify communication networks. Therefore, there was a section of the questionnaire that asked each respondent to identify the source of information. An example of this request is as follows:

> From whom did you first receive the information? Please place the source's code number (from your code sheet) on this line.

As indicated in question 1 of Exhibit 9.1, each respondent is sometimes given a code book with every other person's name in it. The individual's code number differentiates between management and operators, between line and staff, and among different organizational levels and functions. For example, in Davis's original audit, "141116" meant, respectively, management (1), fourth level (4), line (1), belt factory (1), and Joe Smith (16) (1953, p. 305). The chief reason for the code was to make tabulation easy; however, another important consideration was to make naming the source seem less personal. The assumption was that somehow people feel less threatened by writing down a number than a name.

From the data concerning sources, it is possible to plot group interactions, directions of communication flow, types of information initiated by certain people or groups, and limited communication networks. If several ECCO logs are used, it is possible to check the consistency of the network across messages.

Identify location possibilities

Because some auditors have wanted to know the physical location of the respondent when receiving information, they have asked questions such as the following:

Where were you when you first received the information? Please check one.

    _ At my desk or other location where I carry out my job duties.
    _ Elsewhere in the room where I work.
    _ Outside this room but still working.

___ Away from my unit but still working.
___ Away from my unit while not working (coffee break, etc.)
___ Away from the building and while not working. (Pacilio and Rudolph, 1973)

ADMINISTERING THE QUESTIONNAIRE

Since the average time for filling out ECCO logs is about three minutes each, they can be filled out at one's work location with a minimum of interference to the work flow. Therefore, the easiest way to distribute the logs is to give them personally to the respondents or to distribute them by mail. If several logs are to be completed at once, however, the response rate may be improved by assembling groups in a conference room.

For logs to be useful, the auditor must know who the respondents are. Therefore, respondents must sign their names or sign code numbers particularly identified with them. Again, the reasons for the codes are to ensure confidentiality and to make tabulation easier.

Rudolph (1972, p. 7) suggests eleven guidelines for administering the questionnaire.

1. Visit with the subjects when distributing and collecting the questionnaires.
2. Use as little of the respondents' time as possible.
3. Instruct the subjects on how to respond to the questionnaire prior to the first administration.
4. Learn as many of the subjects' names as possible and use them whenever given the opportunity.
5. Make a point of assuring the anonymity of each participant (if it seems necessary).
6. Impress the subjects with the importance of their individual answers to the success of the study.
7. Encourage questions about the project and attempt to answer them.
8. Allow an appropriate amount of time for questionnaire completion.
9. Develop employee interest and participation by requesting information for messages or communication episodes to be studied.
10. Make sure the participants realize that an "I don't know any of the information" answer is just as important as an "I know it all" answer.
11. Keep abreast of any developing problem with the instrument and be ready and willing to make necessary changes.

ANALYZING THE DATA

The instrument is simple, and the analysis need not be difficult. The following steps have proved to be useful.

1. Screen the responses. Like other questionnaires, this one will not be filled out completely by everybody. Some will be unsigned and, therefore, will not be useful.
2. Tabulate individual responses so that a frequency distribution and percentages can be compiled. The subprogram FREQUENCIES has been successfully used for this (Nie et al., 1975, pp. 218–219).
3. Arrange the data into predetermined groupings such as work units, scalar levels, or functional divisions. Cross tabulations can be useful in making these comparisons. Sanders (1976), for example, created 2 × 2 comparison tables for all variables. In this way she compared Department A with Department B on the frequency of receiving messages.

A crosstabulation is a joint frequency distribution of cases according to two or more classificatory variables. The display of the distribution of cases by their position on two or more variables is the chief component of contingency table analysis and is indeed the most commonly used analytic method in the social sciences. These joint frequency distributions can be statistically analyzed by certain tests of significance, e.g., the chi square statistic, to determine whether or not the variables are statistically independent; and these distributions can be summarized by a number of measures of associations, such as the contingency coefficient, phi, tau, gamma, etc., which describes the degree to which the values of one variable predict or vary with those of another.

(Nie et al., 1975, pp. 218–219)

4. Since the data associated with ECCO is nominal data, use nonparametric statistics for analysis.
5. Compare units. Some comparisons can be validly determined just by quick examination. However, there are also more elaborate and objective ways to make such comparisons. Davis devised the following formulas for determining the (1) receipt factor, (2) accuracy factor, (3) initiation factor, and (4) interaction factor.

The formula for the *receipt factor is* $R = MR/SR$, where MR is the number of messages received, SR is the number of ECCO surveys returned, and R is the percentage representing the receipt factor. Exhibit 9.3 demonstrates how the receipt factors of various groups can

EXHIBIT 9.3   Comparison of Units on Receipt Factor

	Message 1			Message 2			Total		
	SR	MR	R(%)	SR	MR	R(%)	SR	MR	R(%)
Sales	12	11	92	13	8	62	25	19	76
Personnel	10	9	90	10	8	80	20	17	85
Production Group A	46	45	98	40	25	62	86	70	81
Production Group B	33	30	91	33	15	46	66	45	68
Top Management	12	12	100	12	10	83	24	22	92
Total	113	107	95	108	66	61	221	173	

be compared. Not only do the groups differ in terms of the two messages received, but in this instance it is fairly obvious that the two messages are processed quite differently. Salience of the messages is likely to be a factor in obtaining these results.

The formula for the propensity of messages to be communicated accurately is $A = AR/MR$, where MR is the number of messages received, AR is the number of messages received accurately, and A is the percentage representing the *accuracy factor*. Representative data are presented in Exhibit 9.4.

The *initiation factor* is measured by the formula $I = IR/MR$, where MR is the number of messages received, IR is the number of messages initiated, and I is the percentage or initiating factor. IR is obtained by tallying the answers to the question, "From whom did you first hear the message?" The higher the initiating factor, the more active the person or group was in communicating the message to others. Construction of a table for the initiating factor (see Exhibit 9.5) would be similar to those for the receipt and accuracy factors.

EXHIBIT 9.4   Comparison of Units on Accuracy of Messages

	Message 1			Message 2			Total		
	MR	AR	A%	MR	AR	A%	MR	AR	A%
Sales	16	14	88	12	10	83	28	24	86
Personnel	18	15	83	18	10	56	36	25	86
Production Group A	30	25	83	28	19	68	58	44	76
Production Group B	45	36	80	18	9	50	63	45	71
Top Management	12	11	92	11	6	55	23	17	74
Total	121	101	84	87	54	62	208	155	

EXHIBIT 9.5   Comparison of Individuals on Initiation Factor

	Message 1			Message 2			Totals		
	MR	IR	I%	MR	IR	I%	MR	IR	I%
President	4	15	375	3	2	67	7	17	242
Foreman, Section A	9	2	22	9	3	33	18	5	28
Foreman, Section B	19	17	89	25	7	28	44	24	55
Sales Manager	50	5	10	40	6	15	90	11	12
Personnel Manager	58	5	8.6	35	9	26	93	14	15
Unidentified Colleague		2							
Total	140	46	33	112	27	24	252	71	

A rank order of the totals demonstrates that the president is initiating the communication of these two messages and that foreman B is also very active.

Another important aspect of communication is the interaction among different units in the organization. An *interaction factor* is computed by the formula $INT = RO/MR$. MR refers to the number of messages received in an area. RO is the number of messages received from outside that unit, and this is obtained by identifying the unit of the source and the unit of the receiver. INT represents the percentage identified as the interaction factor. The number of messages received from outside the unit may be subtracted from the total number of messages received to obtain the number of messages received from *within* the unit. Exhibit 9.6 presents data for the interaction factor.

Another possibility is to use these data to plot the actual linkages among the units being audited. For example, one could determine whether the eleven messages coming from outside Production Group A tended to come from one other unit or from many units.

6. Plot networks. It is possible to plot networks by hand from the ECCO analysis. Sometimes information flows through a single-strand channel, with one person telling a message to only one other person. Another pattern to identify is a cluster in which, for example, person A tells three people a message, and one of them passes it on to others.

EXHIBIT 9.6   Flow Within and Between Units

	Top Mgt. f%		Sales f%		Personnel f%		Production A f%		Production B f%		Total f%	
Within	8	89	11	79	0	0	19	63	22	76	60	71
Between	1	11	3	21	2	100	11	37	7	24	24	29
Totals	9	100	14	100	2	100	30	100	29	100	84	100

EXHIBIT 9.7   Comparison of Units' Channel Usage

Channel	Top Mgt. f%		Personnel f%		Sales f%		Prod. A f%		Prod. B f%		Total f%	
Telephone	0	0	1	20	6	29	0		2	.05	9	8
Informational Interaction	2	17	1	20	8	38	22	69	30	77	63	58
Organized Meeting	10	83	1	20	7	33	4	13	1	25	23	21
Memos	0	0	1	20	0	0	0		1	25	2	2
Organization House Organ	0	0	1	20	0	0	6	18	5	13	12	11
Total	12	100	5	100	21	100	32	100	39	100	109	100

Unfortunately, such charting can be time consuming if many people are involved. To combat this, Walter Stewart of Ohio University has designed a computer program to make the task quicker and more complete. Called the ECCO Analysis Program, it can process data from organizations with more than one thousand employees. Furthermore, it has been validated against hand-computed networks (Stewart, 1982). Stewart's program increases the utility of ECCO as an audit technique simply because it reduces the time and energy necessary to analyze the data.

7. Check media usage. It is easy to prepare a frequency distribution to differentiate the usage of each channel listed on the ECCO log. The channels can then be rank ordered to get a sense of how widely they are used. Additional information can be obtained by comparing different units' frequency of usage. Compute a table for each message featured, similar to the one shown in Exhibit 9.7.

On the ECCO log, one can begin to determine the compatibility of a message to given channels. Of particular importance is plotting how the informal channels work in this organization.

8. Check the message's locus of receipt. The procedure for determining this is much like the preceding one. The auditor simply lists all the options and then computes the frequency of location for each unit being audited.

9. Note the timing of each receipt. Again, a frequency distribution can demonstrate how quickly messages are circulated. To make this information particularly useful, it can be related to the channel used. For example, some auditors have learned that the informal channels are often faster than the formal ones.

DRAWING CONCLUSIONS

The adaptability and flexibility of ECCO analysis allow many different focal points, and an auditor perhaps must be selective. The previous discussion has already suggested areas that can be audited beneficially. Nevertheless, the following findings from other audits may be instructive.

ECCO has been particularly useful in analyzing the informal channels. Marting (1969) found no significant differences either between line and staff employees or between hierarchical levels. Knippen (1970), however, found that employees at higher levels had significantly more information than those at lower levels in a retail chain store. In his audit of branch banks, Lee (1971) discovered that the informal channels primarily flowed downward and were slower than the formal channels.

Second, information blockage has been pinpointed. Davis (1964) was able to specify that downward communication was blocked by certain levels in a manufacturing management group. In another audit, Christie and Oyster (1973) described how clique ownership of information restricted the flow of informal messages. Similarly, Davis (1964) identified some functional groups that were consistently isolated.

Channel adequacy can also be assessed. For example, Bailey (1974) noted that the two messages received by the fewest number of respondents were the only two received through Medium A. This finding would lead one to believe that this channel was not very effective in disseminating information generally.

Downs traced the patterns among graduate students to discover how information was processed among them. Two liaison individuals were identified, and it was determined that location of office was a major reason for their being central to the communication flow. Later, when one of the individuals changed offices, she no longer was central to the communication network.

Perhaps the most frequent use for ECCO analysis has been to examine roles and network structures. Bailey (1974) found three different communication networks operating in a church. Sanders (1976) contrasted the differences among functional and scalar groupings of administrators. She described precisely how they processed types of information.

ADVANTAGES OF ECCO ANALYSIS

The simplicity of the ECCO instrument is appealing. It does not take much time to develop or to fill out the questionnaire. Respondents generally find it easy to answer right at their work stations with minimum interruptions. This means that it is also inexpensive to administer.

The simplicity and quickness of ECCO analysis allows several logs to be administered over a period of time, thus overcoming the snapshot impression associated with longer questionnaires. Easily adaptable to field settings, it can generate large amounts of data about different aspects of communication in a short time.

The ECCO log's brevity makes it feasible to include all employees in the survey. In fact, if one is going to obtain an accurate assessment of how the message spreads, most employees should be included.

LIMITATIONS OF ECCO ANALYSIS

Perhaps ECCO's greatest weakness is the high nonresponse rate. Even though the questionnaire is simple and short, many people simply refuse to fill it out. Their reaction may be no different to other questionnaires; however, there have been some unique reactions to the ECCO methodology. Comments from potential respondents in one organization indicated that they did not want to identify sources. In fact, several protectively said, "We can't give you that information." These were people high in the organization, and for some reason they felt threatened by the likelihood of identifying the sources, even though the message had been released publicly and they were promised anonymity.

Nonresponse creates a problem for analysis. If 30 percent do not answer, as happened in one audit, severe limits are placed on any network construction or unit comparisons.

Respondent honesty is questionable at times. Although people have been open in general, I have experienced situations in which people did not like to admit they had not heard important information. We have toyed with the idea of testing truthfulness by using a false statement, but the risk is too great because we would be giving people false information. In a sense, the ECCO log is a communication channel that not only tests what people know but also informs them of things that they did not know.

Memory is also a limitation. How does one treat the data when there is obviously a mix-up? For example, in an audit of a university administration, Sanders (1976) circulated a message from the Office of Affirmative Action. However, a number of people "remembered" receiving this information in a memo from the top executive. Upon checking, it was determined that the executive had never sent such a memo. Consequently, the respondents must have been confused or forgetful. Whatever the reason, the data were wrong, and any network analysis built on them would have been misleading.

Choice of specific messages is limiting. Although one does try to choose typical or representative messages, there is no way one can assuredly generalize to all messages. Even using fifteen messages, as Bailey (1974) did, does not ensure that one really understands how other messages will be processed. Furthermore, the type of messages investigated may not be the most important ones. For example, the most crucial messages in an organization are those sent to particular people to enable them to perform their jobs. Since the messages on an ECCO log have to be distributed to all people being audited, the specific performance-related messages are often precluded from the study.

Finally, ECCO does not give the comprehensive overview of organizational communication that is grasped by either of the questionnaires reviewed in previous chapters. Therefore, it may be wise to use it as a supplement to interviews, observations, or other questionnaires.

CONCLUSION

This chapter has described the basic ECCO methodology and has pinpointed some of its applications and some of its inherent limitations. Despite some limitations, it is still a valuable audit tool. It covers most of the major elements in the communication process such as sources, receivers, messages, channels, timing, and space. And it is economical, practical to administer, relatively unobtrusive, capable of generating data about the flow of information, and adaptable to any organization.

REFERENCES

Bailey, Paul. "Communication in the Congregation." Master's thesis, Kansas University, 1974.

Christie, Timothy, and Oyster, Eire. "A Communication Audit of the Missoula Bank of Montana." Paper presented at the International Communication Association Convention, Montreal, May 1973.

Davis, Keith. "A Method of Studying Communication Patterns in Organizations." *Personnel Psychology* 6 (1953): 301–312.

Davis, Keith. "Management Communication and the Grapevine." In *Business and Industrial Communication,* by C. Redding and G. Sanborn, 111–113. New York: Harper and Row, 1964.

Knippen, Jay T. "An Episodic Study of Informal Communicaiton in a Retail Chain Store." Unpublished Ph.D. diss., Florida State University, 1970.

Lee, John W. "Episodic Study of Communication in a Geographically Centralized Banking Organization." Unpublished Ph.D. diss., Arizona State University, 1971.

Marting, Barbara J. "A Study of Grapevine Communication Patterns in a Manufacturing Organization." Unpublished Ph.D. diss., Arizona State University, 1969.

Nie, Norman H.; Hull, C. H.; Jenkins, J. G.; Steinbrenner, Karen; and Bent, Dale H. *SPSS: Statistical Package for the Social Sciences*. 2d ed. New York: McGraw-Hill, 1975.

Pacilio, John, and Rudolph, Evan. "An Overview of ECCO Methodology." Paper presented at the International Communication Association Convention, Montreal, May 1973.

Rudolph, Evan. "An Evaluation of ECCO Analysis as a Communication Audit Methodology." Paper presented at the International Communication Association Convention, Atlanta, May 1972.

Sanders, Janet. "Utilization of Lines of Communication Within the Administration of the University of Kansas Described by ECCO Analysis." Ph.D. diss., University of Kansas, 1976.

Stewart, Walter T. "ECCO Analysis Program." Paper presented at the International Communication Association Convention, Boston, May 1982.

Timpano, Doris. "A Study of Communication Networks in Scholars by Means of ECCO Analysis." Paper presented at the International Communication Association Convention, Montreal, May 1973.

10
Diagnosing
Communication Networks[1]

A potential nucleus of any communication audit is a description of the organization's communication networks. A thorough communication audit must not only assess the qualitative nature of an organization's communication climate, it must also assess the structure in which that climate exists. To ignore the communication structure would be like a physician examining only the skin of a patient who has a broken leg. Similarly, organizations can have "fractured, if not broken, legs" in their communication networks. Understanding the underlying skeleton, or structure, of communication is the bottom line when conducting network analyses in a communication audit.

A BASIC RATIONALE

Although audit interviews and surveys give a glimpse of information flow structures, only a direct, dedicated assessment of these networks will allow you to:

    1. Identify *where* information flow is blocked or overloading a communication network.

    2. Identify *who* is blocking or overloading the flow of information, and

    3. Construct *new* structures to reduce information blocks or overloads.

---

[1]This chapter was written by D. Thomas Porter, University of South Florida. Dr. Porter has extensive experience with a variety of network methodologies.

These goals are worthy of any auditor. Their fulfilment, however, can be a complicated task. For example, if we describe the communication contacts within a small department of ten people, the possible permutations of communicative contacts become enormous. In a ten-person department, there are at least ninety different communicative contacts ($10 \times 10 - 10 = 90$) to consider and summarize.

When we consider groups larger than ten people, the pragmatic and scientific analysis problems grow exponentially. Our goal then becomes to simplify this huge set of numbers with a more understandable representation. This is the central goal of network analysis. This chapter presents a pragmatically feasible and scientifically justifiable technique for summarizing such permutations of human contact.

As was pointed out in Chapter 3, the flow of information is vital to a healthy organization. When communication is blocked, decisions are made prematurely, inaccurately, or not at all. When information gluts the communication system, expensive resources are wasted, information overload results, and, again, decisions are made prematurely, inaccurately, or not at all.

This chapter explains techniques designed for communication research and applies to ongoing, "real-world" organizational communication audits. (For a review of technical work on "traditional" approaches, see: Moreno, 1934; Bales, 1950; Barnes, 1972; Shaw, 1964; and Monge and Day, 1976.)[2] These techniques give the auditor several advantages.

---

[2]Traditional approaches to examining communication structure take one of three forms. First, ECCO analysis, discussed in Chapter 9, is useful for some studies but does not always meet the needs of a *comprehensive* communication audit. Second, communication diaries or logs theoretically cover all messages in the system. Because their administrative logistics call for *every* organizational member to note *every* received or sent message and a variety of associated characteristics, employees soon tire of this assessment process, and the truthfulness of the data that are returned becomes quickly suspect. Third, traditional network analyses gives a very detailed description of individuals' information flow, but it, too, has inherent limitations. For one thing, it requires a census to be conducted. This means that *everyone* must fill out the appropriate data collection forms. All it takes to invalidate the whole data set are a few people on vacation, or just one reluctant key individual to avoid filling out the form. For example, in a recent audit, a manager of an important unit refused to be interviewed and did not fill out the demographic data on a questionnaire; therefore, no analysis could be made of his unit. Realistically, in the organizations of the real world it is almost miraculous if response rates are as high as 90 percent, yet validity suffers considerably when even a small proportion of employees fail to respond.

In addition, traditional network analysis is limited because it gives only a general view of communication flow. In an audit of a university, respondents were asked to indicate first their network of "formal" communication and then their network of "informal" communication. Both terms are very abstract and vague. On the other hand, many organizations would profit from an assessment of information flow on a *topic-by-topic basis*. For example, the communication flow about a plant relocation may be blocked internally, but the flow may be glutted with information about compensation and benefits. Traditional network analysis would not detect either problem.

This approach relies on non-census data collection procedures and identifies several message-specific communication networks. The validity of this approach is dependent upon retrieving a random sample, not a census-level data set. *Statistical analysis shows that procedures that use a random sample of organizational members are more valid than even a network analysis with a 90 percent return rate.*

This approach also provides communication structure analyses for a number of different message topics selected by the client organization.

Finally, it provides an empirically derived pictoral map of how information flows on *a given message topic.* Such information has assisted managers in identifying blocks in the communication system on one topic while discovering gluts on another. As a result, the techniques presented here make it easier to get to the two essential points of communication network analyses — understanding an organization's communication structure and providing a data base from which systematic changes can be made in communication structures.

CONDUCTING A SUCCESSFUL COMMUNICATION NETWORK STUDY

To conduct a successful communication network analysis, four key principles must be followed:

1. Collect data in a logistically efficient manner.
2. Analyze data so that the conclusions are scientifically justified.
3. Interpret the data so that the results are intelligible.
4. Integrate the conclusions into the overall strategic plan for organizational communication change and development.

Each of these principles translates into a major step that, when followed, describes how a communication network analysis is conducted.

Collecting data

Planning is very important when considering how to collect data for a communication network analysis. As with other audit methods, there are three issues that must be resolved before collecting data — identifying (1) *who* is to be studied, (2) *what* message topics are important, and (3) *what work groups* are to be assessed. Without careful, strategic decisions regarding these issues *in advance* of collecting data, errors in interpretation and application will be beyond correction.

First, consider *who* is to be studied. What constitutes the network? Although the answer may seem obvious at first, the question can be vexing. For example, are individuals who work for the organization, yet are not a regular part of its structure, part of the network? Consider security or janitorial personnel and temporary clericals contracted via an independent company. Their involvement in the organization could be critical, yet their assessments of the communication flow are rarely considered in communication audits. Furthermore, what about communicative contacts outside the organization? Messages to and from customers, sales representatives, advertising executives, consultants, and the general public are clearly part of an organization's communication system. Yet, collection of data from these individuals could be a logistic nightmare. If external contacts or temporary internal personnel are to be viewed as part of the communication structure, provision for collection of data from them must be made as well. Without such provision, it is not uncommon for a data set to be rife with responses about messages *to* these individuals without any data about how these individuals view messages *from* the communication structure in the organization. Therefore, make sure that reciprocation is as high as possible; for every response from work group A about its communications with work group B, you need information about how B sees communicating with A.

A second issue is the identification of message topics that are key concerns for organizational change and development. By identifying specific messages, you will be able to identify important communication blocks or overloads. Research (Porter, 1979; Porter, 1985) has shown that most messages communicated by people in organizations center around the following central list:

1. How well the person is doing his/her job
2. Job duties
3. Organizational policies
4. Pay and benefits
5. Specific problems faced by management
6. Promotion and advancement opportunities in the organization
7. How the individual's job relates to the whole operation
8. How organization decisions are made that affect one's job
9. How job-related problems are being handled
10. Mistakes and failures of the organization
11. How technological (or social) changes affect the job
12. Complaining about job-related problems
13. Reporting what an employee is doing in his/her job
14. Asking for work instructions
15. Evaluating the performance of superiors/subordinates/peers

Use this list as a guide, but modify it, of course, to match the particular jargon of the client organization. The final list of message topics should also be as specific as possible to the needs of the client organization. For example, I once added to this list, "The acquisition of Tandem Industries." Tandem Industries (a fictitious name) was a recent acquisition, and the organization was particularly concerned about communication blockages or overloads that resulted from this acquisition. As one can readily see, the selection of message topics is critically important for improving the usefulness of analyses. The more specific the message topic, the more specific (and useful) derived conclusions and recommendations can be.

The third and final planning issue for collecting data concerns identifying the actual groups of people with whom you are concerned. In other words, what groups of people *should* be communicating with what other groups? What are the relevant departments or units that *should* be in contact communicatively with each other? The identification of these work groups could come from the official organiational chart. Or, more validly, they could come from problem areas identified from interviews or surveys in other parts of the audit. In either case, the work group identification should be exhaustive and mutually exclusive; that is, all individuals who respond to the data collection forms should be able to identify the work group to which they belong. The list of work groups should be recognizable to every respondent, and each respondent should be able to identify only *one* work group to which she or he belongs. If you find out through pilot testing that a significant number (greater than 5 percent) of respondents work in "more than one work group," your list of work groups is not mutually exclusive. If your list does not cover all work group areas for all respondents, then the list is not exhaustive. Both of these criteria *must* be met.

The data collection form

Once you have identified the *people* included in the communication networks to be studied, the *message topics* of prime importance, and a mutually exclusive and exhaustive list of *work group areas,* a data collection form (DCF) can be constructed. The overall goal is to develop a data collection form that is aesthetically pleasing, easy to fill out, and complete in detail.

The first sheet of the DCF must ask the work group area to which the respondent belongs. In addition, you may ask any relevant demographic questions such as sex, length of employment, job classification, or age. The respondent should be instructed as to the purpose of this survey and told how it differs from the other parts of the survey instrument. These instructions must emphasize the necessity of checking one, and one only, work group; otherwise, the data from the individual respondent is worthless. The remainder of the DCF comprises specific instructions, a list of message topics, and a list of work groups with a rating scale for individuals to indicate how much or how often they communicate (sending and receiving) with other work groups.

Exhibit 10.1 contains a typical example of a model DCF. It is for a communication network analysis of ten work groups. Although it uses the first three message topics from the central list, others can be added as needed. The respondent is instructed to indicate for each message topic and each work group how often he or she "communicates." The scale used in this DCF is a five-point scale where 1 = Never and 5 = Daily. The rating scale used here is, frankly, arbitrary; but it is useful as long as respondents understand it and as long as it goes from low to high degrees or amounts of communicative contact.

The responses to the DCF give the auditor a data set that quantifies how much each work group is connected communicatively with every other work group. From an analysis of these responses, the auditor can see where communication is blocked (or overloaded) about "specific problems faced by management," or "pay and benefits," or anything else put on this message topic list.

Analyzing the data

Assuming that data collection has been successfully accomplished, there are two preliminary judgments to be made before data analysis can begin: the data set must be assessed, first, in terms of its sampling adequacy and, second, in terms of its reliability.

Sampling adequacy. • For every work group identified in Step 1, there must be an adequate number of respondents from that work group: If you have given DCFs to everyone in the organization, you should have at least 50 percent of the respondents in each work group represented in the data set. If not, any communication linkages reported by that work group with less than 50 percent returns must be cautiously interpreted. If you have randomly selected respondents from each work group to fill out the DCFs, you need at least seven to ten representatives from each work group of fifteen to twenty people. When these criteria are not met, the sampling adequacy of the network data set prevents all but the most crude statistical analyses.

Reliability. • The statistical value of "reliability" ranges from 0.0 to 1.0, where 0.0 indicates no consistency internally or over time and 1.0 indicates perfect consistency. There are two factors that affect a communication network data set's reliability (see Porter, 1977, and Porter, 1978, for technical papers on reliability). First, the agreement of respondents across work groups about how often (or much) they send or receive information affects reliability. If the President's Office respondents say they communicate with Corporate Staff "daily" and Corporate Staff respondents say they communicate with the President's Office "periodically," there is an important inconsistency to be resolved; there is low reliability about the communicative link between the President's Office work group and the Corporate Staff work group. Therefore, one can have little confidence about the quality of this linkage estimation.[3]

Additionally, the number of respondents within a work group also affects reliability. For example, consider two work groups—the Los Angeles

---

[3]Serious discrepancies occur when there is greater than a 20 percent differential between work group linkage values. For example, if the message topics are scaled on a range from 1 to 5, a differential greater than 1.0 (5 × .20) between the work group linkage values indicates a serious lack of reciprocation.

EXHIBIT 10.1   Sample Data Collection Form

Listed below are a series of message topics about which the company regularly sends and receives messages. For each message topic, indicate how often communication (sending or receiving) occurs. When responding, please use the following rating codes:

> Never, print a "1"
> Seldom, print a "2"
> Occasionally, print a "3"
> Periodically, print a "4"
> Daily, print a "5"

If you communicate (sending or receiving) with the work area:

Be sure you have put a number (1, 2, 3, 4, or 5) in each and every space.

WORK AREAS

MESSAGE TOPIC:	President's Office	Corporate Staff	Marketing	Los Angeles Sales	Chicago Sales	Cleveland Sales	Accounting and Finance	Indiana Manufacturing	New York Manufacturing	Personnel
1. Pay and benefits										
2. Promotion and advancement opportunities										
3. Specific problems faced by management										
...... continue list of Message Topics as desired										

Sales group with twelve respondents and the Chicago Sales group with ninety-two respondents. The ninety-two respondents will be more reliable over time than the group of twelve respondents. It is somewhat similar to a classroom test. In this case, each respondent is equivalent to a multiple-choice test item. The greater the number of test items, the greater the consistency over time. Assuming all other factors are equally internally consistent, a twenty-item test will be less reliable than a one hundred-item test. If a person makes one clerical error on the twenty-item test, it constitutes 5 percent of the total score. If one makes a similar error on the one hundred-item test, the effect is almost negligible.

Examining network data closely, we can see at least two sources contributing to errors of reliability of a data set: (1) the degree to which work groups disagree about their linkage strength (link reciprocation) and (2) the proportion of people who fail to respond to their DCF. When work group A says it communicates with work group B "occasionally" and work group B says it communicates with A "periodically," there is error in the reporting of their linkage strength. When work group C fails to be represented adequately or does not report contact when contact in fact exists, error is also introduced.

In order to provide estimates of reliability for network analyses, the following formula is useful:

$$\frac{2r}{1 + r} \; P^2 = \text{Reliability}$$

where r = Correlation of reciprocation, and P = Proportion of total DCFs returned.

For example, consider an average correlation of .72 between work group linkage values. In other words, if we took the linkage values of work groups A through G (seven groups), constructed correlations between these two sets of values (e.g., A's links to C and C's links to A), and averaged these seven correlations, we would have the "correlation of reciprocation" ($r = .72$). If one hundred people were sampled and ninety-two returned DCFs, the proportion of DCFs would equal .92(P). Thus the reliability of this data set would equal the following:

$$\frac{2(.72)}{1 + .72} \; (.92^2) = \frac{1.44}{1.72} \; (.8464) = .71 = \text{Reliability.}$$

In most cases, a reliability coefficient of .65 or higher is acceptable. If .65 is not reached, extra attention must be paid to collecting a greater proportion of DCFs; that is, follow up by getting more people to cooperate and return their DCFs.

In this formulation, reliability is functioned by the degree of reciprocation (average correlation between work group linkage values) and the proportion of respondents providing input. The P value serves to adjust the reliability estimate according to the absence of information (a source of measurement error). The *P* value is squared because the effect of absent information in the network analysis context is exponential.

Compiling the actual network

Once we have assessed the sampling adequacy and the reliability of the network data set, actual analysis can begin. The overall goal is to create a geometric map of how work groups are connected communicatively. Figure 10.1 illustrates one such output for a given message topic, the "acquisition of Tandem Industries." Although the interpretation of Figure 10-1 is discussed in the next section on interpreting data, simply remember that the closer the dark circles, the closer the communicative linkage. Figure 10.1 shows, for example, that the Accounting work group and the Human Resources work group are very far apart communicatively on the acquisition of Tandem Industries; in other words, these two work groups had little communication contact on this message topic.

The procedures used to create Figure 10.1 come from a statistical technique called smallest space analysis. For a complete technical description of how to execute the statistics described in the example that follows, see Norton (1980). You will note that Norton's actual data are employed to illustrate how smallest space analysis is used for communication network analyses. To show how these statistics operate, assume we are considering the communication linkages between only four work groups:

FIGURE 10.1   Information Flow Analysis

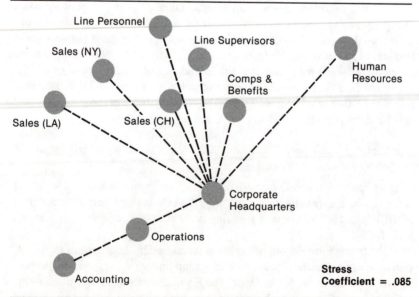

1. Los Angeles Sales Group (LA)
2. Chicago Sales Group (CH)
3. New York Sales Group (NY)
4. Headquarters, Corporate (HQ)

If we put the rank of their average linkage values in a "rank table," it may look like this (Norton, 1980, p. 312, Table IV):

	LA	CH	NY	HQ
LA	–	δ 12	δ 13	δ 14
CH	4	–	δ 23	δ 24
NY	2	6	–	δ 34
HQ	1	5	3	–

The purpose of the rank table is to weigh interactions so that a *visual* configuration of these work groups matches the numerical values provided by the work groups.

Then, *arbitrarily* place the work groups in a two-dimensional space (Dimension I and Dimension II). For example, the coordinates table might look like this (Norton, 1980, p. 313, Table V):

	Dimension I	Dimension II
LA	4.00	3.00
CA	8.00	3.00
NY	3.20	5.60
HQ	2.00	3.00

A visual representation of these *initial* geometric coordinates would look like the table on page 176. (Norton, 1980, p. 313, Figure 1).

If the initial visual placement of the work groups is fairly close to the relationships reflected in the rank table, fewer adjustments (iterations) will be necessary to reach a "best fit" – the fit between the communication linkage data and the visual map of that linkage data.

Next compute all possible distances between the four work groups, using the Pythagorean theorem for right triangles. These geometric distances are calculated for each relationship (e.g., between HQ and LA) by the following equation (Norton, 1980, p. 313):

$$d_{ij} = [\sum_{a=1}^{m} (X_{ia} - X_{ja})^2]^{\frac{1}{2}}.$$

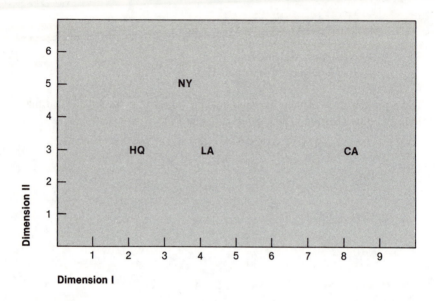

For example, the distance (d_{23}) between CH and NY is calculated as follows (Norton, 1980, p. 314):

$$d_{23} = [(8.00 - 3.20)^2 + (3.00 - 5.60)^2]^{1/2} = 5.46.$$

Once this is done for all possible distances, a table like this is created (Norton, 1980, p. 314, Table VI):

	LA	CH	NY	HQ
LA	–	d_{12}	d_{13}	d_{14}
CH	4.00	–	d_{23}	d_{24}
NY	2.72	5.46	–	d_{34}
HQ	2.00	6.00	2.86	–

The goal is to get these *visual* distance estimates as close as possible to their numerical source—LA, CH, NY, and HQ communication linkage values. To see whether or not these distances are sufficiently accurate, a "stress test" is calculated (Norton, 1980, pp. 314–316). The amount of stress tells whether these *arbitrary* dimension points are useful and how much to adjust them to get an acceptable fit. The initial coordinates are adjusted by creating a correction set of new coordinates (c_{ij}) such as those in the following calculation (Norton, 1980, p. 316):

$$\text{If } i = j, \text{ then } c_{ij} = 1 + \sum_k \frac{d^*_{ik}}{d_{ik}}$$

$$\text{If } i = j, \text{ then } c_{ij} = 1 - (d^*_{ij}/d_{ij}).$$

For example, the correction adjustment for HQ would be 3.91 (instead of 4.00 in the initial configuration).

$$HQ_{44} = 1 + \frac{2.00}{2.00} + \frac{5.46}{6.00} + \frac{2.86}{2.86} = 3.91.$$

Doing this for all possible distances gives a new set of coordinates for Dimension I and Dimension II (Norton, 1980, p. 317, Table XI).

	Dimension I	Dimension II
LA	4.00	3.00
CH	7.99	2.94
NY	3.08	5.67
HQ	2.16	3.01

Once these new coordinates are used for LA, CH, NY, and HQ, an accurate picture of their communication relationships becomes possible.

After constructing all these averages, place them in the appropriate places in a "table of relationships." See Exhibit 10.2 for an example of such a table. In Exhibit 10.2 the numbers in the upper right half of the table represent the average rating between the particular work group combinations. For example, the rating of 3.15 between the President's Office work group and the Personnel work group indicates that the strength of their communication link is somewhere between "occasionally" and "periodically." Please remember, of course, that there is no magic to these numbers. They have meaning only when compared to the other numbers in the table. Assessing the *relative* strength of these numbers is a major value of smallest space analysis.

The next step is to rank order the strength values in the upper half of the table in Exhibit 10.2. This means assigning a "1" to the largest or strongest communication link, a "2" to the next strongest, and so forth. The lower left half of the table in Exhibit 10.2 has these ranks. For example, the strongest communication link (4.78) is between the Chicago Sales work group and the Indiana Manufacturing work group. Note the rank of "1" in the table. The weakest link (rank = 45) is found between the Cleveland Sales work group and the Personnel work group (linkage value = 1.32). The function of these ranks is to weigh the strength values in order to obtain a geometric configuration of how these numbers fit together. In other words, these ranks tell us what work groups are most closely linked communicatively. Without these ranks, smallest space analysis cannot assess whether or not the geometric map of communication structure (see Figure 10.1) is accurate.

Interpreting the data

Before discussing strategies of interpreting data, it is important at the outset to clarify our goal in network analyses. Until the numbers become a geometric map of the communication structure *and* are given meaning, we

EXHIBIT 10.2   Sample Table of Relationships and Ranks*

Work Group Area:	President's Office	Corporate Staff	Marketing	Los Angeles Sales	Chicago Sales	Cleveland Sales	Accounting & Finance	Indiana Manufacturing	NY Manufacturing	Personnel
President's Office	*	4.14	3.78	3.98	3.75	4.21	4.25	3.79	3.81	3.15
Corporate Staff	10	*	2.75	2.58	2.49	2.67	2.01	2.65	2.71	2.99
Marketing	17	29	*	4.01	3.73	3.89	2.11	3.12	3.32	1.75
Los Angeles Sales	12	33	11	*	1.51	1.45	3.55	4.51	4.55	1.34
Chicago Sales	18	34	19	40	*	2.02	3.41	4.78	4.66	1.47
Cleveland Sales	9	31	14	42	36	*	3.47	4.52	4.23	1.32
Accounting & Finance	6	37	35	20	22	21	*	3.01	2.78	1.97
Indiana Manufacturing	16	32	25	5	1	4	26	*	1.43	3.95
NY Manufacturing	15	30	23	3	2	7	28	43	*	4.22
Personnel	24	27	39	44	41	45	38	13	8	*

*The values in the upper half of the table are average rating values between the particular work group areas where "1" = "never communicate" to "5" = "communicate daily." The values in the lower half of the table are the rank order of the values in the upper half of the table.

do not have *information,* we only have *data.* We need information (data that has been given meaning) if we are to make intelligent, scientifically justified recommendations about the organization. Thus the emphasis of Step 3 is on giving meaning to the numbers and their corresponding geometric maps. Without this meaning, we cannot proceed to Step 4, the real payoff for network analyses in a communication audit.

Three strategies should be used to interpret data from a network analysis. (1) Examine the numbers for statistical and organizational problems. (2) Inspect the visual map of communication relationships (e.g., Figure 10.1) for "surprises," for it is in these surprises that you learn more about the client organization and its communication flow. There is no point in collecting communication network data if your sole purpose is to confirm what you already know. (3) Generate specific recommendations not only about the overall communication flow but also about communication relationships between specific work groups.

Examine the numbers. • There are three problems that the *numbers* provided by network analysis can help detect in the communication flow of the client organization. First, examine the numbers for discrepancies in reciprocation values. For example, let us say that the Los Angeles (L.A.) Sales group reports that it communicates with Chicago Sales an average of 3.5 (on a 5-point scale). Chicago, on the other hand, reports that it communicates with the L.A. Sales group an average of 2.4. There is a serious discrepancy here, an important lack of reciprocation. There are several potential interpretations for this unacceptable anomaly. It could be a simple problem of sampling adequacy. Perhaps one of the sales groups was not adequately sampled – either because there was insufficient response from one group or because nonrandomly selected respondents from one group were more (or less) eager to report communications with the other work group. On the other hand, the L.A. Sales group may, in fact, communicate more with Chicago than Chicago wants to admit. For whatever reason, Chicago thinks the connection is not as strong. Needless to say, without qualitative data (from the interviews or climate surveys) it would be difficult to figure out which interpretation is correct. Hence, there is an absolute necessity of collecting other data besides network data. Otherwise, you have collected data with little opportunity to turn it into information.

Second, examine the numbers for strong and weak communication links. For example, inspect in detail those three or four work groups that have the highest communication relationship values. Exhibit 10.2 indicates that the L.A., Chicago, and Cleveland Sales groups have close connections with the manufacturing work groups of the organization. The specific message topic being traced in the data of Exhibit 10.2 was "Hiring a new vice president for Manufacturing Operations." As such, these strong communicative links make sense. In addition, contrast the relatively weak links between the Corporate Staff work group and these same work groups. Several interpretations are possible. First, perhaps Corporate Staff, like many corporate staffs, is out of the mainstream of key decisions. Often corporate staffs are viewed and treated as decision implementers, not decision makers. On the other hand, these communication strength values may simply reflect gossip about "Who's going to be the new vice president?" In either case, qualitative data collected elsewhere in the audit can assist in deciding which interpretation makes most sense.

Third, examine the numbers for sampling adequacy. As emphasized several times in this chapter, each work group must be adequately sampled in terms of numbers of respondents and respondent representation. If only 4 percent of the L.A. Sales work group provides communication strength ratings and Chicago provides 11 percent, then by definition we will have a more accurate picture of Chicago's communication links than L.A.'s. If at all possible, follow up with L.A. to increase the group's respondent rate. In addition, an examination of key demographics from the first page of the DCF can be used to assess the other side of sampling adequacy—respondent representation. For example, if you know that Personnel is composed of 63 percent women and if 48 percent of the respondents from the Personnel work group are women, the communication strength values Personnel reports will be biased toward male perceptions. While this imbalance may not matter on one topic, it may on another. Therefore, it is critical that, whenever possible, you follow up with additional efforts to balance the respondents' data with known organizational demographics.

Although these data inspections and follow-up procedures may be tedious, they are critical nonetheless. Respondent under- or overrepresentation *will have an effect* on your conclusions. Unfortunately, without data inspection for sampling adequacy and appropriate follow-up procedures, you will not even know where or how your conclusions were affected. There is no point in collecting communication network data, wasting your time and the client organization's resources, if those data lead to faulty conclusions. And they will—without detailed data inspection and appropriate follow-up action.

Look for surprises. • Surprises come in a variety of forms. As you inspect the visual representation of communication flow (e.g., Figure 10.1), consider initially two types of surprises. First, look for closeness where communicative distance is expected. Second, look for distance where communicative proximity is expected.

The geometric map in Figure 10.1 illustrates several of both types of surprises. For example, consider the communicative distance between Accounting and Corporate Headquarters. The acquisition of a new company should directly involve Accounting; yet, relatively speaking, the communicative distance between the two groups is large. In addition, consider the relative noncentrality of Operations. While Corporate Headquarters should be in a communicatively central position (and it is), Operations should also be centrally located.

Some distances are not surprising. Tandem Industries was located physically nearest Chicago, and, as such, Chicago Sales is "communicatively close" to Corporate Headquarters on *this* message topic. An alternative interpretation here may be that Chicago Sales is also closest physically to Corporate Headquarters (thirty miles). Resolution of the correct interpretation would come from other communication audit data sources.

It is also clear that Human Resources, on this message topic, is relatively isolated. This may be as it should be, but perhaps Human Resources should be more communicatively close, given the impact of adding a union company to a predominately nonunion holding company (the client organization).

Some of the communication linkages are strong and should be strong. For example, the closest work groups communicatively are Line Personnel and Line Supervisors. This is as it should be. Some of the communicatively strong relationships are relatively weak, and perhaps should be. Consider the linkage between Line Personnel and Accounting. The linkage is weak and should be weak, relatively speaking. While these latter interpretations are not surprises, they do confirm the validity of the geometric representation—an important feature if we expect the client organization to take the results of the network analysis seriously.

Generate Recommendations.   The process of generating recommendations is a result of "examining the numbers" and "looking for surprises." From examining the numbers, we could generate at least two recommendations.

We found out from interviews that the lack of reciprocation between Chicago and L.A. Sales was due to Chicago Sales thinking of itself as superior in comparison to L.A.; that is, Chicago accounted for 76 percent of the sales of the client organization's primary product line and was closest to the action—it was within thirty miles of Corporate Headquarters. Recommendation:

> Transfer two key personnel from Chicago to L.A. to "help" L.A. sales increase sales and reduce the competitiveness between two groups that should be cooperating.

From the numbers we also found Corporate Staff had weak communicative connections to a large proportion of the other groups. From interviews we found that Corporate Staff personnel believed they were "left out" of several key decisions and that the President's Office and Accounting thought Corporate Staff should be left out. We also learned that Corporate Staff was often required to implement aspects of acquisition decisions and was held accountable for said implementation. Recommendation:

> If Corporate Staff is to be held accountable for the results of an acquisition decision, it must be kept informed of decisions regarding acquisitions *as they are being made.*

From looking for surprises, we could make at least two recommendations from the visual representation of communication relationships. The visual map in Figure 10.1 showed that Accounting and Corporate Headquarters were communicatively distant. From the climate survey we found much lower job satisfaction in Accounting. From interviews we learned that Accounting personnel were suffering from an acute sense of job insecurity. Preliminary investigation of the client organization and interviews with Corporate Headquarters personnel disclosed that the client was suffering from severe fiscal stress (cash flow); yet it was committed to a growth-through-acquisition/diversification program. Recommendation: None.

The fiscal parameters of the client were beyond our expertise as a communication audit team and were deemed to be the true cause of problems, not communicative distance per se. In other words, business problems were causing communication problems, not communication problems causing fiscal stress.

From the visual map of communication relationships we found Operations to be out of the communicative mainstream. Analysis of the demographics of Operations personnel revealed that almost all respondents had had their positions less than one year. From follow-up interviews we learned that Operations was a new organizational entity and did not, as we first suspected, suffer from a high turnover rate. Recommendation:

> Since Operations is a new organizational entity and is left out of key decisions regarding the acquisition of Tandem Industries, Operations and Corporate Headquarters should be housed physically in the same building.

Although there are certainly more recommendations that could be derived from both the numbers and the visual map, there are three principles illustrated by the recommendations presented. First, they reflect all of the available data sources. None of the recommendations presented here could have been made in their current form or with assurance without qualitative data from other sources. Second, the fact that there is a communication disturbance does not mean that there are communication-related reasons for such a disturbance. It is better at times to just back away. Third, the recommendations reflect simple common sense. It often takes complex diagnostic tools such as the communication audit assessment tools to bring about common sense recommendations. Sometimes our common sense becomes apparent only when we have "data" to support it.

In summary, interpreting the data comprises three strategies: examining the numbers, inspecting the visual map for surprises, and generating recommendations. The goal of interpreting communication network data is to give meaning to the numbers. We need information (data given meaning) to effect Step 4—integrating the recommendations into the overall strategic plan for organizational communication change and development.

Integrating recommendations

In Step 4, the presence of an overall strategic plan for organizational communication and development is assumed. If the client organization does not have such a plan, some of the recommendations may obtain more (or less) effectuating resources than they deserve. How to assist a client in developing its plan is beyond the scope of this chapter, but there are four key elements that should be part of any plan of organizational communication change and development.

First, there should be an actual, articulated communication policy. It is morbidly fascinating to note organizations that articulate policies about coffee breaks but have nothing but unstated (and often ambiguous) policies about how, where, when, and with what effect communication shall be accomplished.

Second, the communication policies should be *communication* policies. Organizations have a tendency to act on the premise that all problems are derived from communication problems. Some communication policies really concern who's where in the heirarchy of the organization. Such policies may be useful for following the chain of command and may have a direct effect on communication, but they are not communication policies per se.

Third, the communication goals should have specific, measurable or observable indices of fulfiillment. As Yogi Berra said of the Yankees in 1957, "If you don't know where you're goin', you'll probably get there." Unless the results of goal fulfillment are measurable or observable, no one can be held accountable for (or committed to) the goal's fulfillment or lack thereof.

Fourth, the communication plan should have contingency plans integrated throughout. If one plans for a communication crisis, it is no crisis— it's a managed problem. Things do go wrong. If there are no plans to deal with errors, then the plan only works when things go right. Contingency planning is not only good management; it is plain, good common sense.

Beyond the assessment of the communication plan for these four elements (or the development thereof), another major hurdle the communication auditor must overcome is gaining management ownership of the recommendations. If the client organization (management *and* nonmanagement personnel) does not feel as if it "owns" the recommendations, the client will see what it wants to see, do what it wants to do—instead of seeing and doing what needs to be done. In short, without client ownership of the recommendations, there is no commitment to following through on the recommendations' implementation.

Client ownership comes through the client participating in the whole process of creating recommendations. An effective way to do this is to select individuals from all levels of the organization, have them examine the data in detail, and, most importantly, have them help shape the final recommendations. If the client views the recommendations as *your* recommendations, not only is there the danger of selective attention to several key recommendations, there is the potential for the client ignoring your final report. Client owner-ship is the only answer to this potential failure.

Once a communication plan is assessed or developed and the client is integrated into the process of developing the recommendations, the next step is to assess the priority of each recommendation. Prioritization is accomplished by categorizing each recommendation into that part of the communication plan for which it has the most import. If the recommendation does not logically fit anywhere in the plan, consider what may be wrong with the plan. Perhaps the communication plan needs to be modified; it may not cover the issue underlying the particular recommendation. If the plan *is* comprehensive, the recommendation may not be of sufficient importance to deserve organizational resources to implement. Again, client integration in these priority checks is absolutely necessary. No involvement in prioritization leads to no commit-ment of personal and organizational resources for the recommendations' implementation.

When discussing recommendations and action plans for their im-plementation with the client, be wary of two types of "solutions." First, avoid recommendations that call for committees, task forces, or action teams to im-plement the recommendation. Such groups can easily get bogged down and should be avoided as a general rule. There are, however, circumstances under which such action teams are appropriate. If the task implied by the recom-mendation requires a high degree of creativity and a high degree of commit-ment or involvement to its implementation, *and* if there is sufficient time and other resources for the action team to accomplish its task, such a team may be appropriate.

Second, avoid making recommendations where communication is not a central part of the problem diagnosed. Given the pervasiveness of communication-related issues in the organization, it is easy to go beyond one's level of expertise in organizational change and development. It is also easy to forget that not all organizational problems are *communication* problems. Avoid such recommendations, even though communication may be an effect (as opposed to cause) of the underlying problem.

CONCLUSION

The goal of communication network analyses is to understand the underlying structure of an organization's communication flow. To accomplish this goal, data must be (1) collected in a logistically defensible manner; (2) analyzed in a scientifically and pragmatically justified manner; (3) interpreted in a qualitatively integrated manner; and (4) integrated into an overall plan for organizational communication change and development.

The success of these steps depends on integrating all data sources into recommendations, considering at all times the client's needs—from data collection to recommendation integration—and involving the client in the entire process. Without client involvement, not only will many recommendations be irrelevant and misleading, but the client will not *own* them—the analysis will become "just another consultant's report on the shelf." As an auditor you have an ethical and professional responsibility to see that this does not happen.

REFERENCES

Bales, R. F. *Interaction Process Analysis: A Method for Studying Small Groups.* Reading, Mass.: Addison-Wesley, 1950.

Barnes, J. *Social Networks.* Boston: Addison-Wesley, 1972, pp. 1–29.

Monge, P. R., and Day, P. D. "Multivariate Analysis in Communication Research." *Human Communication Research* 2 (1976): 207–220.

Moreno, J. L. *Who Shall Survive? A New Approach to the Problem of Human Interrelations.* New York: Beacon Press, 1934.

Norton, R. W. "Nonmetric Multidimensional Scaling in Communication Research: Smallest Space Analysis." In *Multivariate Techniques in Human Communication Research,* edited by P. R. Monge and N. J. Cappella, 309–331. New York: Academic Press, 1980.

Porter, D. T. "Reliability Made Simpler: Program PIAS." *CEDR Quarterly* 8 (1978): 7–11.

Porter, D. T. "The Development of an Estimation Procedure for Network Analysis." Published paper presented to the Buffalo Conference on Organizational Communication. State University of New York at Buffalo, 1977.

Porter, D. T. "The ICA Communication Audit: 1979 Organizational Norms." Paper presented to the annual convention of the International Communication Association, Chicago, May 1979.

Porter, D. T. "The Validity of Communication Needs Assessment." *Journal of Applied Communication Research* 13 (1985): 59–69.

Shaw, M. E. "Communication Networks." In *Advances in Experimental Social Psychology,* Vol. 1, edited by L. Berkowitz. New York: Academic Press, 1964.

11

Phase 5: Final Analysis and Interpretation

Collecting data using the methods described in Chapters 4 through 10 can be interesting and creative, and the process of data collection can be scientifically planned to meet rigorous research standards. There are general rules to be followed concerning the sampling of respondents, the design of questionnaires, and the strategies of interviewing. By following these rules, the auditor can be confident of the audit product so far. However, the audit is incomplete without a conversion of data into conclusions through skillful interpretation. And, in contrast to the data collection procedures, no one has been able to delineate completely and specifically how interpretation ought to be performed. Therefore, this chapter describes the nature of interpretation, suggests a process that facilitates effective interpretation, and identifies some common issues and problems. Because some aspects of interpretation were discussed for individual methodologies, this chapter will focus on a general diagnosis when all data from all resources are brought together.

THE NATURE OF INTERPRETATION

After a professor made a presentation to a group of executives on her research in international business, an executive from IBM asked her to explain one part of the results. When she replied that she could not do so without doing more basic research, the whole room erupted in laughter, and the executive turned to me and said, "Spoken just like a true academic!" Many years of graduate education not only impart knowledge but also, perhaps inadvertently, condition one to be "reasonable," to accommodate multiple points of view, and to feel uncomfortable about taking a stand. This well-intentioned humility can cause problems at the interpretation stage of an audit because it generates a fear of being wrong. To interpret is to try to make sense of or to understand something in a particular way; as understanding increases, the auditing process becomes worthwhile and valuable.

The following description of the process of interpretation by Weick and Daft offers useful prospectives to consider (Cameron and Whetten, 1983, pp. 74–78). Interpretations:

1. are like trying to construct a reading or manuscript that is foreign, faded, full of sllipses, incoherencies. . . .
2. . . . inform and modify that which they are intended to explain. Interpretations interpret interpretations rather than events.
3. . . . utilize special knowledge, sympathy, or imagination.
4. . . . are like acts of translation from one language to another.
5. . . . focus on elapsed action . . . [which] precedes cognition.
6. . . . are quasi-historical.
7. . . . construct environment rather than discover it.
8. . . . are reasonable rather than right.

At first glance, these views of interpretation appear to be negative. They suggest that interpretation is not a very exact science, and such lack of definition may seem wishy-washy. Nothing is further from the truth for the knowledgeable professional auditor. Nevertheless, implicit in these statements is the notion that different auditors may interpret the audit data differently. Indeed, the auditor who is particularly trained in networks and structures may view the problems as being caused by ineffective organizational structures. The auditor with expertise in interpersonal communication will perceive that the deficiencies are caused by imperfect interpersonal relationships. Admittedly, selective perception takes place among the auditors. Nevertheless, if the auditors are competent, the different interpretations may contribute much to an understanding of the organization. This does not mean that the one auditor should back away from his or her interpretation. What really separates better interpretations from poorer ones is the "degree to which the interpreter has knowledge or imagination to provide a plausible rendering of events that might have generated the present display" (Weick and Daft in Cameron and Whetten, 1983, p. 75). In summary, the process of interpretation requires the *construction* of an answer that makes practical sense, rather than the *discovery* of the right answer that already exists in the environment. Adopting this frame of reference frees auditors to develop their own systematic approach to interpretation.

ESTABLISH A SYSTEMATIC
APPROACH TO INTERPRETATION

Most of us have pet systems for developing solutions to problems. Many of us were trained in the five steps of the Dewey's reflective thinking pattern.

1. Define the problem.
2. Analyze the problem.
3. Set up criteria for a solution.
4. List alternative solutions.
5. Choose a solution.

This pattern has had a profound influence on organizational and group decision making. One of its greatest contributions has been its emphasis on defining the real problem before being solution-oriented.

Another interpretive route to reaching conclusions in communication audits was developed by DeWine, James, and Walance (1985). The following example illustrates the six steps in their process.

1. *Problem Identification:* Employees indicate they have insufficient information about personnel policies.

2. *Objective:* Employees should more fully comprehend the policies relative to their jobs.

3. *Method:* Two changes would address this problem: (a) development of a Policies and Procedures Manual; and (b) distribution of the manual to all employees.

4. *Reality:* Limited resources within the Personnel Department make the development of a manual unlikely. Therefore, a modification of the idea may be implemented.

5. *Implementation:* A representative small group of employees should meet with the Personnel Director to identify issues that need clarification. These employees can then begin to work on parts of a manual.

6. *Evaluation:* Once the recommendation is implemented, effectiveness could be assessed by: a survey six months later; discussion of the policies in employee appraisals; or questions about new policies in the organization newsletter.

The particular system that I have found useful is similar to those advocated by Dewey and DeWine, with some important modifications. Basically, it involves eight steps: (1) synthesize all data, (2) develop focal areas, (3) identify and define problems, (4) identify organizational criteria for success, (5) consider the organization's stages of development, (6) form tentative conclusions, (7) finalize the conclusions, and (8) make client-centered recommendations. In the discussion that follows, each one of these steps will be described in detail, along with some of the problems inherent in each.

Synthesize all data

Whereas Dewey and DeWine both start their analyses with problem identification, the interpretive process actually begins with a close examination of all the data collected, and few aspects of the auditing process are more challenging or more troublesome than integrating the results of qualitative and quantitative analyses. In some ways, the synthesis process is as much intuitive art as science. Experience will help you refine your own synthesis process, but the following sections list some of the guidelines and concurrent problems that we have found useful.

Use data from all instruments. • Unlike the researcher who knows exactly how information is going to be used from the start, an auditor does not know exactly how information will be used until after it has been collected and examined. Ostensibly, all data may yield significant information about the organization. On the other hand, one knows from the start that much of it will have to be discarded as unimportant; one just does not know which part. Decisions concerning data's importance can only be made after thorough examination of it all.

A common problem at this point is the tendency to rely too heavily on data from one method at the expense of the other methods. Particularly, auditors sometimes rely too heavily on questionnaire or quantitative data, simply because they feel more comfortable dealing with numbers. The attitude seems to be, "If I can count it, I am on safer ground." This is not necessarily good auditing technique, so one should look for ways that the different findings reinforce or contradict one another.

Reconcile contradictions. • Resolve differences by searching deeper into the reasons that the methods yielded different kinds of information. Presumably, you have developed an accurate description of the organization; therefore, contradictory information may be accounted for by the differences among the methodologies.

For example, in an audit one of our strongest findings from the questionnaire was that upper management was perceived negatively by subordinates. Estimates of management on trust, sincerity, encouraging differences of opinion, concern for employees' welfare, and recognizing outstanding performance were significantly low. Yet the interview data did not support this critical view. The conclusion from the interview data was that although subordinates did not see superiors as much as they might have liked, they understood the demands under which upper management was working. In the case of such contradictions, it is necessary to decide which interpretation is more representative. In this particular example, upper management may have come off worse in the questionnaire because it was the one item that all employees had in common; thus negative comments about it were magnified. But because the interview data suggested that employees had some appreciation of upper management's problems, we tempered our conclusions.

Avoid the halo effect. • A "halo" refers to the tendency for one thing to become so big or so important that all other estimates are somewhat biased by it. For example, when auditors work in teams, members sometimes tend to emphasize the information obtained personally, and that information becomes more important than other types of information. For example, two auditors once conducted an interview that was particularly enlightening and enjoyable to them. In the group analysis sessions, they let that one interview bias their every observation; in fact, that is all they wanted to talk about. Finally, this dysfunctional pattern was pointed out to them, and they began to consider other information more objectively. It takes considerable self-discipline to overcome such a halo effect.

Use other auditors' work carefully. • Audit teams frequently divide up the analyses so that people work from summaries written by other people. Make certain that these summaries are complete, *using verbatim comments whenever possible.* After the first round of interviews in one audit, all summaries were given to an interviewing team of three people. The team quickly learned that the initial summaries were too sketchy and that the other auditors' understanding of what had been written during the interviews was different than the team's interpretations. Consequently, a quick training program was implemented, and all summaries were rewritten to be more explicit and more usable.

Keep negative information in perspective. • This was mentioned earlier, but it is worth repeating. The ultimate objective of an audit is a realistic appraisal of both strengths and weaknesses. There is a common tendency, however, to focus almost exclusively on the negative; tackling problems seems to be more interesting and more challenging. Therefore, the negative must be kept in perspective, balanced with the positive. Also keep in mind that most organizations must work fairly well to be able to stay in existence.

On the other hand, another potential problem (although less common) is the tendency to downplay the negative. It is not uncommon for beginning auditors particularly to be intimidated by managers or to want to please the managers by emphasizing the positive. This tendency must be overcome. Although it may be interpersonally pleasing, it damages the realism of the audit.

Develop focal areas

The most disconcerting characteristic of most audits is the sheer amount of information generated. When you begin to combine data from several of the audit instruments covered in this book, the result can be an information overload that is easily overwhelming. The essence of a general communication audit is to search for as much information as possible; then, when the information is obtained, some important analytic and interpretive questions, such as the following, have to be answered:

What are the needs of the organization?
What areas are really important?
What gives the most useful diagnosis of the organization?
Of all the things that might be mentioned, what are the areas that can yield the greatest improvement for management?

Such questions lead to the beginning of a focus for interpreting the data. Chapter 3 discussed many areas to explore, but not all are equally applicable for every audit. Therefore, three suggestions that may be helpful in developing important focal areas are presented.

Brainstorm. If there is an audit team, it should spend time discussing the results and what they mean. There will be disagreements, and much time can be consumed, but the time is not necessarily wasted. Remember that the nature of interpretation is *constructing* a case, not discovering it. Therefore, these discussions can be invaluable in refining one's thinking. Even when conducting audits alone, I have found it useful to discuss some of the findings with trusted colleagues. Presenting the ideas to others forces me to refine and clarify my insights.

Allow time; do not rush. • Interpretation requires an incubation period. All the information needs to be digested and integrated, and this cannot be done quickly. If a team is involved, group discussions are important. Progress may seem slow sometimes, but the process is important.

Remember that not all problems are communication problems. • Communication may indeed be the process by which organizational problems are solved, but not all problems are necessarily communication problems. If employees are dissatisfied with their benefits, for example, communication is not likely to change that. Or consider the plight of one of the best plant managers with whom I have worked. He developed a thorough team approach in a new plant. Within five years it was a showcase in the large international organization. One innovation had been that employees were paid for what they knew, not what they did. The system encouraged employees to train for several jobs, and each time they learned a new one their salaries could advance. The system worked so well that management and employees thought it effective. However, the plant manager could see a problem looming on the horizon. So many employees liked their jobs that there was little turnover. However, as people got to the top of their pay scales and learned all the jobs associated with that team, there was nothing else they could do to earn more. Therefore, the plant manager fully expected the organization's next great challenge to be the dissatisfaction of the longer-term employees. He planned to keep the communication channels open and did discuss it with employees, but this problem is potentially so complex that it cannot be defined merely as a communication problem. The implication of recognizing noncommunication for the auditor is profound. In a communication audit, one must stay with what one knows.

Identify and define problems or strengths

"Problem definition by its very nature is an ill-defined, complex, and ambiguous problem in its own right. . ." (Kilmann and Mitroff, 1977, p. 150). As you examine all the audit data you begin to *sense* problems. Then, after the intuitive sensing comes the necessity to identify more specific areas. The actual process of defining a problem is an exercise in creativity. There are decisions about how best to express the problem and what terms best represent the essence of the auditor's insights. Often at the beginning is a nebulous notion about what is wrong, and somehow you must work through the vagueness to refine your grasp of the problem.

It has already been pointed out that problem definition is linked to some concepts of organizational effectiveness; in other words, the problem is that gap between current practice and the expected or desired level of performance. But the gap must also be in an important area for it to be considered a problem for the entire organization.

In defining problems, there are five errors that can be made: (1) not discovering a problem that actually exists, (2) identifying a problem that does not exist, (3) treating all problems as communication problems, (4) trying to solve the wrong problems, and (5) failing to probe deeply enough to understand the problem. Each of these can be addressed in the following ways.

Make your search comprehensive. • An audit is more like a fishing net than a fishing line. Try to make the area covered as general as possible so as not to miss anything; in other words, try to "catch" as many problems as possible. This is why several methodologies are desirable. The "catch" must be examined comprehensively. Some problems will grab immediate attention, but do not let them deter you from examining more subtle areas.

Determine whether an observation really is a problem. • If one does does not do this, there is a likelihood of *solving the wrong problem.* For example, we normally expect problems to occur if organizational roles are not clear. In one organization, we found widespread disagreement about a certain manager's role. We asked whether or not this led to any real communication problems. After much discussion, we concluded that it did, because this influential person was violating a number of organizational values. In another instance, we discovered a lack of communication between two units in the same department. The presumption was that they *ought* to be communicating, but actually the organization was not suffering as a result of their lack of communication. Consequently, we had to admit that their decision not to communicate was not a problem. Similarly, in a network analysis, having certain people described as "isolates" sounded bad, but it turned out that these people neither wanted nor needed to be integrated into the organization. Hence, they did not cause a problem.

Test different ways of characterizing problems. • Kilmann and Mitroff (1977) propose the following methodology for problem definition.

1. Formulate several, if not many, different definitions of the problem situation.

2. Debate these different definitions in order to examine critically their assumptions, implications, and possible consequences.

3. Develop an integrated or synthesized problem definition by emphasizing the strengths or advantages of each problem definition while minimizing the weaknesses or disadvantages.

4. Include in the definition process those persons who are experiencing the problems, who have the expertise to define problems in various substantive domains, whose commitment to the problem definition and resulting change program will be necessary for that program to be successfully implemented, and who are expected to be affected by the outcomes of any change program that attempts to solve or manage the perceived problem (p. 150).

This methodology contains excellent suggestions for guaranteeing a sensitive analysis of the organization. Step 1 requires breaking up some of the cognitive maps developed from first impressions of the organization. Furthermore, managers who employ an auditor often have a definite problem in mind. In such cases, it takes a kind of self-assured discipline to explore problems in ways that differ from management's viewpoint. In other words, an auditor should consider management's definitions but avoid being swayed by them. Finally, of all the previous steps, step 3 is probably the most difficult to achieve, but trying it can liven up the auditors' meetings. In an audit of a university, five auditors spent many hours sharing insights and hammering out problem definitions. The process is tiring but is very fulfilling when the synthesis finally occurs.

Probe the nature of the problems fully. • Probe as deeply as you can into the root causes of the problem. Every problem has sub-problems, roots, tributaries, or contributing factors. (See Figure 11.1.) Most of us start by defining problems superficially, but it is a mistake to end with a superficial definition. And although it may be wise to keep our explanations to others simple, we certainly should not be willing to leave our understanding of problems simple. For this reason, the communication analyst will often work with liaison members of the organization at this point, testing out ideas and refining definitions.

FIGURE 11.1   Probing the Nature of a Problem

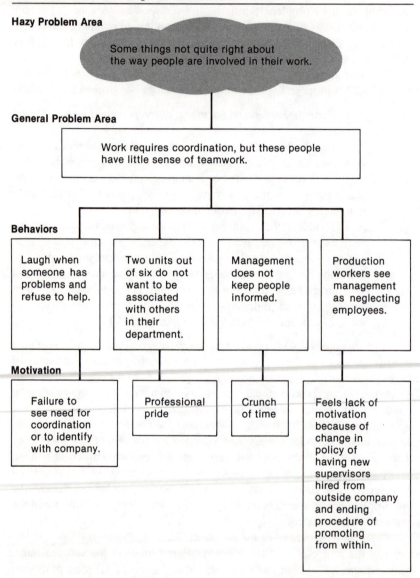

Hazy Problem Area

> Some things not quite right about
> the way people are involved in their work.

General Problem Area

> Work requires coordination, but these people
> have little sense of teamwork.

Behaviors

| Laugh when someone has problems and refuse to help. | Two units out of six do not want to be associated with others in their department. | Management does not keep people informed. | Production workers see management as neglecting employees. |

Motivation

| Failure to see need for coordination or to identify with company. | Professional pride | Crunch of time | Feels lack of motivation because of change in policy of having new supervisors hired from outside company and ending procedure of promoting from within. |

For example, when one finds, as I did, that the communication climate in a manufacturing plant had deteriorated in recent months, one obviously wonders why? A "poor climate" was really a symptom of several other factors affecting relations in the plant. It was important to note those contributing factors because they were part of the problem. Several things that had happened to reduce employees' identifications with the plant were pinpointed – a 50 percent increase in output that put strains on workers, a new hiring policy, and a recent reorganization. The relevant communication factors were examined for each. At the end, we had a very specific understanding of the problems that had reduced the health of the communication climate.

We have defined problems as the gap between current performance and the performance that is desired. Although the identification of effectiveness criteria is implicit in the definition of a problem, it is useful to make these criteria explicit.

Identify criteria of organizational effectiveness

Defining organizational effectiveness is a wicked problem; the major hurdle to solving wicked problems is to formulate the problem (Cameron & Whetten, p. 268). Different theories lead to different measures of effectiveness, and the best criteria for assessing organizational effectiveness varies with:

1. whose perspective is used,
2. the domain of activity on which the judgment is focused,
3. the level of analysis being used,
4. the purpose for judging effectiveness,
5. the time frame being employed,
6. the type of data (subjective or objective) being used for judgments, and
7. the referents against which effectiveness is judged (Cameron and Whetten, 1983).

Although effectiveness is a loosely defined concept, it is absolutely necessary for the auditor to discover the referents against which effectiveness is being judged *in the organization being audited.* Organizations are political arenas in which competing interest groups vie for control over resources, and perceptions of effectiveness reflect the demands made by critical constituencies. For example, in one audit we discovered a case in which management had invited professional workers in two units to participate in determining space arrangements in a new facility. Management considered the participation as demonstrating effective communication. However, employees in both units were very angry because not all of their advice was taken, and they characterized the communication as ineffective. One representative said, "They should not have asked us if they were not going to take the advice." As an auditor, how does one reconcile these different interpretations?

There can never be, nor is it desirable to have, one simple approach to effectiveness. Knowing that there is not one *right* answer can have a freeing quality; on the other hand, it also can increase the tension to discover what is really important about organizational communication. The discussion that follows pinpoints several of the referents against which effectiveness can be judged. In each case, the assessment of effectiveness gaps is the basic means of identifying a problem; in other words, a problem occurs when there is a difference between what the organization wants and what it actually has.

In making these comparisons, auditors may be wise to make their judgments descriptive. "The elements of the process are two-fold: (1) the presence of objective measures that compare actual behavior with some kind of standard, and (2) the communication of the standard, the measure, and the judgment to the recipient" (Filley and Pace, 1976, p. 67).

Organizational comparisons. • In the final audit reports, managers have typically wanted to know how their organization compares with others. They apparently believe that if others are doing better than they are, they must have problems. Such "norm-referred appraisals" take place when a judgmental interpretation compares one organization with other comparable members (Filley and Pace, 1976, p. 67). These comparative judgments give a basic frame of reference for effectiveness, and that is why the data banks for the ICA and Communication Satisfaction (Com Sat) Questionnaires, discussed in Chapters 6 and 7, are such useful tools. Obviously, what one knows about other organizations offers some comparative standards. However, audits should be cautioned against comparing different types of organizations too readily or comparing organizations that operate under different circumstances. Within the same large company, for example, the communication within a Florida plant differed in some significant ways from that in a plant in Minnesota, and regional differences had to be taken into account.

Internal organizational comparisons. • Similarly, one way of identifying problems is to make comparisons among units within the same organization. If one unit has more success communicating than does another unit, we look for ways of improving the second. For example, when several plants in the same large organization were audited, the comparisons among them became useful tools for offering suggestions to the individual plants. The reasons for the communication successes of Plant A allowed us to make suggestions for Plant B. In most audits, we make similar comparisons among shifts, work units, managerial levels, and pay classifications. This is a means of identifying exactly where communication problems are.

Comparisons with stated goals. • Much has been made about the importance of goal-setting in appraising individuals. It does not take much imagination, therefore, to realize that the same process can be useful at the more general organizational level. The problem is that one will rarely find these goals stated specifically or explicitly at an organizational level. More often, they are vague encouragements to "emphasize communication." However, if the auditors search, they may find definite goals. In an audit of a service organization, the chief executive handed the audit team a statement of values and goals for the organization and asked that the audit be oriented toward how well the organization was achieving them. "Communicate clearly and appropriately" was one of the values, and in the audit results it ranked lowest of the twelve values listed. This helped in the definition of problems. In such cases the *incongruency* between goals and performance is in itself a problem. By using a priori goals as standards of effective communication, the members agree on the definition of "good" communication in advance. "Thus, it escapes the arbitrariness of an externally imposed standard" (Filley and Pace, 1976, p. 68).

Comparisons with past performance. • One standard for effectiveness is to ask, "Where are we today relative to where we were?" This book began by recommending periodic audits, because the auditors can work from a sense of progress over time. In one audit it was significant to discover that the ratings of communication climate had gone down significantly in a manufacturing plant. We probed vigorously to discover that increased pressure to produce had precipitated real tensions and had created a feeling among employees of not being informed of what was going on. Furthermore, increased demands on the managers' time had made them less accessible. It was, therefore, not only the auditors who were comparing the present with the past; the employees registered their reactions on the same basis.

"Change score analysis" over time is useful because it prompts a thorough examination of why changes for the better or for the worse occur. In making these interpretations, however, the auditor is challenged to look at the total system and to avoid making simplistic cause-effect inferences. Finally, although comparisons with past performance give some insight into the organization, it still needs to be analyzed in terms of outcomes and compared with other organizations. Organizational improvement may not be sufficient if others are improving more or producing more.

Outcomes. • Chapter 3 dealt at length with outcome variables of satisfaction and productivity, because they are ways of measuring communication success. Unless there are severe environmental crises, the tendency is to view inadequate communication as a root cause for either morale or productivity problems and to see improved communication as a means of solving these problems. In this arena, the question is "what works?" If something is not working well, change it. Again, attention must be directed to the fact that many variables other than communication affect productivity and satisfaction; nevertheless, the auditor can look for direct links between organizational communication and organizational outcomes.

Desirable characteristics. • Communication effectiveness is often judged in terms of normative ideals, that is, those that are assumed to be characteristic of properly functioning organizations. For example, the Com Sat Questionnaire assesses eight communication factors, and it assumes that employees should be satisfied with each one. Consequently, one way to measure effectiveness is to rank order all factors in terms of what employees find most satisfying. When we did this in one audit, we found, for example, that all the means for all eight factors fell in the satisfied range. However, the mean for the Personal Feedback factor rated lowest. In fact, the mean score fell close to the mid-point, "neither satisfied nor dissatisfied." Since feedback is one of the most important types of communication and since it was ranked lower than less important types of communication, we concluded that the organization was not providing it as effectively as it should.

The same ranking pattern can be used with any audit instrument. All individual questions in each section of the ICA Questionnaire were rank ordered in an audit of a chemical plant to determine what relations were not as effective as others, what channels were not as effective as others, and so on. The most effective were identified as strengths; the least effective were mentioned as potential problems.

The value of these "content-referenced evaluations" depends on a proved connection between behavior and outcomes and on the recipient's acceptance of that connection (Filley and Pace, 1976, p. 68). When a certain form of communication has been demonstrated to lead to a desired goal, controlling the communication assures that the goal will be achieved. Its chief limitation is that different contingencies allow other alternatives of communication behavior to achieve the same goal.

Consider the stage of organizational development

Although organizational comparisons have merit, every auditor must be sensitive to differences among organizations. Research studies comparing types of organizations usually report some similarities but also pinpoint some major differences. These differences reinforce the contingency approach to organizational communication that advocates viewing each case as unique. One area of contingency that we have found to be especially important is the organization's stage of development, or organizational age. Greiner (1972) maintains that organizations evolve through various stages of development, and each growth area creates its own crisis. He points out that it is important to know what stage of development the organization is in and to realize that *each new solution breeds new problems in the long run.* In other words, the organization never stops evolving.

One important implication for the communication auditor is that the same rules of communication do not apply equally to all organizations. For example, the interactive patterns are much simpler in some small organizations than in large, well-developed organizations. The president of a successful insurance company reminisced about the early days of the organization when he had access to everyone. With success had come more demands on his time, and with greater numbers of employees had come a reduction in the time he could spend with any one. He was no less competent in communication as the organization grew, but circumstances dictated changes. Similarly, I audited a manufacturing organization that had a successful and profitable history. However, a new plant manager decided to modernize it through improvements. Within a year, the plant experienced an increase in productivity of 50 percent as the organization moved from one stage to the next. The new creative approach led to a crisis in leadership, and some employees experienced difficulties. Nevertheless, as an objective outsider I could forecast that in time the plant manager's innovations would be helpful. The problem was the transition period — a time that is probably always going to be somewhat painful for an organization.

As a final example, an audit of a consulting firm again revealed the importance of keeping the evolutionary perspective. This nationally known company had been developed by one man and was still family controlled. As it grew, the founder decided to move toward professional managers. The audit was conducted during a transition phase, and it was helpful to interpret the findings in terms of the organization's evolution from a one-man operation to a firm with a diversified approach to management. Some communication problems arose because of sudden changes in management and moving part of the staff to another location. In assessing the current communication practices, we also had to be cognizant of where the organization was heading.

Form tentative conclusions

If there are a number of ways that a problem can be phrased, there are even more ways that improvements can be suggested. These different solutions will have relative weaknesses and merits that need to be examined.

Look at the implications of your conclusions. • Particularly, relevant costs should be examined. For example, one of the most widely advocated solutions to communication problems is to have more meetings. Now, meetings can be important communication vehicles that offer excellent communication opportunities; however, when you compute the employees' downtime and salaries, the cost of any meeting may determine how useful it is. Furthermore, if employees believe that they already go to too many meetings or that their current meetings waste time, more meetings are not going to solve a problem. In another instance, formalizing job descriptions was touted by an auditor as the answer for solving a problem involving ambiguous roles. Although job descriptions can be useful, many managers resist having formal, explicit job descriptions because they are too restrictive and cause other kinds of problems. Therefore, in this case management would have rejected that suggestion. A good communication vehicle may not always be acceptable when one considers people's reactions, time pressures, or costs.

Check assumptions. • Although assumptions are implicit in everything we do, we often have difficulty stating them. Furthermore, when we are able to state them explicitly, we do not always like what we hear. For that reason, analyzing the assumptions at both the problem identification and the conclusion stages can facilitate a greater understanding of the interpretive process.

Kilmann (1984) advocates a process of "assumptional analysis." When different conclusions are given for the same problem, the analyzers are divided into teams, with each team discussing one of the conclusions. Each team's assignment is to make a list of the assumptions underlying the conclusion. After this is accomplished, the teams regroup, reveal their lists of assumptions, go through a process of challenging the assumptions, and finally prepare a matrix of assumptions divided into "certain–uncertain" and "more important–less important" categories. They then begin to synthesize the assumptions in order to improve their conclusions.

Use intuitive powers. • Intuition is not something to be avoided; in many ways, it is akin to creativity. Interpretation requires mental leaps from data to conclusions, and this requires that you go beyond mere descriptive statements.

Beware of the false cause-effect trap. • Just because one thing precedes another in time does not mean that the first thing caused the other. And just because you are conducting a communication audit does not mean that a lack of communication caused all the problems. Throughout the book, I have tried to emphasize that organizations are complex, and any conclusions drawn about the organization must reflect an understanding of that complexity. Tom Porter (1986) coined a phrase "cauffective" to help deal with these cause-effect problems.

> This "need" to separate myopically causes from causes and, more importantly, to attribute "cause" *or* "effect" to events can be disastrous. This is particularly true with communication in organizations. Too many communicative acts are both cause and effect and neither. . . To say a given act is the *"cause"* is clearly subjective assignation. With systematic events, *"cause"* is simply the "effect" of a previous "cause," ad infinitum. . . *Cauffective* acts are the best way by which to conceive of communication in the organization (p. 5).

Finalize your conclusions

The interpretive process described here should lead to basic conclusions about the organization. Although the preceding discussion has a decided problem orientation, the final conclusions should reflect strengths as well as weaknesses. They should be general statements, amplified with specific rationales explaining why you think they are true. They should also cover only the most important items; do not try to cover everything in the conclusions.

The following is a statement of a conclusion from one audit.

Results indicate an inconsistency between the statement of values by upper management and the ways these values are perceived by staff. Upper management espouses a belief in an open culture and is very concerned that company values are incorporated into company and employee behavior. However, many employees did not feel that these were effectively carried down through the ranks. (A rationale was then provided.)

Make client-centered recommendations

One of the temptations of auditors is to substitute their own values for those of the organization or management. This is a grave mistake. The recommendations should always address the practical realities of the organization. Is it practical or workable? Is it desirable? And is it cost efficient?

As an auditor, I seek answers to these questions in preliminary discussions with managers. Because they know the job far better than I do, I have tentative discussions with them in which we explore one another's thinking. This is basically a form of process consultation, discussed in Chapter 2. It also leads directly into the final phase of the audit: feedback.

A FINAL NOTE

Basically, interpretation is a process of constructing theory about organizational communication. "The fate of all theory is to be either ignored or improved" (Mackenzie, 1986). Many readers may consider this a shocking statement, but it represents the reality of theoretical development. In no organizational discipline do scholars have enough "theoretical truth" to make prediction exact. In fact, there are many theories about organizational design, organizational behavior, and communication, and each theory focuses on different elements and relationships. Furthermore, each one is (or should be) undergoing constant development. Mackenzie (1986) exemplifies the proper scholar by claiming that his theories are the best that he knows today but "this belief is tempered with the awareness that when it is examined in 1992, it will be found wanting just as the 1976 version looks primitive when viewed in 1984" (p. 12). Nevertheless, one must use whatever theory one has. The ultimate test of any theory is whether it works, that is, whether it is usable, useful, and relevant when applied. In this sense, communication theories have been applied with great success in communication audits. Furthermore, the fact that theories are incomplete does not deter our attempt to understand as much as we can from our current theoretical perspective.

Since there are many theories, the auditor seeks to be so well informed that theory can be used judiciously. Consider the example of "openness." Every source I know encourages openness in communication. It is supportable by theory and by research studies. But "openness" has no absolute meaning, and experience teaches that certain forms and certain amounts of openness can be detrimental. It simply is not always wise to expose everything one is thinking. "Openness" is always a matter of degree. Therefore, I must ask how what I know about open communication can be used to the best advantage.

Furthermore, the state of the art is such that no umbrella theory of communication exists. Therefore, each problem in the organization may require me to use different kinds of theories, always watching for contradictions and inconsistencies. Research has told us much about the use of channels, supervisory-subordinate relations, and other communication phenomena, even if the findings have not been developed into full-blown theories.

In reviewing the communication research on feedback and on the relationship of communication to productivity and satisfaction, I found that a great deal of information has been generated in all three areas. A knowledge of such information can be helpful to me in interpreting audits. Nevertheless, no definitive explanation of any of the three areas exists. Competent auditors need familiarity with current theories and research as well as the motivation to seek greater explanatory and predictive insights. Once the interpretation stage is completed, the auditor is ready to prepare the final report.

REFERENCES

Cameron, Kim, and Whetten, David A. *Organizational Effectiveness.* New York: Academic Press, 1983.

DeWine, Sue; James, Anita C.; and Walance, William. "Validation of Organizational Communication Audit Instruments." Paper presented to the International Communication Association, Honolulu, May 1985.

Filley, Alan, and Pace, L. A. "Making Judgments Descriptive." In *The 1976 Annual Handbook for Group Facilitators,* edited by J. W. Pfeiffer and J. E. Jones. LaJolla, Calif.: University Associates, 1976, pp. 12–130.

Greiner, Larry E. "Evolution and Revolution as Organizations Grow." *Harvard Business Review* 50 (July 1972): 37–46.

Kilmann, Ralph H., and Mitroff, Ian. "A New Perspective on the Consulting/Intervention Process: Problem Defining versus Problem Solving." In

Proceedings. Orlando, Fla.: Academy of Management, 1977, pp. 148–152.

Mackenzie, Kenneth D. *Organizational Design.* New York: Ablex Publishing Co., 1986.

Pfeffer, J. *Organizations and Organization Theory.* Boston: Pitman Publishing Co., 1982.

Porter, D. Thomas. "Contributions of Systems Theory to the Study of Organizational Communication." International Communication Association, Chicago, May 1986.

Webb, Eugene; Campbell, Donald T.; Schwartz, R. D.; and Sechnest, Lee. *Unobtrusive Measures: Nonreactive Research in the Social Sciences.* Chicago: Rand McNally, 1966.

Weick, Karl, and Daft, Richard. "The Effectiveness of Interpretation Systems." In Cameron, Kim, and Whetten, David A., *Organizational Effectiveness.* New York: Academic Press, 1983.

12
Phase 6:
The Final Report

The data have been collected, and the interpretation has been made. Throughout these processes, the managers have been interested observers and participants. Now it's payoff time, and the final feedback report is the most important step in the entire audit. It is the reason the audit was conducted; all the hard work has led up to this moment. Therefore, this final phase should be accorded great care. This is not just another report; it is *the* report—the one opportunity that the auditor has to discuss the issues and make important points. Furthermore, although it marks the end of an audit, it is not necessarily the end of the relationship. In fact, it often is the *beginning* of a longer term relationship if one is to help the organization implement solutions to problems. The nature of that relationship depends in large part on the reaction to this report. Therefore, one cannot overemphasize the importance of this final report. With that in mind, this chapter explores the options for preparing the most effective report possible and provides specific guidelines for communicating the report.

The final report must be a superb form of communication about communication. This is often a real test for communication scholars. An IBM manager recently described it this way. Upon completion of her Ph.D. in Communication, she took a job with IBM that called for her to supervise communication. She says that she suddenly realized that she knew how to *analyze* a meeting, but she did not know how to *run* one. Auditors who propose to audit communication practices also need to be able to practice what they preach.

PREPARING THE REPORT

Although there are several considerations in preparing an effective audit report for the clients, all of them must be interpreted with one overriding consideration in mind: effective feedback requires sensitivity to the client's abilities to process the information in the report.

Feedback affects performance. That is the general conclusion drawn by Downs, Johnson, and Barge (1984) in their review of research studies, and the point is true for organizations as well as for individuals. However, the research also cites many instances in which feedback has had either little or a negative impact. Therefore, the dominant consideration for designing the report is determining how the feedback can be given effectively to these people under these circumstances.

Stay within the original boundaries set at the beginning of the audit. Review the expectations announced by the organization's representatives, as well as the benefits that you promised. What were the selling points used to get the client to agree to the audit? These become the ultimate criteria for judging what goes into the report. Furthermore, make certain that the report covers all stipulations of the consulting contract.

Manage the message

Choosing what to present in the final report and how to present it often takes a great deal of consideration. The end product should be a complete and professional document. (See Exhibit 12.1 at the end of this chapter.)

Be thorough. • At a minimum the report should include the following:

1. Statements of purpose.
   a. Identifies major thrusts of the diagnosis.
   b. States the limitations of the audit.
   c. Describes the particular client system concerned.
   d. Provides historical background for the study.
2. Review of the procedures for data collection.
   a. Includes copies of all instrument used.
   b. Describes the sampling techniques for collecting responses.
   c. Indicates the formats used in collecting data.
3. Summary of raw data obtained for each question.
   a. Includes separate sections for each kind of data. For example, summaries from interviews and questionnaires may be written separately.

b. Reports information in a descriptive, nonevaluative way.

c. Pinpoints any problems with data, such as absences of responses.

4. Description of analytic procedures.

a. Describes statistical manipulation of raw data.

b. Summarizes results of the analysis.

c. Provides narrative descriptions of tables.

d. Amplifies results with relevant examples or details to make them meaningful to the client.

5. Conclusions about strengths in, and obstacles to, communication.

6. Recommendations for future development.

Arrange the report systematically and attractively. • As with all other management communication, the physical arrangements affects the receptivity to the presentation. This report must be as professional in appearance as possible. Keep it physically attractive, typed with lots of white space. Arrange headings for easy reference. Start each reaction on a new page. Place the entire report in an attractive loose-leaf notebook. Leave the pages loose for maximum ease of reference but have dividers that clearly mark each section. Use charts and graphs to add explanatory power. Certain key statistical data will stand out more if they are presented using some type of graphic display.

Limit the number of conclusions. • Do not tell everything you know; choose the essential findings. Remember that the report is basically an exercise in case building. Most audits obtain more information than it is possible to comprehend in a short one to two hour report. Some of the criteria for making the choices include the following:

1. Keep the conclusions to the agreed-on purposes of the audit.

2. Relate them to the goals of the organization.

3. Choose only the most important findings. Even some areas that are significant statistically are not significant organizationally.

4. Emphasize those problem areas where change is possible.

5. Be prepared to rank order the areas of concern in terms of their importance.

Provide examples. • Although it is important to document all conclusions, it is imperative that you *go beyond numbers.* For each conclusion draw supporting data from each method used. Furthermore, a descriptive example is one of the most influential ways of giving feedback (Nadler, 1979).

Keep problems and strengths in perspective. • It is important that auditors remain neutral, objective, and realistic. It is also important that the report be realistic, conveying the best overall estimate of the state of the organization. The tendency to focus only on problems has been discussed before in detail; however, it should be especially avoided in the report. Care should be taken not to overwhelm clients "with negative findings that leave them with disproportionate feelings of helplessness and, therefore, unable to act" (Levinson, 1972, p. 496). A viable organization is going to have many strengths, and these should be recognized in the report. Such a balance will increase your own credibility and make people more receptive to the total feedback presentation.

Remember also that sometimes there are positive and negative sides to the same feature. In one organization, all data indicated that "communication relationships between supervisors and subordinates are quite positive." However, we also concluded that "the extent to which supervisors know and understand the problems faced by subordinates was one area of dissatisfaction—with 40 percent indicating dissatisfaction on the survey." Pointing out both sides raises questions, but it also increases the likelihood that the audit is fine-tuned, valid, and accurate.

Emphasize variability in responses. • When a teaching assistant once told a student that she could read with rapt attention for an hour or so, the student countered that she could not possibly do this because the research showed the average attention span was ten minutes. For that student, the average had come to represent the total reality, and individual differences were disregarded. This tendency is both unfortunate and misleading in terms of representing the organization.

One reason I provide frequency distributions for answers to questionnaires is to show the variability of responses. If there is a 1 to 7 scale for questions on a questionnaire, it is likely that the responses will cover at least a spread of five points on most questions. Why is this important? Sometimes we forget that averages do not tell the whole story, that they lose sight of individuals. For example, if the average response to a question was 3.4, there may still have been a number of people who answered 1 and some others who answered 5. These individuals need to be remembered.

Maintain anonymity of respondents. • Since anonymity was promised in the initial stages of the audit, it should be maintained. Care must be exercised to avoid revealing information inadvertently. Any specific examples need to be disguised; and if critical incidents are reported, positions as well as names may need to be camouflaged.

Even the presentation of numerical and statistical data must be reviewed. If demographic data are presented, it may be undesirable to break down answers into groups of fewer than eighteen people, because someone may be able to guess how an individual answered. Consider my dilemma in the audit of an airline. A high-ranking manager had five subordinate managers reporting to him. Each of them indicated great dissatisfaction with the same aspect of communication. To report the responses on the questionnaire in a normal frequency chart would have told him exactly how each subordinate had answered. To prevent this, we had to report the results in a different, nonquantitative way. The findings were described narratively as "most" respondents feeling a certain way.

Note limitations. • Every audit will be limited in terms of completeness or in the ability to generalize what can be drawn from the data. Although there is no need to be apologetic or defensive, these limitations need to be clearly spelled out to remind both the auditors and the managers how the data can be utilized.

A common limitation that needs to be acknowledged is the fact that many audits are based primarily on perceptual data. Unless they have done extensive observation, auditors rely on what people tell them about the organization. One hopes these perceptions are valid, but sometimes they are contrary to the truth. When this is discovered, however, the disparity in itself may constitute a communication problem.

Another common limitation is the underrepresentation of some units. In a recent audit, only one person from a unit returned a questionnaire, and no interview could be arranged with the manager of that unit. Therefore, what could be said about communication either in or with that unit was restricted by lack of data.

Make well-developed recommendations

The rationale for audits includes not only reinforcing what the organization does well but also forecasting problems and pinpointing beneficial ways to change. It is in the latter area that recommendations become important. If there are significant problems, the auditors may have the insights and expertise to point toward corrective actions. In doing so, recommendations must never be made cavalierly but with the recognition that the well-being of the organization is at stake.

Keep recommendations consultative. • In keeping with the process model of consulting, make tentative recommendations that essentially comprise areas for discussion. Since the managers will have to implement any new changes, they will provide important input as to what may or may not be effective.

Consider cost. • Consultants may not be able to compute the actual costs of a proposal, but they should be aware that manpower, downtime, social activities, publications, meetings, and training are expensive items. If there are several potential solutions to a problem, expense may be an important consideration. In one audit, the plant manager talked about the need for training the supervisors, but the production schedule made it unlikely that they could take off even three hours a week. Training would have been costly in terms of instruction, but the important cost to the plant manager was the fact that the supervisors would be unavailable to their subordinates during the training.

Assess priorities. • The 20/80 rule so adaptable to personal performance reviews is equally applicable to audit recommendations. Essentially, it requires one to assess priorities in selecting the 20 percent of those things an organization may do to improve that will achieve 80 percent of the improvement desired. In addition, it would be wise to eliminate any recommendation that does not have a high probability of success.

Examine your own values and biases. • Some consultants seem to have the same proposal for any problem. One prominent writer saw participative management as the ultimate solution. Others recommend meetings, quality circles, or training as standard solutions. In a sense, these recommendations fit the auditors' biases, but do they always work? Although we can never get outside our own values, we can ask ourselves whether the organization should be bound by these values and to what extent can we frame solutions consistent with organizational values.

Perfection is illusive. • As Greiner (1972) has pointed out, every solution carries within it the seeds of new problems. This thought is not meant to paralyze actions or discourage making recommendations. It does, however, suggest that for every recommendation it is important to anticipate what new problems may be encountered. If we change organization's structure, for example, we take something away from those with a vested interest in the current structure. Will that fact create problems? A public utility learned that it did the hard way. The new structure looked good on paper, but it caused many serious problems once it was implemented.

COMMUNICATING THE REPORT

Thoughtful preparation of the written report thoroughly acquaints an auditor with the material that should be presented to the clients. But being well informed is not enough to ensure a successful interaction with the client about the report. Consequently, the following discussion suggests ways of maximizing the potential for success.

Choose appropriate report context

There are basically two options: to give the report to a group of managers all at once or to give it to the manager in charge of the audit. There are organizational politics involved, and I usually follow whatever method the organization prefers. My preference is to brief the manager first and to brief the management group later if they desire. This gives the greatest flexibility in dealing with the managers' responses. In a variation of this method, a group of auditors of a university once prepared a general report for the management group and then met individually with the deans to give each one a report tailored to his or her particular domain.

Use multiple channels

A combination of oral and written reports should be used because the two kinds of reports can reinforce one another. The oral report permits the auditor to set expectations, to explain the report, and to highlight what is most important. The written document can be more detailed, and managers can examine it in depth at a different time. Under no circumstance, however, should you send a written report without an opportunity to first present it orally.

Arrange an exact sequence

Levinson (1972) describes an excellent arrangement for reporting back to clients. First, he presents the report to the client responsible for bringing him into the organization. They set aside two hours for the report, and Levinson reads the report aloud while the executive listens and makes notes for later discussion.

> I want him to be sensitive to the way I present matters so that he does not find himself in embarrassing or difficult circumstances because of the way I have phrased things. I make it clear that I cannot change the substance of my findings, but I emphasize my need to have his help in stating what I have to say in the most advantageous way (p. 497).

The client then takes the report to read overnight. Finally, Levinson meets with the client in a two-hour session on the next day for further discussion. After this process is completed, the auditor is ready to present the results to other groups in the organization.

Use a process-oriented discussion

My preferred consulting sytle is process-oriented in that I collaborate with managers throughout the audit process. This extends even into the feedback phase. The oral report should be more of a discussion than a formal presentation. It is a good idea to use an exploratory approach rather than a selling approach. Be receptive to questions and do not rush through the points. Even at this stage, ask questions of the managers to facilitate discussion. Each group may offer suggestions about presenting the materials to other groups.

The discussion of the recommendations is of particular importance. When auditors identify problems and make recommendations, they give their best thoughts. Nevertheless, there may be many ways of solving perceived problems, and the auditors' recommendations may stimulate discussion of new possibilities. Above all, the auditors should avoid trying to tell the managers how to run the organization. Their job is to collect the data, summarize it in a meaningful fashion, offer tentative recommendations, and facilitate a discussion so that the best organizational action can be determined.

Involve the audit team

The director of the audit may handle the entire presentation. However, another option is to assign team members leadership roles in the presentation and discussion. Both methods can be effective. The latter has an advantage of bringing out different orientations while "rewarding" or recognizing the team members for their efforts.

Adapt to the clients

Throughout the audit process, auditors should have been able to gauge certain characteristics about the managers hearing the report. It is important to consider variables such as education, degree of interest in the project, levels of understanding, and observer biases.

An important aspect of adaptation includes focusing on what is happening emotionally to the clients during the presentation of the report, and certain stages are quite predictable. Initially there will be some tension, because people do not know quite what to expect or may fear the worst. Second, there can be resistance to the negative information in the report. Scapegoating, rationalizations, and even attacks on the auditor are common in this phase. After a while people tend to relax and become more attentive if they find the substance of the report helpful. Finally, productive discussions will lead to consolidations behind the report and the desire to plan future action around its implications. The following specific behaviors are useful ways of adapting to clients.

Give assurances. • Even some highly skilled managers are nervous when it comes time to hear the results. There is always the possibility of some embarrassment when it comes time to discuss the organization's shortcomings as well as the strengths. For that reason, I always take the time to review the entire process that was used and set a very nonthreatening tone.

Answer questions. • Regardless of how well prepared you are, it is important that you take the time to answer the managers' questions. There have been times when I have moved from one point to a second, only to find that someone has been thinking all the time about a previous point and has a question. You must be flexible and take the time to develop each point to the clients' satisfaction.

Deal gently with resistance. • Most of the time, managers are receptive to the audit reports. They believe that they will learn from the process and are willing to listen enthusiastically. However, there are people who overtly or covertly resist what they hear. This is not so surprising when one considers the evaluation content of the report. Academic auditors, accustomed to being detached from their research data, must realize that because an audit report can have important ramifications for the managers' work lives and careers, they cannot be detached about all this. Therefore, expect some resistance and respond with genuine consideration. There is nothing to gain by setting up the report time as a confrontation to prove who's right. Some actual forms of resistance are pinpointed in the following paragraphs.

"Your data is not valid.": One president kept referring to "your" data throughout the report as if we had somehow manufactured the data out of thin air. He seemed to be trying to divide the organization from the report. Ironically, this happened during what was perhaps the most complete audit in which I have been engaged. Without being defensive, it was important to make careful allusions to the findings and how they had been obtained.

"I already knew that" is a response that can be an accurate affirmation, or it may be a way of belittling the report. Obviously, no audit will discover only things that the managers did not know; the best managers *ought* to have a feel for their organizations. These people usually are happy to have their own perceptions reinforced.

"I'm under attack.": There are times when the report has negative implications for managers listening to it. They sometimes begin to consider the report—and perhaps the reporter—as a personal affront. When these cues begin to appear, maintain a supportive climate and provide an opportunity for these feelings to be ventilated. Do not minimize the results, but make certain that the discussion stays on a factual basis.

"What do all these numbers mean?": This question is often legitimate, but one way to resist the report is to avoid understanding it. On occasion, respondents can protest too much. The auditors must never lose their patience in giving explanations.

Demonstrate appropriate modeling behavior

The audit presentation is, in itself, an important communication vehicle. It is a challenge to the auditor to demonstrate how effective communication is accomplished. His or her own activity can become a model that people in the organization can emulate.

> . . . the behavior of the consultant should be a model for how he [sic] wants the organization to go about its problem-solving activity: *by joint engagement with authoritative leadership around open examination of mutual problems for collective solutions toward more effective organizational functioning.* He must demonstrate that he does not fear hostility; that he stands confidently for his findings despite differences; that he is willing to be cross-examined about what he has learned and how he has learned it, together with the assumptions he has made; that he is willing to be appropriately corrected and to have his conclusions modified by new data. (Levinson, 1972, p. 501).

Distribute a separate report throughout the organization

One of the greatest inhibitors to participation in audits is the fact that employees rarely hear the results of the surveys in which they participate. Frequently, they feel cheated out of information. To overcome this problem, employees should be told from the outset that they will get a report, and it should be distributed. The following points can guide you in preparing such a report:

1. Keep the report to one to two pages.
2. Highlight the basic findings.
3. Keep it simple, because most people are not interested in great detail.
4. Have management screen it. Auditors are not in the business of creating communication problems, and sometimes they learn things that management would not want publicized.
5. Thank the employees for participating.

This chapter has emphasized basic considerations for presenting an acceptable audit report to the client organization. The entire book has been oriented toward that end. With the conclusion of the presentation of the audit report, the audit project is completed. Somehow it seems an oversimplification to say the process is ended, because the auditor has received two challenges. First, although the auditing phase may be completed, the consulting phase may not be over. As was pointed out, managements usually have some rationale for conducting a communication audit, and that rationale generally includes a desire for improvement or change. Conducting a successful audit provides such great insights into the organization that the auditors are uniquely equipped to become important consultants for introducing changes for improvements. This task can be even more demanding than conducting an audit.

Second, in conducting an audit, auditors are not only analyzing an organization, but they are also analyzing their own theories and thinking patterns. In other words, they get challenged mentally, and their knowledge gets tested in very practical ways. For me, this has been one of the greatest benefits of conducting audits.

EXHIBIT 12.1   Partial Final Report of Communication Audit at ACME

INTRODUCTION

The communication audit was undertaken to describe the communication process as it presently exists in the St. Louis office and to identify some of the major strengths and weaknesses of this process. In order to interpret this data accurately, it is necessary to keep the following items of information in mind.

Nature of the data

In addition to our observations, we are dealing with perceptual data of employees. Our information was gathered from (1) a Communication Satisfaction Questionnaire, (2) a Communication Experience Questionnaire, and (3) in-depth interviews. Therefore, we describe how employees perceive communication within the organization. Some of their perceptions *may or may not be an accurate description of what actually happens within the organization. However, it is important to understand that the way people perceive a situation serves as the basis for their own actions within that situation.*

The information came from a large sample of the employees, First-round interviews were conducted with 32 employees from throughout the organization. Upper management, nearly all the managers, and a selection of supervisors and staff members were interviewed.

Following the fiirst-round interviews, questionnaires were distributed to all employees based in the St. Louis office and to approximately 25 full-time employees. A total of 67 questionnaires were returned, which indicates a return rate of over 76%, well above the average.

The questionnaire was divided into five sections. The first section was designed to ascertain level of satisfaction with eight facets of communication in the organization: corporate perspective, personal feedback, organizational integration, relation with supervisor, communication climate, horizontal communication, media quality, and relation with subordinates. The second section addressed satisfaction with communication channels. The third section asked respondents to rate the importance, quality, accuracy, and timeliness of interdepartmental communication. The fourth section was concerned with the enactment of company values. The fifth section on the questionnaire solicited a "Communication Experience" from employees. The employees were to describe an instance of a work-related experience in which communication was particularly effective or ineffective. Thirty-four responses were received and analyzed.

Finally, second-round interviews were conducted with 23 employees at various levels of the organization. The interviewer focuses on information about company values, day-to-day feedback, yearly appraisals, and the effectiveness of information exchange.

Analysis of the data

As with most analyses, results show that there is a wide range of responses to any given question. Therefore, each conclusion drawn needs to be interpreted with due regard to the tendency for variability in the responses. We have, however, identified areas of general concern to Acme employees.

Our methods included: 1) theme analysis (a form of content analysis) of the interview data and communication experiences; 2) frequency counts; 3) *means* (the average score of a question) and *percentages;* and 4) multiple analysis of variance tests (an analysis to determine the significance of rating differences between groups in the organization).

Overview of communication concerns

This report focuses on six major areas, which are briefly described below:

I. *Communication with Upper Management*
This section highlights information on timeliness, downward and upward communication, and perception of company values.

II. *Communication Relationships Between Supervisors and Subordinates*
This section deals with the satisfaction of subordinates in terms of their communication relationships with supervisors.

III. *Communication Relationships with Coworkers*
This section includes information on work group compatibility and information sharing between employees.

IV. *Performance Feedback*
This section deals with the degree of employee satisfaction with day-to-day feedback, yearly appraisals, and the in-house training program.

V. *Communication Systems Coordination*
The section focuses on interdepartmental communication, the clarity of job functions, and the perceived decision-making process.

VI. *Overall Satisfaction with Communication*
This section explores the extent to which individuals feel a strong personal identity with the company, the extent to which people feel that their personal development is encouraged, and the extent to which people feel support for their personal and professional needs.[1]

I. COMMUNICATION WITH UPPER MANAGEMENT

Overview of findings

Most of the personnel expressed *satisfaction with the intentions* of upper management in regard to communication. Comments revealed a great deal of respect for these intentions and for upper management as individuals. Certain areas of communication were perceived as problematic, however. In this respect, most of the *dissatisfaction seemed to center around the lack of appropriate channels and systems for disseminating necessary information and feedback.* Also evident was a feeling that persons in upper management were unaware of the things needed from them that would enable staff to do their jobs and to feel more valued as members of the organization.

The topics covered in this section are: 1) Timeliness of Information Dissemination; 2) Perception of Company Values; 3) Informal Power Structure; 4) Downward Communication; and 5) Upward Communication.

Timeliness of information dissemination

According to data gleaned from the questionnaire, *timeliness of information from administration to other departments seemed to be the major concern.* This was

[1]Note that this only gives the first section of a full report.

especially significant as an issue since importance of information was, on the whole, rated highest. As such, there seems to be a discrepancy between the realization that upper management has the information necessary for persons to do their jobs well and the perception that that information is not always received at the time it is needed.

This finding was corroborated by the interview data. The consensus of the interviews was that *upper management needed to make and communicate decisions more quickly.* There were perceptions that management does not follow through on things planned, that staff only hears about "start-ups" but little about "conclusions." Sometimes promises just "drop from sight." One person stated that one "never gets a direct answer to a question in less than three months." While this particular statement may have been an extreme sentiment, it seemed to echo the general feelings that *"crises have to occur before things are acted upon."* The employees felt that one of the consequences of this lack of timeliness was the *strengthening of the grapevine,* which often, according to some, predated official channels by "two days." Most agreed that grapevine information was also distorted and they would prefer getting the real story from the official channels. In addition, some persons stated they would like more advance information on things that affect jobs and income—like tape sales, system changes, free ticket policies, etc.

Questionnaire findings on perceptions of importance/timeliness

(The highest rating on the questionnaire was 1 (very great). The lowest was 7 (very little). Thus means, or averages, closer to 1 indicate more satisfactory ratings.)

	Mean	Rank Order	
Importance of Information	2.7	1	(highest rating)
Accuracy of Information	2.9	2	
Quality of Information	3.4	3	
Timeliness of Information	3.9	4	(lowest rating)

Perception of company values

Upper management espouses a belief in an open culture and is very concerned that company values are incorporated into company and employee behavior. However, *many employees, while realizing that the values were important to upper management, did not feel these were effectively carried down through the ranks.* Staff felt that while upper management understood how values were to be incorporated in the daily running of the company, lower staff did not. One person said he/she did not remember all the values but did remember a meeting where the value list was passed out by the president and the general manager. Most were not sure what was to happen as a result of this meeting.

Results indicate an inconsistency between the statement of values by upper management and the ways these values are perceived by staff. The values of creating and sustaining an atmosphere of trust and openness and communicating clearly and appropriately seemed to cause interviewees most pause. They felt that although upper management talked about openness, there was, at times, a feeling of eliteness and secrecy in upper ranks. One person mentioned that when A, B, and C go into a room to discuss something, he/she wondered, "What are the Big Three gossiping about today?" Another person, while agreeing that there was a lack of communicating appropriately and clearly, felt that the lack was not on purpose. In fact, a majority of those interviewed felt that upper management simply did not realize the need for passing on information in a timely and complete manner.

Some supervisors and department managers were not sure how they themselves affected decision making. They felt upper management listened, but they were not sure what they did with what they heard. Some persons felt people were afraid to speak out—either to give ideas or to disagree—because they were still fearful of the things that happened in the "old days" when it was felt people could get fired for being out of line. *Most felt that the present management wanted creativity but since little verbal feedback was given they were not sure how innovative ideas from staff would be handled.*

The questionnaire ranking of company values was generally corroborated by interview data. According to the questionnaire, persons felt that the organization stressed that ACME was a profitable operation that sought to be BEST and to provide superior quality service. In addition to these values, most of those interviewed also felt ACME nurtured enthusiasm, and some felt there was an entrepreneurial atmosphere. "If you want to try something (and you know what you are doing) you can." A few persons mentioned that there was a supportive tolerance for mistakes made in efforts to "try out new things."

In summary, *the company is looked upon as providing a quality product and attempting to provide an atmosphere in which innovation and enthusiasm can maintain that quality. However, the attempts by upper management to support staff participation are not always clearly perceived by staff members* as being communicated equitably.

Questionnaire ranking of values

Be profitable	2.5	1	(highest rating)
Being the BEST	2.7	2	
Provide pleasant environment	2.8	3	
Achievements are team effort	2.8	3	
Emphasize cooperation, not competition	3.1	5	
Respect for the individual/trust	3.2	6	
Nurture worker needs/growth	3.2	7	
Encourage innovation & creativity	3.3	8	
Create environment of achievement	3.6	9	
Communicate clearly and appropriately	3.9	10	(lowest rating)

Informal power structure

In addition to the formal power structure that includes the three upper managers and the formal managerial and supervisory hierarchy, *there seems to be an informal power structure* made up of persons that are either consulted because of their recognized expertise and enthusiasm or are included because the persons themselves have sought to give input. One staff person said, "If you want it, you've got to go for it." The interviewees who mentioned the informal structure did not seem to have any problems with it; however, *the researchers saw some potential conflict in terms of company values.*

Some of those identified in the informal power structure were not as enthusiastic about participative management as was formal upper management. In fact, one of the persons involved in the informal power structure mentioned he/she felt that the sheet on company values should be re-ordered to put profit considerations at the top. He/she felt the management training and involvement were nice but that little would come of it, that people do not change and the company should be run by more conventional business strategies. He/she felt the present bent toward participative management was a natural reaction to the opposite extreme of no participation enacted by the previous management.

Another person in this informal power structure felt that too many persons were asked for input on decisions and that there were too many meetings that did not accomplish anything. *There was an indication that some of those involved in the informal power structure felt profit motive and participative management were incompatible.*

Since the questionnaire identified the values of profit making and being the BEST as receiving highest priority at Acme, perhaps either the informal power structure is more influential than would appear *or the company needs to consciously build a rationale that relates profit and participation/openness as supportive concepts and not mutually exclusive or opposing functions.*

Downward communication

Most of the interviewees acknowledged that Acme was in a state of flux, that many of the present ambiguities could be worked out, and that there generally was a genuine attitude of care and respect pervading the workplace. Because, however, there is a perceived lack of feedback, *many are not sure what upper management wants.* For example, a few persons said that upper management would like for staff to write up memos on problems according to a particular format—with solutions and alternatives included with the statement of the problem—but that this is not specifically communicated to everyone. Some felt that upper management did not understand how departments worked so they did not always respond appropriately. Customer Services appreciated the time P recently spent in their department to view first-hand how things operated, and they felt this should be done on a regular basis.

Many staff felt they *would like more verbal feedback and encouragement from upper management.* Sometimes they felt suggestions and efforts went unnoticed or unrecognized. Other persons felt that upper management would not always follow through when they had promised to get back to someone. In general, the personnel saw upper management putting forth efforts toward openness. However, they also felt that these efforts would be enhanced by a more systematic procedure and an awareness of the importance of information to the staff. Most felt that *upper management made a point to listen, but that the breakdown came in the follow-up and feedback phase.*

Upward communication

In terms of upward communication, employees indicated that creativity and suggestions were encouraged, but, as mentioned before, they would like more feedback to reinforce this atmosphere and to let them know where they stood. A few employees felt that it was proper if they gave suggestions.

II. SATISFACTION WITH SUPERVISOR/SUBORDINATE COMMUNICATION RELATIONSHIPS

Overview of findings

According to questionnaire and interview data, *communication relationships between supervisors and subordinates are quite positive.* In fact, of the eight factors considered in the first section of the questionnaire, these two factors received the highest satisfaction ratings. Despite these high ratings overall, *two departments appeared to have some problems in this area.*

Relationships with supervisors

The five questions concerning relationships with supervisors involved attention given (78% satisfied), trust (87% satisfied), guidance offered (76% satisfied), response to new ideas (82% satisfied), and the ideal amount of supervision (82% satisfied). This factor provided an overall mean of 2.42 (1 = high satisfaction, 7 = low satisfaction), which illustrates the satisfaction felt.

During the interviews, many persons cited examples of positive relations with supervisors. One person appreciated that tasks were explained clearly and that patience was shown when she attempted new things. Several made the comment that their supervisor's door was always open. The following comment was typical: "X is very receptive and tries to help out to get things done. He's very easy to talk to—very open." Another spoke of the real effort her supervisor displayed to keep in contact with her through weekly meetings where issues could be discussed and questions answered. As a result of one of those discussions, a method was devised to answer high priority needs: when the supervisor finds a note in her chair, she knows it requires an immediate response.

Subordinates generally felt they were respected, listened to, and taken seriously. They enjoy the fact that their input is valued and that their supervisors are available "when they need them." They spoke of supervisors trying to create a positive (win/win) atmosphere and responding to information received. Words like "open," "valued," "responsive," "involved," and "superior" indicated the general attitude of the interviewees.

The extent to which supervisors know and understand the problems faced by subordinates, however, was one area of dissatisfaction (40% indicated dissatisfaction on the survey). It seems that some supervisors are perceived as not following through, ignoring requests for information and suggestions for improvement. Other comments indicated that supervisors, at times, may assume facts rather than asking a knowledgeable subordinate for the information.

Relationships with subordinates

The five questions about relations with subordinates concerned responsiveness to downward communication (92% satisfied), anticipation of information needs (71% satisfied), lack of communication overload (50% satisfied), responsiveness to evaluation and feedback (92% satisfied), and acceptance of responsibility for accurate upward communication (92% satisfied). The overall mean for the five questions was 2.62 (1 = high satisfaction, 7 = low satisfaction). On the whole, supervisors saw subordinates as responsive to, involved in, and concerned with their positions at Acme. One supervisor noted a subordinate's increase in productivity after being given corrective feedback.

On the other hand, there was also a comment about subordinates' incompetence and some concern about trust of certain subordinates. It was interesting to note that there was far more data concerning subordinates' perceptions of supervisors than supervisors' perceptions of subordinates.

Concerns with departments

Although work unit relationships is a general area of satisfaction at Acme, *there are two departments that appear to have some problems:* AB and CD. The findings about relationships between personnel and supervisor in CD indicated some inconsistencies. While some spoke of engaging in social functions after work, others spoke of "hidden hostilities." Several mentioned that the supervisor "treats us like kids" and demands that permission be asked to go to the bathroom. Another reported that the supervisor was "overbearing" and didn't seem to care about her subordinates. In many of these statements, however, persons tried to clarify that they were not so unhappy with the person as with her management style.

It should be noted that CD was an area of concern from several perspectives throughout the audit. CD personnel had the perception that as a unit they were not respected by the rest of the organization. Some people in the department attributed this to "the low pay they received." Others felt that their need for timely information, dictated by the nature of their job, may have put them at odds with other departments from time to time.

The information on AB was somewhat conflicting and could not be pursued, as the department head was not available for the second interview. Although the information from the questionnaire indicated an overall mean of 2.5 on Relationships of Supervisors, interviews revealed evidence of some divided loyalties, with some subordinates going to one person and some to another.

V. COMMUNICATION SYSTEMS COORDINATION[2]

A key element in the efficient and effective functioning of an organization is the coordination of its communication systems. Our communication audit of Acme revealed information about three aspects of the organization's communication systems: *interdepartmental communication, clarity of job functions and organizational structure,* and *communication channels.*

[2]Sections III and IV of this report were deleted to save space.

Interdepartmental communication: overview of fiindings

Overall, our analysis of interdepartmental information flow at Acme has revealed more strengths than weaknesses. Strengths lie in the *accuracy* and *quality* of information sent interdepartmentally. Weaknesses appear to center around the *timeliness* of that information.

Examining the strengths and weaknesses of specific interdepartmental links has led us to some conclusions about the varying information needs of the departments.

First, CD *has a high need for information from all departments with the exception of AB.* The amount and immediacy of information needed may explain why this department finds problems with the timeliness of much of the information it receives.

Second, *two departments apparently rely very little on information from other departments; neither AB nor EF rated the importance of information from any other department as great or very great.* Since only one person from EF responded to the questionnaire, we may choose to discount this information, particularly since the coming changes in budgetary procedures will require more information exchange between EF and other departments. It is more difficult to explain the independence of AB. Perhaps it is related to the physical separation of that department from the others in the company.

Interdepartmental communication: results for each department

Orientation • Analysis of the data from the first round of interviews suggested that information flow between departments was sometimes problematic, especially in terms of timeliness. Consequently, this area was probed more specifically in both the questionnaire and the second round of interviews. Questionnaire respondents were asked to rate the information they received from each department on its importance, quality, accuracy, and timeliness. Interviewees were asked to name the other departments whose information was most important to their work, as well as to discuss their satisfaction with the information from those departments. This information, in combination, provided us with a picture of the interdepartmental communication relationships in operation.

In this section we report the results and the implications of our investigation of interdepartmental communication. As an audit team, we agreed that the strength or importance of the communication link between departments should serve as the focus of our interpretation of the factors of quality, accuracy, and timeliness of information: when one department's successful performance depends upon the information it receives from another, it is crucial that the information received is accurate, timely, and of a high quality. Consequently, this report pinpoints the quality, accuracy, and timeliness ratings each department received from those departments whose mean rating of the importance of its information was Very Great (1) or Great (2). In most cases, ratings of quality, accuracy, and timeliness are lower than the importance rating. This is probably not too surprising: when we view information as highly important, we may tend also to view its quality, accuracy, and timeliness as not quite equal to its importance.

Where questionnaire results indicate a serious discrepancy between the rating of quality, accuracy, or timeliness and the importance rating one department received

*from another, we suggest that the two departments meet to examine their information
exchange practices in an effort to improve the information flow.*

Clarity of job functions and organizational structure: overview of findings

Analysis of the audit data indicates a *lack of clarity of job functions and
organizational structure* at ACME stemming primarily from the rapid growth and change
the organization is experiencing. This situation has implications for *information flow,
decision-making strategies,* and *conflict resolution procedures.* It is also apparent that
upper management is sensitive to this situation and is taking some steps to address the
problem. *However, we believe that the problem can only be fully alleviated by the formal clarification of both job functions and organizational structure.* We recommend
that this formalization be made a high priority.

Job Functions, organizational structure, and information flow

Interviews and communication experience accounts reveal that an area which
affects communication systems coordination is the clarity of job functions and organizational structure. As a result of the rapid changes ACME is experiencing, this clarity
is lacking. The first evidence for this lack is found in the information we gathered on
job descriptions. Employee coments included: "We write our own." "It is somewhere,
but it needs to be rewritten because tasks have changed." "I was given some written
material, but it was vague as to specifics." And, "I have a list of tasks in my employee
file, but I think it's outdated." One department manager is trying to develop job descriptions for his department, for, he said, "Up to this time, it [the department] has been
run very loosely." *His reason for developing the descriptions is to let other departments know the responsibility of his department so that information can be exchanged
on a timely basis.* In fact, this appears to be the primary reason why job descriptions
may be needed in the company, since most employees were not really concerned that
they had no "written" set of responsibilities. Each employee seemed reasonably clear
on what was expected of him or her. *However, in listening to descriptions of interdepartmental relations, it became clear to us that the lack of job descriptions resulted in
employees not knowing specifically what others do, when they need to do it, and what
information they need to do it.* As one employee stated, "others are not aware of my
responsibilities. This [awareness] would be helpful, since the company is growing so
rapidly. One thing that happens as a result of this is that other departments assume
what goes on in another department and a lot of times these assumptions are either
negative or just not true of the real situation." While it may be difficult to arrive at
written job descriptions that will be valid for any length of time in a company which
is in flux, our analysis indicates a need for some clarification of job functions. *This
situation may be one cause of the poor ratings on timeliness of information dissemination discussed in the previous section.*

*This lack of clarity of job functions appears to extend even to top manage-
ment,* with administrators indicating some "fuzziness" and "cross-over responsibility."
It is also reflected in some confusion over the organizational structure. For example,
it was mentioned by a supervisor that the company is too big for the once informal
ways of communicating. This person felt an understanding of the organization's hierarchy

would help persons "get along better." In *two departments, there appears to be some confusion about the chain of command. Data processing* is unsure about YZ. Consequently, they are unsure about how to interpret apparent "orders." AB employees also reveal some uncertainty about their manager, with some of the employees going to one person and some to another for their needs. An employee in another department commented that this is a "company where you have to feel your way around more." Several staff members mentioned the need for clearly defined lines and channels of communication and an accurate organizational chart.

Job functions, organizational structure, and decision making

Lack of clarity of job functions and organizational structure has implications for *decision making,* as well as for information flow. As one supervisor noted, "If something is used in a crisis and works, the company fails to formalize the procedure for the next crisis." Thus, *the ambiguous structure steers the company toward a reactive approach to day-to-day decision making.* Related to this are comments from managers that suggest more key people need to be involved in decision making. This suggests the need for a clear organizational structure to identify the "key" people for each decision.

Job functions, organizational structure, and conflict resolution

Conflict resolution methods also appear to be affected by the clarity of organizational structure. On the questionnaire, 38% of the respondents indicated some dissatisfaction with the "extent to which conflicts are handled appropriately through proper communication channels" (Question 27). *The lack of clear channels may be one cause of this dissatisfaction.* In the second round of interviews, we directly addressed this question. While responses revealed satisfaction with the way conflicts are handled within individual departments, they also revealed ambiguity about conflict procedures beyond the departmental level. Comments included: "I am not sure how conflict is resolved in the organization because I really only deal with my immediate supervisor." "There is no kind of grievance procedure. No official way to file a complaint. If you dare to go past your immediate supervisor, you're really in trouble." Other comments indicated that the company is taking some positive steps to improve the handling of conflicts, however, through Supervisory Training and the Employee Attitude Survey. *Establishing a clear organizational structure and job functions may also help to clarify conflict resolution procedures.*

Communication channels: overview of findings

Analysis of the information on communication channels indicates a generally *accep ⸱le level of satisfaction with all channels* across the company. *In-house organizational members are most highly satisfied with one-on-one meetings, the newsletter, and memos. Sales are most highly satisfied with telephone conversations, the newsletter, and memos and group meetings.* While information from the interviews and communication experiences helps to explain these ratings for some channels, it does not explain either the reason for the success of the newsletter or the dissatisfaction with the bulletin board. Acme may wish to further investigate these two areas in order to maintain satisfaction with the former and increase satisfaction with the latter. Information on *memos* was ambiguous; although many found them useful, others believe they could be used more efficiently and selectively. There was no ambiguity regarding group meetings, however. *Employee comments reflected a desire for more company-wide meetings and manager meetings.*

In-house staff perceptions of channels

Communication channels represented a third area affecting communication systems coordination. Questionnaire responses indicated the following mean satisfaction ratings for channels. *Channels are ranked according to level of satisfaction, with the channel receiving the highest satisfaction rating listed first.*

Channel	Mean	Rank
One-on-One Meetings	2.8	1
Newsletter	3.0	2
Memos	3.3	3
Group Meetings	3.4	4
Telephone Conversations	3.5	5
Bulletin Board	3.6	6
Other (Grapevine—2 responses)	7.0	7

Information from the interviews offers insights into the attitudes behind these ratings. *When asked what channels were most useful on a day-to-day basis, most persons cited face-to-face and the informal hallway communication* because "it's quick and memos are sometimes complicated." *Memos are still a popular means of communicating, particularly with managers.* Most stated that they trusted the information they received from memos and felt no need to question its "authenticity." Some staff members criticized others' extensive use of memos, however, as well as the lack of an efficient "memo format."

Satisfaction with group meetings ranked fourth. This ranking seems to reflect a desire for *more meetings* rather than a complaint about the meetings that are held now. A good number of employees indicated interest in more meetings as a place to express their ideas, as a source of information, and as a means of company identification.

Interview comments do not completely reflect the negative questionnaire ratings the *grapevine* received from two individuals. Although management is concerned about the grapevine, many staff consider it helpful since it is often their most timely means of getting information on what is happening. As stated earlier, one staff member said it predates formal channels by two days. Many, however, also feel the grapevine distorts information. For example, when one person was fired, the information was passed through the grapevine as a sudden decision. According to supervisors, though, the decision was the result of four months of negotiations with this person.

VI. OVERALL SATISFACTION WITH COMMUNICATION

Overview of findings

The data collected from the first and second rounds of interviews and the questionnaire were analyzed to determine the overall level of satisfaction people were indicating they felt with the communication process. This satisfaction was looked at in terms of the extent to which individuals felt a strong personal identity with the company, the extent to which people felt that their personal development was being encouraged, the extent to which people felt support for their personal and professional needs, and the extent to which certain communication factors distinguished between those people who are satisfied with their jobs and those who are dissatisfied. In the following section, each of these indicators will be examined and possible reasons for different levels of satisfaction will be discussed.

Personal identity with the company

The comments made during the first and second round interviews indicate that *people generally feel highly involved in the organization.* Reasons given for this high degree of involvement include the statement "I love my job," having a high level of responsibility, an involvement in the decision-making process, and a feeling of confidence that the supervisor will take comments and suggestions made seriously. *Generally, people indicated an increased level of involvement as they were given more responsibility and greater influence in the decision-making processes in the company.* Top managers' visits and the sharing of company and personal news in the "Acme" newsletter were both mentioned specifically as occasions which make the employees feel that they are worthwhile members of the organization. In fact, the need to feel worthwhile and important to the organization was frequently expressed by those interviewed.

The high level of involvement expressed in interviews was not found in the results from the questionnaire. When asked the "extent to which the company's communication makes me identify with it or feel a vital part of it," 26 individuals rated themselves satisfied, while 23 rated themselves dissatisfied, with a mean of 3.8. This dissatisfaction may be a result of not having a high level of responsibility or influence in decision making, if the comments made in the interviews are representative. Several who indicated a currently high level of involvement had previously felt uninvolved or less involved when they had lesser responsibilities or had supervisors who did not include them in the decision-making process.

Personal development

One of the company's values states that we "develop ourselves and those with whom we work . . . at all times." People's perceptions about company encouragement of personal development and enactment of the values were explored in the questionnaire and in the second-round interviews. The results of the questionnaire were not highly significant (a mean of 3.4), with 30 people indicating that personal development was encouraged and 11 indicating that there was little encouragement of personal development.

Statements from the interview indicate that while people are encouraged to develop themselves, to propose their own solutions and to make their own decisions, to be creative, and to move within the company, there is also a feeling that some supervisors really prefer that decisions be cleared with them first. Uncertainty and frustration were felt as a result of this discrepancy. It was also stated that while personal development was encouraged in the form of in-house-training and the opportunity to attend other seminars, people were not rewarded adequately for their achievements.

Support for needs

It was widely reported in the interviews that people feel both personal and professional support for their needs from co-workers, supervisors, and upper management. Individuals reported that *the general atmosphere at Acme is one of warmth, caring, and friendliness.* People said that they felt that the doors of both their immediate supervisors and upper management were always open. People reported that *personal relationships at Acme are satisfactory, as is evident by "the laughter, the liking and loyalty" shared by those within the company.*

Amount of communication

People were also questioned concerning the "extent to which the amount of communication in the company is about right." A significant level of dissatisfaction was reported, with 25 people stating that they were dissatisfied and 22 people stating that they were satisfied, giving a mean of 3.9. Whether the dissatisfaction was caused by too much or too little communication was not indicated on the questionnaire. However, the comments made during the interviews indicate that *while some feel that there is too much information, more people believe that there is too little.*

Those who felt that there is too much communication state that people are overloaded with administrative trivia, with too many reports, phone calls, interviews, etc.

Those who felt that there was too little communication reported that they needed more information about what is going on in the rest of the company. They stated that they did not know what other departments were doing and that other departments did not understand their functions and needs. Suggestions for resolving this problem included company-wide meetings, sharing of general information about what is happening in the company, an increase in company-wide functions outside of work, a sharing of job responsibilities, and interdepartmental meetings to clarify informational needs. *The most commonly proposed solutions were more company-wide and departmental meetings.*

Job satisfaction

A final area examined to determine the overall level of satisfaction with communication at Acme was the extent to which the perceptions of those who were satisfied with their jobs differed from those of the individuals who were dissatisfied with their jobs.

The results of the questionnaire indicated that 40 people felt somewhat satisfied, satisfied, or very satisfied with their jobs while 14 people felt indifferent, somewhat dissatisfied, dissatisfied, or very dissatisfied, giving a mean of 5.4 and indicating a strong feeling of job satisfaction. It is normal for 1/3 of the employees in any organization to report dissatisfaction with their jobs. The percentage of employees expressing dissatisfaction in this questionnaire was slightly under 33%. In addition to the normal work routine, the period of rapid growth and change that Acme has been undergoing during the past six months may have been an influencing factor in people's responses. When asked specifically about job satisfaction over the past six months, 14 people felt that it had remained the same, 23 reported that it had gone up, and 17 people reported that it had gone down, with a mean of 2.1, indicating that, on the average, satisfaction had increased.

The factors which distinguished those individuals who are satisfied with their jobs from those who are dissatisfied include: personal feedback, organizational integration, communication climate, and relations with supervisors.

Those who are satisfied with their jobs report that they are more satisfied with the level of recognition of their efforts and with the way that problems in their particular jobs are handled than those who are not satisfied with their jobs. In addition, those who are satisfied with their jobs report being more satisfied with the information they receive about department goals and policies and about job requirements than those who are dissatisfied with their jobs.

In terms of communication climate, those who are satisfied with their jobs report more satisfaction with the communication ability of others in the organization and with the way in which conflicts are handled appropriately through proper channels than do those who are not satisfied with their jobs. Those who are dissatisfied with their jobs report more dissatisfaction with the extent to which they feel that their supervisors trust them than do those who are satisfied with their jobs. While this difference in the feeling of being trusted is not great, it is statistically significant and indicates an area which distinguishes between those who are satisfied and those who are dissatisfied with their jobs.

Those with different levels of job satisfaction were also distinguished in terms of relations with the supervisor, specifically in terms of the extent to which the supervisor offers guidance for solving problems and is open to new ideas, and the extent to which the amount of supervision given is about right. Those who are satisfied with their jobs are significantly more satisfied with each of these factors than are those who are dissatisfied with their jobs.

Significant differences between those who are satisfied and those who are dissatisfied with their jobs were found in the extent to which people are also satisfied or dissatisfied with the compatibility of their work groups, and the extent to which the communication in the company is perceived as basically healthy. Those who find their jobs satisfying are satisfied with the compatibility in their work groups and find the communication in the organization to be healthy, while those who are dissatisfied with their jobs are significantly more dissatisfied with work groups and organizational communication.

In summary, those people who are satisfied with their jobs are more satisfied with the information they receive concerning job requirements and job performance, are more satisfied with the communication ability of others in the organization, with the level of trust and guidance they receive from their supervisors, with the compatibility of their work groups, and with the "healthy" communication in the organization than are those who are dissatisfied with their jobs.

REFERENCES

Downs, Cal W.; Johnson, Kenneth; and Barge, Kevin J. "Communication Feedback and Task Performance in Organizations: A Review of the Literature. In *Organizational Communication Abstracts,* edited by H. Greenbaum, R. Falcione, and S. Hellwegg. Beverly Hills, Calif.: Sage, 1984.

Greiner, Larry E. "Evaluation and Revolution as Organizations Grow." *Harvard Business Review* 50 (July 1972): 37–46.

Levinson, Harry. *Organizational Diagnosis.* Cambridge, Mass.: Harvard University Press, 1972.

Nadler, D. A. "The Effects of Feedback on Task Group Behavior: A Review of Experimental Literature." *Organizational Behavior and Human Performance* 23 (1979): 309–338.

SUBJECT
INDEX

Administration, 88
Agenda, 57
Analysis, 9, 51, 90, 107, 119, 138, 158, 186
Anonymity, 63, 89
Assumptions, 6, 120, 129, 199
Audit agreement, 21

Benefits, 5

Cafeteria approach, 4
Change score analysis, 197
Channels, 33, 103, 209
  formal, 33
  informal, 34
  multiple, 34, 209
Client relationship, 14, 211
Climate, 70, 113, 194
Communication functions, 34
Communication model, 27
Communication Satisfaction Questionnaire, 112, 197
Comparisons, 107, 109, 122, 196
Conclusions, 77, 199, 206
Confidentiality, 13, 63
Consultant, 3, 11
Content analysis, 16, 125, 141, 146
Contract, 22
Control, 5
Coordinated Management of Meaning, 38
Correlation, 93, 129, 173
Costs, 13, 17, 18, 43, 80, 199, 208
Cover letter, 86
Critical incident, 16, 133
Cross-tabulation, 158

Data bank, 109, 122, 196
Demographics, 95, 107, 170, 207
Design, 4
Diagnosis, 3, 7, 9
Diaries, 16, 167
Difference scores, 107, 110
Directionality, 31, 36
Downward communication, 31, 97, 218

ECCO, 151
Effectiveness, 192, 195, 197
Ethics, 11
Evaluation, 4, 9

Factor analysis, 112, 122
Feedback, 7, 9, 28, 114, 127, 204
Filtering, 28
Final report, 14, 204
Finances, 13
Focus, 16, 25, 81, 190
Formal channels, 6, 102

Goals, 196

Halo effect, 190
Horizontal communication, 31, 97, 113

Informal channels, 6, 156
Information, 30, 97, 173, 179, 190, 202
Initiation, 9, 11
Innovation, 35
International Communication Association Survey, 96, 198
Interpretation, 74, 100, 107, 110, 146, 178, 186, 205
Interview guide, 51
Interviews, 16, 18, 49, 170

Job Description Index, 42
Job satisfaction, 42, 73, 129, 182

Liaison, 15, 193
Load, 30

Maintenance, 34
Managing an audit, 9
Media, 33, 106, 113
Minnesota Satisfaction Questionnaire, 42

Models
medical, 15
process, 15
purchase, 14
Motivation, 35, 70

Network, 16, 38, 160, 166
Norms, 4, 109, 196

Observation, 16, 33, 134
Open system, 40, 202
Order of questions, 86
Organizational development, 198
Organizational processes, 29

Perception(s), 5, 18, 51, 110, 207, 212, 216
Pilot test, 170
Planning, 9, 11, 13
Probe, 61, 70, 193
Problem definition, 192, 206
Process perspective, 26, 210
Productivity, 43, 129
Professionalism, 3
Publicity, 20
Purpose, 12

Qualitative data, 74, 125, 179, 182, 189
Questionnaire, 16, 80, 136, 151
Questions, 58, 60, 81, 83

Rank order, 1, 106, 121, 178, 197
Rationale, 5
Recommendations, 184, 188, 201, 208
Records, 71
Relationships, 36, 103, 179
Reliability, 108, 171
Report, 204, 209, 213
Response, 83, 207
Roles, 38
Rules, 37

Sample, 18
random, 63
representative, 63
size, 19, 20, 80
Sampling, 19, 20, 63, 66, 80, 171, 174, 179
Satisfaction, 41, 94, 118
Schedule, 68
Scope, 12, 82
Semantic differential, 85
Smallest space analysis, 174
Stratified, 19, 66
Structure of interviews, 62
Structure of work, 29
Style, 37
Synthesis, 74
Systems, 2
Systems theory, 39

Task processes, 29, 34
Tenure, 94
Theory, 201
Time, 19, 30, 50, 87, 191
Timeliness, 5, 102
Training, 9, 70

Upward communication, 31, 43, 97, 114, 218

Validity, 18
Values, 208, 217
Verification, 5
Volunteers, 67